Media Persuasion in the Islamic State

MEDIA
PERSUASION
IN THE
ISLAMIC STATE

NEIL KRISHAN AGGARWAL

COLUMBIA UNIVERSITY PRESS   *NEW YORK*

Columbia University Press
Publishers Since 1893
New York   Chichester, West Sussex
cup.columbia.edu
Copyright © 2019 Columbia University Press
All rights reserved

Library of Congress Cataloging-in-Publication Data

Names: Aggarwal, Neil Krishan, author.
Title: Media persuasion in the Islamic State / Neil Krishan Aggarwal.
Description: New York, NY : Columbia University Press, 2019. |
Includes bibliographical references and index.
Identifiers: LCCN 2018038378 (print) | LCCN 2018053978 (e-book) |
ISBN 9780231544122 (e-book) | ISBN 9780231182386 |
ISBN 9780231182386 (cloth : alk. paper)
Subjects: LCSH: IS (Organization) | Qaida (Organization) | Zarqawi, Abu Musab, 1966–2006. |
Mass media—Political aspects—Middle East. | Jihad—Psychological aspects. |
Violence—Psychological aspects. | Persuasion (Psychology) |
Religious milvitants—Psychology.
Classification: LCC HV6433.I722 (e-book) | LCC HV6433.I722 A392 2019 (print) |
DDC 363.325—dc23
LC record available at https://lccn.loc.gov/2018038378

Screenshots of IS media filmed before 2006 were recovered from
internet archives and are thus of limited quality and resolution.
All material used under Section 107 of the US Copyright Act.

Columbia University Press books are printed on permanent
and durable acid-free paper.
Printed in the United States of America

Cover design: Lisa Hamm
Cover image: © Sebastien Salom-Gomis/SIPA/1502111843
(SIPA via AP Images)

Once extralegal organizations begin to mimic the state and the market by providing protection and dispensing justice, social order itself becomes like a hall of mirrors: at once there and not there, at once all too real and a palimpsest of images, at once visible, opaque and translucent. What is more, this doubling, this copresence of law and disorder, has its own geography, a geography of discontinuous, overlapping sovereignties.

—Jean Comaroff and John L. Comaroff,
Law and Disorder in the Postcolony, 2006

A brave new world was being created at hectic speed. Commentators optimistically suggested that, in the age of satellite television and the internet, traditional forms of repression—censorship, imprisonment, torture, and execution—could no longer secure a police state's power; they might even be counterproductive. State control of information and communication had been subverted by blogs and mobile phones; YouTube provided the means to expose, in the most graphic and immediate way, the crimes and violence of security forces.

—Patrick Cockburn,
The Rise of Islamic State, 2015

Contents

Acknowledgments

Several colleagues have graciously publicized my work: Dinesh Bhugra, Kamaldeep (Kam) Bhui, Vaisakha Desai, Carol Gluck, Byron Good, Mary Jo Delvecchio Good, John Horgan, James Jones, Laurence Kirmayer, Michael Norko, Jerrold Post, and Chuck Strozier. Thank you.

Friends continue to offer unyielding encouragement: Hussein Abdulsater, Ravi DeSilva, Yusuf Iqbal, Matt Melvin-Koushki, Ramya Parthasarthy, Samir Rao, Nabilah Siddiquee, Wheeler Thackston, and Parvinder Thiara. My research assistant Kryst Cedeño graciously went through a prior draft to check all references.

I can't ever express enough gratitude to Columbia University Press. Jennifer Perillo commissioned the book as my original editor, and Stephen Wesley offered vital encouragement throughout the review process.

The Truman National Security Project, Columbia University's Committee on Global Thought, and McGill University's Advanced Summer Institute in Cultural Psychiatry have given me venues to try out ideas.

My family continues to furnish plenty of love: Niraj Nabh and Anshu Kumar; Manu, Reema, Asha, and Roshan Aggarwal; Madhu and Krishan Kumar Aggarwal; and of course, Ritambhara, Amaya Ishvari, and Amoha Devi.

Finally, Muhammad Fraser-Rahim of the Quilliam Foundation, Mia Bloom, Kam, Ravi, Dad, and Ritambhara: thank you for intervening at various points when IS's texts emotionally overpowered me. Two anonymous peer reviewers went through a prior draft and made clear what was missing: my own engagements with, and analyses of, this material. I'm grateful to them for pushing me to give this text everything I have.

Media Persuasion in the Islamic State

ONE

Studying Islamic State Discourse as Mediated Disorder

A HANDSOME soldier in fatigues sings into the camera. His voice is bold, unpolished: He shakes his head to convey the intensity of his emotion rather than modulate his rhythm or volume as a more seasoned singer would. Were it not for his black shirt, his mahogany skin would blend into Iraq's desert landscape. His scraggly hair connects to his unkempt beard. He looks to be in his twenties. He sits with two others dressed in fatigues. Their raw vulnerability—a band of brothers singing at leisure to escape the interminable destruction of a war that has lasted more than a decade—contrasts with images of troops atop armed vehicles before and after this shot.

They sing the refrain, a single word repeated four times:

Jundullah. Jundullah. Jundullah. Jundullah.

Soldier of God.

A caption identifies the handsome soldier as Abu Talha Al-Yamani. The location: west of the city Samarra in Salahuddin province in Iraq. The camera pans to an armed convoy of men smiling, raising their right index fingers to heaven, driving slowly so the camera can record their exaltation in these moments free from battle. Abu Talha sings the next verse: "We will never swerve from the course of faith. Our path is the straight path from the Quran's guidance." The English doesn't capture the beauty of the original

Arabic: The assonance of "a" sounds alternate with the clear consonance of "n" sounds in the first three lines.

A	ba	dan	la	na	na	hīd	(1)
A	ba	dan	la	na	na	hīd	(2)
A	na	khu	ta	ti	ma	ni	(3)
Dar	bu	na	dar	bul	qa	wīm	(4)
Dar	bu	na	dar	bul	qa	wīm	(5)
Mi	nal	hu	dal	qu	ra	ni	(6)

Short verses in easy Arabic that even I, a non-native speaker, can learn. But easy does not mean simple: The lines are crafted in strict meter with two iambic feet (la-na na-hīd) marching closely behind one anapest foot (a-ba-da). Poetic discipline mirrors military discipline.

Abu Talha sings a second verse, pointing to the sky and smiling: "The martyr goes to the paradise of God from His path without ever swerving." As he sings, a new image flashes on screen. A bloodied body.

The juxtaposition of the soldier's voice singing with the image of the corpse is jarring. Is this Abu Talha? Are his comrades OK? What has happened to Abu Talha's family and friends? Do they know he may be dead?

Then the chain of thoughts begins. Abu Talha was just starting his life. He looks like me. Why are we, America, still bombing innocent children in Iraq? I hate to say it, but they have a point. We've been there forever and call such deaths "collateral damage." A life on the path of God, full of conviction, surrounded by comrades in arms, fighting tyranny in self-defense, free from the encumbrances of demanding relationships and the hyper-connected modern world. Like Abu Talha, my life could be celebrated after my death, filmed for eternity.

Hours later, I'm walking with my family at Chelsea Piers in Manhattan. It's a Saturday afternoon. My children ride the carousel, and as a cool breeze envelops us, I think back to the men on their trucks who smile, point to heaven, and embrace martyrdom. For hours, I feel this psychological dissociation, physically present with my family but distraught over Abu Talha's fate. *Jundullah*, I hum to myself. *Jundullah*. I know the lyrics now; I've heard them dozens of times. I mull over what might be the morality of this situation. Should witnessing Abu Talha's death, a point in life that we normally share only with our most loved ones, commit me to some sort of action? My life in New York feels insignificant and meaningless.

The cognitive dissonance alarms me. I would never pick up a gun and go abroad to fight for a group that has enslaved thousands of women and children (Callimachi 2015a), destroyed priceless antiquities (Stack 2015), and captured an area the size of Jordan (Chulov and Borger 2015). At one point, it ruled over four million people and a third of the territory in Iraq and Syria, earning millions of dollars from smuggling oil on the world market (Sprusansky 2014). And yet, I suddenly appreciate the motivations to do so. I process this contradiction. Through its beautiful bellicosity, the video appeals to my emotional self. Maybe it was the hours of videos I had watched beforehand that primed me for this moment. Maybe it was the grueling monotony of raising very young children. I—a Hindu-American cultural psychiatrist, an infidel whose beheading the Islamic State (IS) would undoubtedly love to film, a scholar who has written extensively against terrorism—have my first bitter taste of radicalization.

If IS's media elicits these reactions within me, what about its sympathizers? Why is its media so seductive? Finding answers to these questions is crucial given the high stakes involved: The wars in Iraq and Afghanistan alone have cost the American economy more than $3 trillion (Stiglitz and Bilmes 2008). As of this writing, conflicts with IS have produced more than 220,000 Iraqi and five million Syrian refugees, as well as more than three million Iraqi and six million Syrian internally displaced persons (Office of the United Nations High Commissioner for Refugees 2017a, 2017b). The U.S. Department of State (2015) estimated in February 2015 that more than twenty thousand foreign fighters from one hundred countries had migrated to Syria and Iraq to join groups like IS. What can cultural psychology and psychiatry bring to this discussion that advances the goals of counterterrorism?

The Need to Understand the Psychology Behind Militant Media

I have written this book to analyze the psychological mechanisms of media persuasion and the cultural identity of IS and its precursors. In my earlier books, I justified the analysis of militant media by invoking the American government's restrictions on travel to the Middle East and communicating with militants. I maintained that such restrictions only drive our need for independent scholarship and that texts on the internet are legitimate primary sources for bypassing these restrictions. Throughout this book, I use *text* to mean "any configuration of signs that is coherently interpretable by some community of users," including written, audio, and visual media (Hanks 1989, 95).

My defensive posture in favor of textual analysis has changed since I began writing this book. We now know of numerous attacks in which the video and audio lectures of Anwar Al-Awlaki, Al Qaeda's English-speaking Yemeni-American ideologue, have been implicated: Nidal Malik Hasan's shooting in Fort Hood, Texas, in 2009; Faisal Shehzad's failed Times Square attack in 2010; the Tsarnaev brothers' bombing of the Boston Marathon in 2013; Syed Farook and Tashfeen Malik's shooting in San Bernardino, California, in 2015; and Omar Mateen's shooting at a gay nightclub in Orlando, Florida, in 2016 (Conway 2012; Shane 2016). We also know that, through its online media, IS has inspired attackers around the world previously thought to be "lone wolves" not under any organization's command structure (Callimachi 2017), pushing the U.S. government to disrupt IS's online presence (Sanger and Schmitt 2017). The War on Terror has inspired new forms of cultural media that intersperse reality and fantasy, as militants spread fear by filming deaths and invite others to join in the killing as if they were playing group video games (Aretxaga 2002; Al-Rawi, 2018). This raises essential questions for me as a cultural psychiatrist: Why is militant media so successful at inspiring violence? What kinds of cognitive reaction do militants want to trigger? How can we develop tools to analyze the media of militant groups in general?

If we needed further justifications for studying online media, we now have rigorous research that verifies the importance of analyzing militant texts. In an exhaustive review of 298 studies comparing the beliefs, attitudes, and behaviors of participants exposed to certain types of narrative versus participants not exposed to those narratives, Kurt Braddock and James Dillard (2016) found that (1) narratives could be reliably characterized as cohesive, causal sequences of events based on the purposeful actions of characters; (2) the beliefs, attitudes, and behaviors of the people in the studies who had been exposed to the media in question started to align with the messages of the narratives; and (3) the participants in the studies were affected irrespective of the form of the narrative, whether a written document or audiovisual film. This landmark study verifies the importance of studying militant communication. The question now is this: How does such messaging work?

Kurt Braddock and John Horgan (2016) have argued that militant narratives induce certain psychological mechanisms that should inform our process of constructing counter-narratives. For example, Abu Talha is a parasocial character, a human who appears in the media (like celebrities, athletes, and other public figures) to whom a media consumer responds as if they were in a typical social relationship (Giles 2002). We know that when individuals develop attachments to parasocial characters and perceive similarities with them, they can forge relationships at a distance and feel transported into their world (Brown 2015). I admired Abu Talha's bravery and perceived a physical similarity with him, and these factors transported me into his world. I was shocked, even saddened, at his death. This inculcation of emotion, I contend, is one way that IS persuades recruits. I wrote a book on the Taliban's texts (Aggarwal 2016) and never felt attached to its characters even though it produced videos in languages I speak natively. IS media is persuasive in a different way. What can a sustained engagement with the group's media teach us about its multifaceted approach to language and persuasion?

In the great works on IS published so far, none has placed the group's media front and center to analyze the cultural and psychological processes of its changing discourse. To take a few examples, Abdel Bari Atwan (2015) and Jessica Stern and J. M. Berger (2015) have covered the group's online activities but did not isolate the specific psychological mechanisms of persuasion through which IS media inspires attacks. Atwan (2015) writes of IS's English-language periodical: "Issue four of *Dabiq* called on Western followers to attack in the West. Almost immediately, in May 2014, twenty-nine-year-old Mehdi Nemmouche opened fire on visitors to the Jewish museum in Brussels, Belgium, killing three" (189). The cultural psychiatrist wants to know what about this particular media is so persuasive in inciting violence. Similarly, William McCants (2015), Brian Fishman (2016), and Fawaz Gerges (2016) have examined aspects of the group's evolution but have not focused on its changing media discourses throughout history to incite violent thoughts, emotions, and behaviors, which prove its capacity to adapt and refine its persuasion strategies. Finally, and perhaps most foreign to scholars outside the field of mental health, none of these studies has related shifts in the group's cultural identity to the psychological processes involved in persuasive messaging. These are not criticisms: No author can cover all aspects of a complex phenomenon like terrorism. Instead, it points to the potential academic and policy contributions that cultural psychiatrists can make to a science of militant persuasion, messaging, and counter-messaging through a systematic analysis of these variables.

Patrick Cockburn's (2015) passage in the epigraph reminds us that IS has disseminated narratives to attract recruits though the internet, thus circumventing Iraqi and Syrian state controls on information. IS challenges claims of governance made by the Iraqi and Syrian governments: As an extralegal organization with territorial control that competes with nation-states (Comaroff and Comaroff 2006), IS markets itself as a provider of protection, dispenser of justice, and fashioner of a new social order based on its interpretations of Islamic law. Its competition with the Iraqi and Syrian governments is evident in bureaucratic texts related to governance and administration. Throughout its manifestations, the group has propagated messages of violence to change the thoughts, emotions, and behaviors—that is, the psychology—of people. What's going on culturally and psychologically in these texts such that people respond violently? We don't have to agree with messaging, but we must take these texts seriously if we want policy-relevant research. This is a pressing need since many have ridiculed the U.S. Department of State's counter-messaging as sarcastic and ineffective. Videos that warned would-be militants that joining ISIS would get them killed backfired when such promises were instead perceived as guarantees of martyrdom (Cooper 2016). Hundreds of Muslim scholars and thought leaders have denounced IS as completely unrepresentative of their faith ("Open Letter to Dr. Ibrahim Awwad Al-Badri, Alias 'Abu Bakr Al-Baghdadi'" 2014), but that has not stopped IS's recruitment efforts, media production, or attacks around the world. We need to combat the group's ideas, which is possible only through a deep, longitudinal involvement with its texts.

The Islamic State as Mediating Disorder

The volume of IS media output is overwhelming: The terrorism researcher Aaron Zelin (2015) discovered that IS once disseminated 123 media releases in just seven days, all in Arabic. The second most used language was English, with 8 releases (6.5 percent). Pictures constituted 63 percent of the content (77 releases), followed by videos at about 20 percent (24 releases) and written texts from periodicals such as the English-language *Dabiq* at about 5 percent (6 releases). An analysis of 1.5 million tweets from Syria in 2012 and 2013 during the civil war showed that secular revolutionaries and moderates posted more content than violent Islamists, though IS supporters posted the most Islamist content (O'Callaghan et al. 2014). Slick videos, images from flying drones, and messages posted in many different languages have motivated militants to migrate to IS's territories and expand its caliphate (Shane and Hubbard 2014). IS's online posters respond quickly to developments abroad, especially American policies on Iraq, through dozens of statements each month (Kimmage and Ridolfo 2007). Rapid sharing across Twitter and Instagram networks spread IS's apocalyptic worldview (Berger 2015a), and the disproportionate ratio of audiovisual to literary texts is intended to recruit a new generation of millennial youth who watch, rather than read, texts (Gates and Podder 2015). IS has created a social media application called "The Dawn of Good Tidings" to retweet hashtags on Twitter, and its followers have mastered "Twitter storms" for publicity (Farwell 2014; Stern and Berger 2015). It has repurposed Zello, an application for smartphones and computers for sharing audio files, to disseminate speeches from leaders and sermons from supporters (Weiss and Hassan 2015). After crackdowns on Facebook, YouTube, and Twitter, it switched to using encrypted messaging applications like WhatsApp, Kik, Surespot, and Telegram, through which it publicizes claims for attacks (Berger 2015b; Callimachi 2016). IS has constructed a virtual media empire.

How can we make our way through this material analytically? Given its sheer volume, Zelin (2015) has suggested that only a book could decode the IS archive. I agree. I've discerned distinct cultural and psychological changes in the group's discourse, which have not yet been presented in a systematic fashion, and restrictions remain on the amount of text that can be analyzed. Seven years before Zelin's characterization of IS output, the researcher Anne Stenersen (2008) noted that the number of written instruction manuals, encyclopedias, videos, and online periodicals would be impossible to analyze completely: "To assess the amount of material available online would be very time consuming, if possible at all" (219). Since then, the American government has periodically announced the discovery of thousands of documents occupying terabytes of data inaccessible to the public (Schmitt 2015, 2016a). Just from the Syrian city of Manbij, coalition forces retrieved twenty terabytes of data, equivalent to the contents of more than twenty million books (Schmitt 2016b)!

Since analyzing all the group's texts would be impossible, we can use principles of qualitative research to organize a reproducible, defensible sampling strategy for its texts. I am sympathetic to big-data approaches that are getting off the ground to integrate images and texts through automated data mining and information visualization (O'Halloran et al. 2016), but this serves a different purpose than for qualitative research in psychiatry, which explores and interprets subjective meanings, experiences, and realities from an insider's perspective (Whitley and Crawford 2005). In qualitative research (Patton 2002)—especially the text-based research tradition in cultural psychiatry (Littlewood 1999; Aggarwal et al. 2013)—only one case study may be need for analysis if it deepens our understanding of a unique phenomenon. For instance, analyzing one video known to have sparked violence is more useful in gaining an understanding the psychological mechanisms of persuasion than analyzing many videos whose impact on viewers is unclear. In these instances, single studies can provide us with targets for clear, effective intervention (Riley et al. 2017). In the absence of single case studies that exhibit an obviously unique phenomenon, others suggest that analyzing a minimum of four data specimens can elicit general themes of a cultural phenomenon—in this case, the psychological processes of persuasion that instigate violence— provided the texts come from a distinct cultural group (Guest, Bunce, and Johnson 2006; Onwuegbuzie and Collins 2007). For this reason, I list in each chapter whether a particular text, such as a speech, video, article, or bureaucratic document, is exemplary as a unique case study or is representative of a larger dataset.[1] I deliberately select data that are different—what we call maximum variation sampling—to identify common themes across data (Patton 2002). I believe this technique is more analytically useful, as it allows the researcher to go out of the way methodologically to inspect thematic convergences and divergences in media. I assume that IS's authors constitute a closed self-monitoring group with an identifiable culture and psychology distinct from those of other groups (Shweder 1999a) and that dissemination with the group's imprimatur (such as the flag in its videos) reflects official viewpoints.

It's worth asking: Why has IS produced so much media? I believe it is to mediate disorder, and I use this theory to study the evolution of IS's cultural and psychological discourses of violence. Regarding the term *mediated disorder*, I chose the word *mediated* as it consists of two meanings to explain how disorder occurs. First, *mediated* highlights the group's consistent embrace of cultural media production—jihadist videos, taped speeches, written periodicals, internal correspondence, and bureaucratic documents, among other genres of text—to create psychological responses. Many of us working at the intersection of culture and psychology have been slow to realize that media occupies a central position in our lives (Cartwright and Crowder 2017; Collins, Durington, and Gill 2017). We use the internet to find new ways to work, play, and exist, so treating media as insignificant when it comes time for our research blinds us to how it mediates cultural and psychological activities (Nardi 2015). The internet transforms individual and group identities—how we view ourselves and how others view us—since users position themselves in online communities (Kirmayer, Raikhel, and Rahimi 2013). Such positioning affects thoughts, emotions, and behaviors (Bhui and Ibrahim 2013), as well demonstrated by IS in its successful recruitment of foreign fighters like Abu Talha Al-Yamani ("the Yemeni"), whose nom de guerre indicates that he is not from Iraq or Syria. A 2006 financial spreadsheet from a precursor of the group known as the Islamic State of Iraq (ISI) itemizes expenses for digital cameras and special production equipment (NMEC-2007-632533). For over a decade, IS has recognized that media can alter cultural and psychological life. It's time we caught up.

These cultural media supply different types of data. For instance, videos showcase linguistic and nonlinguistic aspects of culture such as symbols, practices, institutions, and forms of social organization in multisensory fashion, which written texts cannot do (Heath, Hindmarsh, and Luff 2010; Chen 2012). Similarly, non-narrative hymns like *Jundullah*, a genre known in Arabic as *nashīds*, use classical Arabic vocabularies and meters to portray a fantasy life of jihad (Creswell and Haykel 2015). *Nashīds* deal with themes of battle, martyrdom, mourning, and praise, recruiting people through catchy tunes and poetry (Said 2012). Muslim youth in European countries have downloaded *nashīds* from social media, leading to shifts in personal identity toward valuing religion over ethnicity, nationality, and country of ancestry (Rosowsky 2011). Finally, non-narrative bureaucratic documents may not have casual sequences of events, but they list shared meanings, practices, and symbols within institutional contexts (Heyman 2004; Hull 2012). By analyzing how different texts mediate disorder, I triangulate findings across data and minimize biases that could accrue from using a single type of data (Bowen 2009), responding to recent calls for comparing data across media platforms (Conway 2017). The theory of mediated disorder reveals how militant groups like IS aspire to mold individual psychologies through cultural media.

The second meaning *mediated* conveys relates to the fact that, in all cases, we see that IS demands the right to mediate between individuals and society, inhabiting an intermediary position to stir up violence against others. IS's interpretations of Islam demand that individuals reject the nation-state's authority; this approach belongs to a historical trajectory in which traditional religious elites have lost power. The spread of the printing press in eighteenth-century Muslim-majority societies allowed lay citizens to debate the meanings of Sharia—the corpus of texts that constitute Islamic law, what Muslims believe to be God's word in the Quran, and the sayings and doings of the prophet Muhammad in collections of Hadith—with unforeseen consequences. Islamic law has gone from a technical type of knowledge requiring expert training that only judges were conversant with to a comprehensive set of habits and practices that many now see as necessary to live life as a good Muslim (Robinson 1993). Islamic legal scholars who formerly exuded authority now compete with individuals who use the internet to publicize their views (Eickelman and Salvatore 2002). This has been true of militants who challenge historical interpretations of religious texts, since there are few barriers to internet access and there are higher degrees of interactivity between producers and consumers of online media than of traditional print media (Anderson 2003; Weimann 2004). Despite their varying geographies and causes, all online militants incite violence (Tsfati and Weimann 2002), and violent behaviors interest mental health professionals like me, since our field was founded to develop risk assessments that separate dangerous populations from civilians (Foucault 2008), a medical function we continue to perform today.

The word *disorder* also has a double meaning. I'm aware that the word can be used to pathologize whole groups of people when used uncritically. That is not my intention. I've addressed the dangers of this approach in the mental health literature elsewhere (Aggarwal 2015), so I do not address the question of pathology among suicide attackers in this book. Instead, I use *disorder* nonclinically to connect individual psychology with cultural context. As the psychiatric anthropologist Byron Good and colleagues (2008) write,

> A benefit of linking "disorders" to "subjectivity" is the potential for increased understanding of the lived experience of persons caught up in complex, threatening, and uncertain conditions of the contemporary world. Such a linking provides a focus on the historical genealogy of normative conceptions associated with order and disorder, rationality and pathology, and brings analytic attention to everyday lives and routine practices instantiated in complex institutions (11).

We may abhor what IS stands for, but our moral commitments do not negate the fact that it has emerged in complex, threatening, and uncertain conditions in the contemporary Middle East. Similarly, Good (2012) has elsewhere described subjectivity as the psychological shaping of selves in relation to culturally distinctive life worlds. *Mediated disorder* focuses our attention on a two-step process that, I contend, is one of IS's primary communication goals: (1) Use media to disorder the thoughts and emotions of individuals; and (2) convince individuals of its cultural justifications to behave violently. This process corresponds to our understanding of violent radicalization as distinct cognitive/emotional and behavioral phases whereby people support militancy *and* act violently (Horgan 2008a, 2009). The term *mediated disorder* helps us characterize the thoughts and emotions that are mediated through texts and that can ultimately persuade people to commit violence.

A Framework from Cultural Psychiatry to Investigate Mediated Disorder

I've mentioned the words *culture* and *psychology* several times. Now it's time for definitions. Both terms have had long careers in the social sciences (Jayasuriya 2008), so it's essential to anchor these analyses in consistent variables that allow for cross-chapter comparison. I accept Paul Rabinow and William Sullivan's (1987) definition of culture as "the shared meanings, practices, and symbols that constitute the human world" (7). As they describe qualitative research, "the aim is not to uncover universals or laws but rather to explicate context and world" (Rabinow and Sullivan 1987, 14). Cultural psychiatry explicates cultural groups on their terms—from a native informant's point of view—before analyzing them against theories from secular, Euro-American, academic contexts (Kleinman 1987; Kleinman 1980; Aggarwal 2015). I also accept the cultural psychologist Richard Shweder's (1999a) broad definition of psychology as "perceiving, categorizing, reasoning, remembering, feeling, wanting, choosing, and communicating" (66). For the purposes of this book, I collapse Shweder's definition into thoughts (perceiving, reasoning), emotions (feeling, wanting), and behaviors (categorizing, remembering, choosing, and communicating). One agenda of cultural psychiatry is "the study of the way cultural traditions and social practices regulate, express, transform, and permute the human psyche" (Shweder 1999b, 1). To do this, we scrutinize thoughts, emotions, and behaviors (psychology) "embodied in socially inherited institutions, practices, artifacts, technologies, art forms, texts, and modes of discourse" (culture) (Shweder 1999b, 26). We represent other cultures as accurately as possible to avoid the biases that erupt from judging others first through our cultural norms and values (Kleinman 1988a). To do this, I reproduce images and quotations to let IS's authors speak for themselves. When the texts are in other languages, I aim for *dynamic equivalence* through translations that make sense, convey the spirit of the original text, have an easy and natural form, and produce similar responses in readers (Nida 2000). To be sure, these conceptions of culture are psychological in nature compared with other social science traditions that theorize culture as emanating from the environment or produced from political and economic structures, but they elicit consistent standards for comparisons across time and place (Good 1994).

My training in cultural psychiatry convinces me of the value of analyzing culture through language. Psychiatrists introduced "talk therapy" to the world (Freud 1990). We have conceived of the conscious mind and the hidden unconscious as structured through language (Lacan 1997). We take language seriously since all our acts of comprehension, diagnosis, and treatment rest on soliciting language and interpreting it in professional frameworks (Kleinman 1996). All humans communicate through language (Sinha 2000), which is the primary means through which people in all societies share meanings (Wan 2012). I accept the philosopher Michel Foucault's (1991) premise that throughout history, people in power have produced knowledge through language that reinforces their social positions, which can be defined as official discourse. Studying discourse by characterizing language use reveals how knowledge is defined, how people jockey for social positions, and how ideas circulate in society (Foucault 1991; Fairclough 1992, 2001), assuming some members in a culture dominate others by controlling communication. I assume that the world inside texts captures the world outside (Fairclough 2001), that texts are socially transmitted if they pass through two or more minds (Farr 1998), and that texts consist of communication practices with the power to persuade others of how to interpret the world (Moscovici 1990). IS controls channels of communication, transmits texts socially, and persuades people of its interpretation of the world, fulfilling these conditions.

Discourse analysis illustrates how people in power use language to influence thoughts, emotions, and behaviors. In political psychology, discourse analysts have shown that language conveys group ideologies and influences public opinion through texts such as newspapers, speeches, and interviews (Gamson and Herzog 1999; Weltman and Billig 2001; Perrin 2005; De Castella, McGarty, and Musgrove 2009; Gray and Durrheim 2013), including within militant groups (Rothenberger, Müller, and Elmezeny, 2018). In political science and international relations, discourse analysis has pushed scholars to disentangle the relationships among culture, ideology, and practices during state formation and exercises of power (Rose and Miller 1992; Barry, Osborne, and Rose 1996; Jessop 2001, 2010; Lemke 2007; Vu 2010). This is a task to which IS is committed, as we shall see from chapter 5 onward when I discuss how the group has shifted its identity toward governance. Finally, scholars of religion have promoted discourse analyses to illustrate how particular knowledge, beliefs, and practices become authoritative over others (Asad 2003; Soares and Osella 2009), a major endeavor for IS since it must find ways to authorize its interpretations of Islam over others. Analyzing textual discourse can demystify the interrelationships among language, culture, and psychology that are transmitted within social groups, including IS.

Discourse analysis is an approach to discovering power-knowledge relationships through language, but it doesn't give us cultural or psychological variables for comparative analysis (Fairclough 1992, 2001). Here, cultural psychiatry offers us a distinctive contribution to investigate IS's mediated disorder. A fundamental dilemma for cultural psychiatrists has been how to analyze thoughts, emotions, and behaviors considered normal or abnormal across societies, especially when people come from backgrounds other than our own (Devereux 2000). Indeed, cross-cultural studies of violence—especially protest suicides or suicide attacks inherently endowed with public meanings—have underscored the need to interpret the cultural justifications for such actions by paying attention to discourse signified in local knowledge categories (Staples and Widiger 2012). To that end, cultural psychiatrists have created the Outline for Cultural Formulation (OCF), a framework to evaluate psychology in cultural context through four domains (American Psychiatric Association 1994, 2013). Based on more than forty years of research, the OCF is the most widely used cultural assessment tool in mental health and provides a comprehensive method to situate the construction of group culture, individual psychology, and social context against the social and behavioral sciences (Lewis-Fernández et al. 2014). In working with populations—even those who invite strongly negative emotions (Winnicott 1949)—we've learned to respond by listening as openly and curiously as possible, processing our personal reactions when they can affect our analyses, and delving into how our responses may be similar to and different from those of others (Kirmayer 2008). Next, I describe the OCF's four domains and the adjustments I make in this book, as illustrated through the example of the video featuring Abu Talha.

1. *Cultural identity*, defined as one's conception of his or her place in the world based on sharing meanings, practices, and symbols with a group (Mezzich et al. 2009). We used to think of cultural identity through demographic traits of group characteristics like race, ethnicity, country of origin, language, religion, spirituality, gender, and age (Lu, Lim, and Mezzich 1995). Over time, we have come to appreciate that identities can be inherited in families, acquired throughout life such as with exposure to the internet, and multiple in nature (Bibeau 1997; Aggarwal 2012; Nesbitt-Larking and Kinnvall 2012). Militant groups try to fuse individual with group identities so that individuals internalize the group's mission of targeting outsiders (Moghadam 2003; Post, Sprinzak, and Denny 2003; Silke 2003; Mishal and Rosenthal 2005; Post 2005; Kruglanski et al. 2009). We can use this domain to trace the specific meanings, practices, and symbols that IS uses to represent insiders—prototypical members who embody group norms, core values transmitted to and demanded of all members—and outsiders (Huddy 2001).

Abu Talha acts as a prototypical member to convey an in-group identity. He sings, "Our path (*darb*) is the straight path from the Quran's guidance." Use of the word *the* rather than *a* before *straight* connotes singularity, that "ours" is *the* only possible path. The single source of religion invoked is the Quran. We don't hear about other ways of making religious meanings to interpret the world, such as nonviolent interpretations of the Quran, exegeses from qualified religious scholars, other texts within the Islamic tradition such as Hadith, or consultation with family or community members. IS jostles for social positioning by communicating that there is only one path possible based on the Quran's guidance to Muslims, which it alone wields the power to interpret.

2. *Cultural conceptualizations of distress*, defined as the communication of specific thoughts, emotions, and behaviors (Mezzich et al. 2009). We've known that explanations come in the form of either narratives with casual sequences of events (Kleinman 1980) or non-narrative expressions that communicate a sense of meaning-making such as colloquial idioms, statements, or analogies between past and present experiences (Groleau, Young, and Kirmayer 2006). I make my first adjustment to the OCF here. We have used the OCF as a research tool to examine psychology in settings in which there is no pathology simply to understand how people construct understandings of themselves, others, and their realities (Hinton and Hinton 2016). Rather than assume there is any "illness" or "distress," I use this domain more broadly to dissect IS's media discourses that propagate violent thoughts, emotions, and behaviors. When there is a narrative structure or multistep argument, I identify initial premises, conclusions, and inferences that link premises to conclusions (Walton 2007). I begin by deductively interpreting all such discourses according to the psychologist Robert Cialdini's (1993) mechanisms of persuasion, which he defines as "social influence," through media communication: (1) drawing contrasts; (2) establishing reciprocity with the audience by offering them something so they feel obligation; (3) using the audience's arguments against it or forcing it to accept initial propositions; (4) presenting evidence of what other people think as social proof to influence actions; (5) liking the person delivering the message; (6) invoking authority; and (7) claiming that the possibility of future scarcity should motivate particular actions in the present. Because each IS text consists of thousands of words that would be impossible to reproduce, I analyze only discourse that relates mechanisms of persuasion to culture and psychology

to balance rigor with transparency in understanding the phenomenon of my central interest (Yardley 2000). I also analyze mechanisms of persuasion specific to each media platform based on the growing recognition in cultural psychiatry that communication consists of *content* at the level of thoughts and emotions, as well as *context*; that is, the medium through which the exchange occurs (Aggarwal et al. 2016).

Abu Talha's video exhibits several mechanisms of psychological persuasion. First, by depicting Abu Talha smiling and singing into the camera, IS tries to cultivate his likeability among viewers. Next, Abu Talha tries to force us to accept his violent thought of attacks leading to salvation: "The martyr goes to the paradise of God from His path without ever swerving." The use of *martyr* indicates that Abu Talha and his comrades expect to be killed, thus deactivating their personal prohibitions against self-death. Since the terror attacks of September 11, 2001, psychiatrists and psychologists have assumed that people who seek out self-death (such as suicide attackers) must suffer from pathology, an artifact of mental health developing within a post-Enlightenment, Christian intellectual milieu that morally and legally prohibited people from taking their own lives lest they violate the will of God (Aggarwal 2015). Instead, IS's fighters have acted as "devoted actors" who sacrifice themselves to defend the group's cultural identity rather than maximize their personal safety or material gains (Ginges et al. 2011; Sheikh, Gómez, and Atran 2016). The text expresses clear determination: "We will never swerve from the course of faith." *Never* implies perennial perseverance, that obstacles will not be hindrances to reaching God. Finally, we have clear social proof of violent behavior in the form of the screenshot of Abu Talha's death.

3. *Psychosocial stressors and cultural features of vulnerability and resilience*, defined as the context of thoughts, emotions, and behaviors in relation to social relationships and institutions (Mezzich et al. 2009). Cultural groups create expectations for how individual members are to think, feel, and behave, which distinguish in-groups from out-groups (Tajfel 1970, 1974; Turner 1982). These expectations circulate interpersonally to define normal versus abnormal psychological phenomena, and cultural psychiatrists look to social relationships to situate unfamiliar thoughts, emotions, and behaviors as transmitted within groups (Aggarwal and Rohrbaugh 2011). Here, I analyze how IS discourse maintains in-group psychological norms within relationships. By employing the first-person plural—"we will never

swerve"; "our path is the straight path"—IS conveys expectations for all its members. Images of men smiling and laughing atop military convoys and the presence of two men in fatigues surrounding Abu Talha reinforce in-group norms of violence as socially desirable. The absence of hierarchy, of leaders dictating to followers, projects a message of egalitarianism.

In cultural psychiatry, we know that social institutions can also dictate how people think, feel, and behave (Saris 1995; Renshon and Duckitt 1997). In IS's text with Abu Talha, there is no discernible institutional presence. However, other texts from IS and its precursors have claimed that it is a state with formal institutions. Administrative, educational, and judicial institutions mold individuals into obedient citizens by delimiting acceptable and unacceptable thoughts, emotions, and behaviors (Abrams 1988). This domain allows us to analyze the critical role of institutions in maintaining violent in-group norms, which will become evident in chapters 6 and 7.

4. *Cultural elements of the patient-clinician relationship*, defined as the psychiatrist's reflections on how his or her engagements affect the analysis. Here is where I make my second adjustment to the OCF, since we are examining texts, not patients, here. As European powers colonized Africa, Asia, and the Middle East from the eighteenth through the twentieth centuries, anthropological and psychiatric research served the desire of politicians and bureaucrats to subjugate foreign populations (Geertz 1973; Littlewood 2002). In recognition that the act of representing foreign cultures and psychologies bears this historical legacy of knowledge–power differences (Foucault 1972; Kleinman 1988b), cultural psychiatrists have warned that biases can taint our analyses (Kirmayer 2008). Instead, our capacity to experience and reflect on emotions can improve our understanding of others (Smith and Kleinman 2010). We do this by first representing the other's thoughts, emotions, and behaviors accurately and then delineating our own academic or personal engagements (Comas-Díaz and Jacobsen 1991).

In texts with protagonists such as videos, I use this domain to understand how IS casts characters to elicit psychological responses within its audiences. William Brown's (2015) systematic synthesis of scholarship on persuasion through parasocial characters specifies four types of psychological mechanism (274–76): (1) *transportation*: the process of becoming wholly absorbed into a narrative during media consumption, which begins when media consumers think and feel like a person in a narrative world; (2) *parasocial interaction*: the process of developing an imaginary relationship with a mediated persona both during and after media consumption; (3) *identification*: the process of conforming to the perceived identity of a mediated persona both during and after media consumption; (4) *worship*: the process of expressing devotion, commitment, and love to a mediated persona both during and after media consumption. In processing my emotions, I acknowledge my absorption in Abu Talha's narrative world (transportation), the development of an imaginary relationship with him during and after media consumption (parasocial interaction), and the sharing—even if ephemeral—of his attitudes toward bravery and fighting injustice (identification). Analyzing the role of persuasion through parasocial characters elevates our understanding of IS's media and supplements other formalized aspects of analysis such as translating Arabic poetry.

To summarize, Abu Talha's video features a prototypical group member who defines Islam strictly through adherence to the Quran's guidance. He exudes positive affect, invokes the Quran's authority, and establishes incontrovertible propositions to justify his act of seeking death. The video features him surrounded by other men to convey that Abu Talha's violent thoughts, emotions, and behaviors focused on martyrdom are maintained in IS's social relationships. Finally, the video invites us to develop a relationship with him and become absorbed in his world such that our thoughts, emotions, and behaviors align with his. This is merely one way that IS uses videos to promote a multimodal experience of sight and sound that mediates disorder, and we will see in the chapters ahead how IS has diversified its portfolio of persuasion over time.

The Layout of This Book

In this book, I use the OCF framework to trace cultural and psychological themes in the media of IS and its predecessors, whereas in my last book, I organized chapters thematically. Why? First, the Taliban has presented itself as a unified movement since its inception in the 1990s, in contrast to IS, which has advertised its changing composition. For example, it made sense to present a psychocultural assessment of Mullah Omar's leadership since he wielded tight control over the Taliban for almost two decades. The same does not apply to IS, whose leadership has changed with the death of its leaders. Zelin (2014) provided an early typology of the group's evolution, which I use to organize the chapters of this book:

- From 1999 to 2004, the *Jamā'at Al-Tawhīd W'al-Jihād* (the Organization of Monotheism and Jihad [OMJ])
- From 2004 to 2006, *Al Qāida Fī Ardu-l Furatain* (Al Qaeda in the Land of Two Rivers,[2] also known as Al Qaeda in Iraq [AQI])
- From 2006 to 2007, the *Majlis Shūra Al-Mujāhidīn* (the Assembly of the Mujahideen Council [AMC]), which created *Al-Dawla Al-Islamīyya Fī Al-'Irāq* (Islamic State of Iraq [ISI]) from 2007 to 2013
- From 2013 to 2014, *Al-Dawla Al-Islamīyya Fī Al-'Irāq Wa'l-Shām* (Islamic State of Iraq and Syria [ISIS or ISIL])
- From 2014 onward, *Al-Dawla Al-Islamīyya* (Islamic State [IS])

Second, we have media from the earliest days of the group, from the OMJ era, whereas the Taliban's earliest texts have not been publicly available. Adopting a chronological framework helps us track the diffusion of the group's identity, the process by which people deliberately spread shared meanings, practices, and symbols within and across generations, as recognized through material artifacts, such as texts (Levitt 1998; Whiten, Caldwell, and Mesoudi 2016). As a cultural psychiatrist, I want to know how IS has built and diffused its culture through its media, persuading people to commit violence. We have thousands of primary sources now—we just need to interpret them without taking the group's culture and psychology for granted. Cultural psychiatry—and its close cousins cultural psychology and psychiatric anthropology—equips us with tools to analyze militant culture and psychology through media in real time, improving our practical understanding of these groups while presenting new horizons for theory development.

In fact, the cultural psychiatry perspective allows us to frame the group's evolution within classic scholarship in cultural mental health (concepts italicized below). We can explore how OMJ created a new cultural identity through *social representations*; how it joined with Al Qaeda to form the AQI through *acculturation*; how it joined with multiple groups to form a *common group identity* during the formation of AMC; how it reoriented shared meanings to include governance during the ISI phase through *identity shift*; how a militant identity diffused institutionally through *cultural group selection* in ISIS territories; and how IS's militant identity has penetrated families through *social suffering*. These are obviously not the only theories in social science that provide a framework for understanding the group; other scholarly traditions and media data may inspire other paradigms. Still, the advantage of this framing is that it allows us to use theories from cultural mental health to analyze other militant groups beyond IS for cross-cultural comparison. We can trace how changes to the group's identity relate to the promotion of violent thoughts, emotions, and behaviors that are reinforced in social relationships and institutions. We've learned from the social sciences that cultural identities shift over time as new meanings, practices, and symbols enter society (Moscovici and Marková 1998; Howarth 2002); that explanations for thoughts, emotions, and behaviors (such as justifications for violence) change in relation to life circumstances (Good and Good 1980; Young 1981; Groleau, Young, and Kirmayer 2006); and that group norms for thinking, feeling, and behaving also evolve, especially as people within groups disagree (Turner and Oakes 1986). By examining the culture-psychology interplay historically, we can determine which shared meanings, practices, and symbols (culture), as well as which thoughts, emotions, and behaviors (psychology), endure (Lewis-Fernández 1996; Lehman, Chiu, and Schaller 2004; Carpenter-Song, Schwallie, and Longhofer 2007) as the basis for persuading audiences. This hones our counter-messaging strategies by targeting stable cultural and psychological traits for maximal impact, and the OCF furnishes us with valid criteria for historical comparison. We'll see in the next chapter that IS's first group, OMJ, had to create a militant cultural identity de novo in response to the 2003 invasion of Iraq to disorder the psychology of its audience.

TWO

The Organization of Monotheism and Jihad

Constructing a Militant Cultural Identity

WHERE DID THE culture of the Islamic State come from? We have little systematic research on the origins of its culture and psychology. This may be because researchers have only recently turned their attention to how militant cultures justify violent thoughts, emotions, and behaviors. Let's take representative examples. David Kilcullen (2007) writes,

> Cultures—organizational, ethnic, national, religious or tribal—provide key links in the global jihad. Cultures determine how each actor in an insurgency perceives the actions of the others, and generate unperceived cultural boundaries that limit their freedom of action. Culture imbues otherwise random or apparently senseless acts with meaning and subjective rationality (612–13).

Thomas Hegghammer (2017) defines jihadi culture as "products and practices that do something other than fill the basic military needs of jihadi groups" (5), acknowledging that "cultural products and practices serve as *emotional persuasion tools* that reinforce and complement the cognitive persuasion work done by doctrine" (16, original emphasis). Samuel Perry and Jerry Long (2016) argue, "The beginnings of a culture offer strong points of identification for its participants" (6), recommending longitudinal studies that trace the effects of past media on current productions.

I agree with these authors, and the Outline for Cultural Formulation (OCF) accounts for culture's relationship to individual psychologies that are maintained as in-group norms through social relationships and institutions. The anthropologists Michael Taarnby and Lars Hallundbaek (2008) note, "Jihadism does not have a religious, cultural or historical origin to draw on. It is an invention despite any insistence to the opposite" (4). Cultural psychiatrists want to know *how* cultural groups arise to understand their psychologies. We treat culture as a process to interpret the world, commonly through social representations that disseminate through institutions (places of work, worship, and leisure), belief systems (science, religion, morality, or philosophy), and languages (Moscovici 1973, 1994; Hogg and Reid 2006). How did IS's first group, the Organization for Monotheism and Jihad (OMJ), deploy social representations to establish a shared culture through which individuals violently interpreted the world?

Moreover, what about OMJ's Jordanian founder, Abu Musab Al-Zarqawi (real name Ahmed Fadeel Al-Khalayleh), was so persuasive? IS members revere him; in the English-language periodical *Dabiq*, an article praises him as his era's "reviver" (*mujaddid*) for implementing a methodology for jihad in strict conformity with Islamic law ("From Hijrah to Khilafah" 2014). Another article views him as a visionary: "Shaykh Abu Mus'ab az-Zarqawi (*rahimahullah*) [may God have mercy on him] anticipated the expansion of the blessed jihad from Iraq into Sham" ("Until It Burns the Crusader Armies in Dabiq" 2014). However, he hardly seems like a group prototype worth emulating. He drank alcohol and was arrested for several crimes, including rape, before traveling to Afghanistan for jihad against the Soviet Union at the age of twenty-three (Gettleman 2006) where he worked on jihadist newsletters (Weiss and Hassan 2015). An interview he gave to Al Qaeda's Al-Furqan Media years later shows how his involvement in media disordered his own thoughts, emotions, and behaviors: "We would get magazines on jihad and [a] few videos that effected [sic] me a lot and made me among those who cared enough to travel to the land of jihad in Afghanistan" (Al-Zarqawi 2006).

After returning to Jordan in 1992, Al-Zarqawi was imprisoned for attempting to overthrow the monarchy and fell under the sway of the scholar Abu Muhammad Al-Maqdisi (Wagemakers 2014). Following his release in amnesty, he plotted attacks against civilians and then fled to Afghanistan in 1999, setting up a camp with hundreds of fighters (Whitlock 2004; Weaver 2006). After the American invasion of Afghanistan in late 2001, he moved between Iraq and Iran to recruit militants for attacks in the Levant. Secretary of State

Colin Powell defended the invasion of Iraq by linking Saddam Hussein to Al Qaeda through Al-Zarqawi, who was convalescing in Baghdad at the time (Marquis 2004). Before OMJ, Al-Zarqawi had participated in at least three other militant organizations (Weiss and Hassan 2015; Gerges 2016), so how did he create a distinct group identity that has endured?

In this chapter, I look at shared representations through a discourse analysis of four texts—two speeches and two videos—in which Al-Zarqawi mediates disorder by appealing to group affiliations. In the first, he addresses his tribe, emphasizing the uniqueness of Islam; in the second, he reminds Sunnis of historical injustices from perceived enemies; in the third, he depicts militants in training; in the fourth, men avenge dishonor visited upon their families during the Iraq War. Through these differences, we can trace common meanings, practices, and symbols that Al-Zarqawi used as social representations to fashion a distinct cultural identity. Starting with OMJ lets us discern which elements of the group's culture and psychology have changed and which have stayed the same in IS's media through the OCF framework.

"A Message to the Tribes of the Banu Hasan"

Al-Zarqawi delivered his first speech on May 1, 2003, after the United States invaded Iraq. The speech is a unique case study in how Al-Zarqawi assembled preexisting social representations to construct a novel militant identity in the group's first media product. In this speech, titled "A Message to the Tribes of the Banu Hasan: Oh Nation, Respond to the Call of God," Al-Zarqawi addresses his own tribe, which claims descent from the prophet Muhammad's grandson Al-Hasan ibn Ali ibn Abu Talib (624–70 CE) and became the ruling elite of Mecca (Weiss and Hassan 2015; Steenbergen 2016). He lifts text from the Quran to begin his message:

In the name of God, the beneficent, the merciful. Praise be to God, the lord of the worlds, the beneficent, the merciful, the king of the day of judgment (*mālik yaum al-dīn*). Peace and prayers of God upon the one who was sent—a mercy for the worlds (*rahma li'l-'ālamīn*), a herald for all people (*nadhīr li'l-nās ajma'īn*)—and upon his family and his companions, the edge of his army (*al-gharr al-mayāmīn*), those who responded to God and his prophet and established the religion (*aqāmū al-dīn*) (17).

Al-Zarqawi (2003) takes key phrases from the Quran—"in the name of God, the beneficent, the merciful" and "king of the day of judgment"—to praise God, a literary technique known as *tahmīd*. The next phrases—"the one who was sent," "a mercy for the worlds"— reinforce Muhammad's exalted status as the messenger of Islam. Certain phrases end with the sound "-*īn*," a style of rhymed prose known as *saja'*, which has been part of Arabic literature since pre-Islamic times and thus reflects the nature of a preliterate oral society that developed rhyming schemes to remember poetry and information (Stewart 1990; Galander 2002). Classical Arabic orations begin with a *tahmīd* to God, praise for his prophet, and *saja'* as a style of persuasion (Qutbuddin 2008). By following this structure, Al-Zarqawi draws upon shared linguistic practices to address an in-group defined through shared meanings of revering God and honoring Muhammad.

Al-Zarqawi (2003) tries to persuade his audience in two key ways. He lays out propositions that he assumed his audience would accept and then invoked the authority of Quranic verses: "Indeed, the prophet of God—peace and prayers of God upon him—was a mercy for his nation, wanting guidance for them. He did not abandon goodness but rather showed them upon it [the guidance]. And there was no evil except to warn them of it" (18). After this, he cited the 128th verse of the Quran's ninth chapter, *Al-Tauba*, verbatim. Next, he states, "He impelled them to comply with His commands—may He be praised and exalted—and interested them in what God had by way of the great recompense and the great reward. He warned them against disobeying Him—may He be praised—and opposing his command" (18). He then cites the 153rd verse of the Quran's eighth chapter, *Al-Anfāl*, verbatim. Al-Zarqawi concludes this section by exclaiming, "God—may He be exalted—ordered his prophet Muhammad—peace and prayers of God upon him—to single out his nation and his tribes with a warning," and then citing the 214th verse of the Quran's twenty-sixth chapter, *Al-Shu'arā*, verbatim. This last thought employs a third mechanism of social persuasion: drawing contrasts with others. By citing Quranic verses stripped of context, Al-Zarqawi follows a tradition in Arabic rhetoric whereby speakers use the Quran to set up an equivalence of contexts between the past and present (Dähne 2001). Al-Zarqawi disorders the thoughts, emotions, and behaviors of his audience with a distinct chain of logic: The prophet meant the best for his nation → this nation must comply with God's commands → God ordered his prophet to distinguish his nation of believers.

Through Quranic verses, Al-Zarqawi exploits strong emotions such as fear of retribution and obedience to God's path.

After articulating these shared meanings of an identity built around religion, he contrasts ethnicities: "Oh nation! God had raised the Arabs with this religion . . . and rescued them with it from the darkness to the light. He took them with it from worshipping idols to worshipping the beneficent. And made them sovereign with it over humankind" (18–19). Since the Quran's revelation, Arab Muslims have linked their religion with ethnicity and language to form a hybrid in-group identity, which grew stronger after conquering and converting others such as North Africans and Persians (Suleiman 2003). He cites an influential scholar to lend authority to his words: "Worship is not limited to prayer, alms, fasting, and pilgrimage but it is greater than that and more encompassing. 'Worship' is as the Sheikh of Islam Ibn Taymiyya—may God have mercy on him—explained it: 'A noun aggregating all that God loves and accepts by way of explicit and implicit words and actions'" (19). Ibn Taymiyya (1263–1328) led an intellectual movement encouraging Muslims to base their understanding of religion only on the Quran and Hadith, rather than assuming that humans can reason through theological uncertainties, in order to avoid unwanted innovations (bid'a) that would deviate from the prophet Muhammad's practices (Abrahamov 1992; McAuliffe 2006). Al-Zarqawi exploits Ibn Taymiyya's reputation for textual orthodoxy to persuade his audience that he is interpreting religious texts correctly.

Al-Zarqawi (2003) named despised outsiders: "The enemies of God sympathize and help those among the polytheists from the east and west, among the Christians and Jews, and make compromises with them based on violating the sacred among the Muslims and their lands" (22). This proposition sets up a binary of "us versus them":

It is the Apache airplanes that bomb the Muslims who are the people suffering at the same time that it is the same airplanes killing our Muslim children and brothers in the womb. This is only to protect the security of Israel and to suppress any movement that has disturbed the sleep of the offspring of monkeys and pigs. Jordan is its safety valve and its firm bulwark. . . . And before this, Afghanistan—what do you know about Afghanistan? Where the people of oneness and faith gathered? To aid this religion and for jihad on the path of God. . . . There, the Jordanian forces fought movement after movement alongside the Crusader forces to extinguish the light of this blessed call. And drive it to its worst. Then, there is Iraq under the oppression of the Christians in their Crusader war (22–23).

With another chain of logic, Al-Zarqawi draws contrasts in identity and fans violent thoughts, emotions, and behaviors: The helpers of God adhere to God's call → they drive out those who attack *our* Muslim brothers and children → their attacks, which Jordan has supported, are intended only to support Israel → Jordan has also supported the Christian Crusaders in Afghanistan who are now in Iraq. Al-Zarqawi portrays jihadists as victims of the nation-state despite fulfilling God's calls. The word "our" before "children" and "brothers" grammatically enlists the audience. Dehumanization is one way that groups contrast themselves with each other during extreme conflicts (Haslam 2006), and to this end, Al-Zarqawi labels Israelis as "monkeys and pigs."

Al-Zarqawi (2003) recommends a single solution. He refers to Ibn Taymiyya's commentary on the eighty-fifth verse of the Quran's fourth chapter, *Al-Nisā*: "Whoso intercedes with a good intercession shall receive a share of it; whosoever intercedes with a bad intercession, he shall receive the like of it" (Arberry 1996, 112–13). Al-Zarqawi (2003) explains, "The intercessor is the one who helps another. And with him it becomes an intercession after it is done one by one. For this reason, it is explained—'a good intercession'—as assisting the believers with jihad. And 'a bad intercession' as assisting the infidels by killing the believers, as Ibn Jarir and Abu Sulaiman mentioned" (24). "Ibn Jarir" refers to Abu Jafar Muhammad Ibn Jarir Al-Ṭabari (839–923), an influential exegete of the Quran who believed that Muslims should emulate the first generation of Muhammad's companions (Stewart 2004). "Abu Sulaiman" refers to Abu Sulaiman Khalid ibn Al-Walid ibn Al-Mughirah Al-Makhzumi (585–642 CE), who reportedly fought a hundred battles, led Muslim armies to victory against the Byzantine and Sassanid Empires, and united the Levant and Iraq under the first caliphate, a system of governance ruled by a Muslim caliph (Akram 2004). Al-Zarqawi invokes the authority of the Quran and Ibn Jarir as mechanisms of psychological persuasion, recalling the prototype of Abu Sulaiman to justify violence.

Al-Zarqawi reinforces violent in-group norms through social relationships in two ways. First, he claims to be a sympathetic guide: "I swear to God, I am concerned that the Hellfire will befall you or that shame and dishonor will befall you on the day that possessions and children will not benefit you [Armageddon] except for what comes from God with a sound heart" (18). The Arabic word for "message" in the title of his speech is *risāla*, a literary genre in which an author provides advice and instruction based on references to the Quran (Allen 2000). Al-Zarqawi jockeys for social positioning by declaring his watch over the audience to ensure compliance with militant in-group norms. As a form of persuasion, he mentions Salahuddin/Saladin (1137/1138–1193), a historical figure who represented in-group norms that his audience's forefathers upheld and who he feels should be emulated now:

> Oh Nation! Come to your religion as it is your glory and your honor and the glory of your fathers and your grandfathers who leaned toward the nobility of self-illumination under the brigade of Salahuddin Ayyubi in Hatin and the nobility of participating in liberating Jerusalem with other tribes. Salahuddin apportioned the lands around Jerusalem to the tribes which participated with him for the sake of protecting them from the Crusaders (26).

The command "Come" insists on action. Lastly, Al-Zarqawi shames his audience by claiming they are not men if they do not act: "Where is your dignity, your manliness, and your concern for piety?" (27).

This is the first text in which the group that would later become IS mediated disorder. Al-Zarqawi's 2003 speech adheres to the style of classical Arabic rhetoric. In following a structure with a *tahmīd* to God, praise for his prophet, and *saja'*, literary tropes influence the style of his messaging. He creates a new cultural identity by positing shared emotions of reverence to God and his prophet, shared meanings of Quranic verses, and shared practices of jihad against multiple out-groups, including the nation-state. There are appeals to in-group identity at various levels: Muslims → Arabs → men. Al-Zarqawi demands that all Muslims fight Jews and Christians as during the Crusades, drawing contrasts to create enemy out-groups. He employs three mechanisms of social persuasion: stipulating propositions for his audience to accept, invoking the authority of Quranic verses and scholars, and highlighting his audience's uniqueness. In doing so, he plays on people's fear of God's retribution, obedience to God's commands, and shame at abandoning manliness. He incites violence by insisting that today's Muslims must emulate triumphant prototypes such as Salahuddin and Abu Sulaiman. Al-Zarqawi (2003) maintains violent group norms by warning his audience that he is watching over them and by exhorting them to fight like their ancestors.

"My Beloved Ummah"

In a speech on April 5, 2004, titled "My Beloved Ummah! The Best Ummah Was Produced for the People," Al-Zarqawi (2004a) addresses an ostensibly different group. Rather than the tribe Banu Hasan, he refers to ummah, the supranational community of Muslims (Roy 2004). This speech is a unique case study in how Al-Zarqawi appealed to a religious, rather than tribal, conception of the world among his listeners. Al-Zarqawi (2004a) introduces a variation on the *tahmīd* by treating the prophet Muhammad as a warrior: "I offer peace and prayers of God upon the one who was continuously fighting, who was sent with the sword between the hands of time to worship God alone" (76).

After asserting a militant identity for the prophet, he asserts a militant identity for his audience. Rather than "I" and "you," he says "we":

We inform you in happiness and companionship, bringing forth the best news about the greatest harm (*nikāya*) and intense massacre from the heroic jihadists against your enemy and their enemy. We praise God. We attack them as they attack us. We assault them as they assault us. We harm them as they harm us (77).

The last three sentences adopt identical syntax, known as parallelism (*izdiwāj*), through the use of antithetical pairs (*tibāq*) ("we" versus "they"), a style of making contrasts in classical Arabic oration (Qutbuddin 2008). Al-Zarqawi (2004a) exclaims, "We are not alone. Our dead are in paradise and their dead are in hell" (77), citing the 104th verse of the Quran's fourth chapter, *Al-Nisā*. This citation is another piece of rhetoric; it appeals to the authority of Islam's holiest text. In the first minute, Al-Zarqawi (2004a) organizes a militant cultural identity by articulating shared emotions of reverence for the prophet Muhammad and shared meanings of violence: God sent his messenger with a sword to fight → we fight the enemy → we go to paradise, and they go to hell. This chain mediates disorder by reassuring the audience that the deceased from among their in-group are guaranteed entry into heaven.

This speech differs from the last in that Al-Zarqawi (2004a) foments violence through different mechanisms of persuasion. Rather than cite the authority of Quranic verses after each proposition, he presents evidence of what other people know as social proof, the knowledge that OMJ's attacks have been successful:

We have torn apart their bodies in a number of areas: the United Nations in Baghdad, the coalition forces in Karbala, the Italians in Nasiriyah, the American forces at the Khalidiya Bridge, the American intelligence agencies in the Shahin Hotel, the Republican Palace in Baghdad, the CIA in the Hotel Rashid, and the Polish forces in Hillah (77).

Enumerating each attack underscores OMJ's multiple victories. Of note, the United Nations bombing led the U.S. Department of State (2004) to declare OMJ a terrorist group. Al-Zarqawi blames the American media for misrepresenting these operations in a contrast between "us" and "them": "We challenge the dishonest American media as it shows the reality of the destruction but hides the ruins which its forces have let loose" (78). As a third mechanism of persuasion, he cites the authority of Ibn Taymiyya: "It is as the Sheikh of Islam Ibn Taymiyya said in his message to the ruler of Cyprus: 'Indeed among the Muslims are people who sacrifice themselves, who exceed the rulers with their horses and knights' " (78).

Through yet another contrast, Al-Zarqawi (2004a) delineates core in-group values:

They tried before to cover up the truth of the battle, to disturb the banner of pure jihad, and they deluded the world that those who rebelled against them were the defeated remnants of the extinct administration and elements of the infidel Ba'athists such that the ummah did not come under the influence of the battle and did not share in the slaughter. This is a lie and dishonest. What it [the ummah] heard was heroism, sacrifice, greatness, and harming the enemies. Rather it was through the grace of God that your sons, and the knights of the ummah from among the migrants (muhājirūn) and helpers (anṣār) were prepared (78).

When Al-Zarqawi (2004a) associates "they" with words such as "cover up," "disturb," and "deluded," he does so to demonize the enemy. By "infidel Ba'athists," he refers to the Coalition Provisional Authority's decision in May 2003 to bar members of Saddam Hussein's Ba'ath Party from government positions and disband the 250,000-strong Iraqi Army, which created a pool of armed, unemployed men hostile to the coalition (Kirdar 2011). In contrast, he lists "heroism, sacrifice, greatness, and harm among the enemies" as core values of his in-group, equating "your sons" with brave knights. Muslims believe that in 622 CE, the prophet Muhammad escaped an assassination attempt at his house by traveling from Mecca to Medina; the Meccans who accompanied him were known as migrants (muhājirūn), whereas the local Medinans who hosted them were known as helpers (ansār) (Watt 1961). By investing new meanings for these terms, Al-Zarqawi draws on Islamic history to support foreign jihadists and their local supporters during the Iraq War, suggesting that Muslims have been attacked at home but can re-create their glorious history of defeating enemies.

To consolidate a Sunni identity, Al-Zarqawi (2004a) makes contrasts with multiple out-groups, beginning with the United States: "America came and it feared the growing Islamic expansion. The song of jihad at its highest volume terrified it. So the world shook and trembled in its grip. And it came to change the foundations of the ummah, to twist the meaning of its position, to change it paths" (79). He accuses the United States of supporting Israel: "America came to maintain the security of its stepdaughter (rabība) Israel and to extinguish any danger that could threaten it" (80). Historically, Arab society conferred social status based on bloodline within the tribe, and stepdaughters occupied a lowly position in the family (Khuri 1981); here, Al-Zarqawi suggests that the relationship between the United States and Israel is one of ignoble convenience. He condemns the Kurds for colluding with the Jews of Israel: "The Zionist client Americans petitioned Jalal Talabani from the murderous faction that follows Mossad living in the streets of Adnan in the center of Kirkuk, which tried quickly to destroy symbols and cadres of the Sunnis" (80). Finally, he denounces the Shia for their animosity toward Sunnis:

It is necessary that you know, Oh ummah of Islam, that the Shia are a religion that has nothing to do with Islam—except as the Jews and Christians included it under the term 'People of the Book'—as they [Shia] have changed the meaning of the Quran, blasphemed the companions of the prophet, and mocked the mothers of believers to the extent of considering the people of Islam as infidels, and they have sought to spill their blood (81).

Through contrasts with negatively perceived out-groups, he attempts to persuade Sunnis, playing on the fear of existential threat to compel action.

Al-Zarqawi (2004a) cites Ibn Taymiyya's authority to convince his audience to fight the Shia, who, he states, have historically supported evil rulers:

> The Sheikh of Islam Ibn Taymiyya was right when he described their state, after he mentioned that they [the Shia] had considered the people of Islam as infidels. He said, may God have mercy on him: "Because of this reason, they have cooperated with the infidels against the Muslim masses, and they cooperated with the Tatars. And they were one of the biggest reasons for the departure of Genghis Khan, the king of the infidels, to the land of Islam. And for the advance of Hulagu to the land of Iraq" (81).

Al-Zarqawi (2004a) quotes his next sentence directly from Ibn Taymiyya: "If the Jews and others become a state in Iraq, the rejectionists (Shia) will become among the greatest of their helpers as they have always supported the infidels among the polytheists, Jews, and Christians" (82). Ibn Taymiyya termed the Shia "the internal enemies of Islam" for supporting Mongol rulers who invaded the Middle East throughout the thirteenth century (Morabia 1978). Al-Zarqawi reminds today's Sunnis that they no longer have defenders:

> The armies of the Ottoman Empire reached the gates of Vienna, but they stopped there, turned around, and returned to protect the Muslims in Baghdad and defend against an assault of the rejectionist [Shia] Safavid state which had shed blood and tore apart holy places. They destroyed mosques and tired out the souls of the Sunnis (83).

Al-Zarqawi's reading of history taps into a legacy of Sunni frustration. Sunni Islam was the official religion of the Ottoman Empire (1299–1923), Shia Islam was the Persian Safavid Empire's (1501–1736), and both states supported their religious communities in the territories that coalesced into Iraq after World War I (Tripp 2002). During the British occupation of Iraq after the dissolution of the Ottoman Empire (1918–1932), Sunni Arabs allied with other Sunnis, Shia Arabs allied themselves with Iran, and Kurds struggled for autonomy (Zubaida 2002), crystallizing three constituencies that continue to have separate political aspirations (Marr 2012). Al-Zarqawi mediates disorder by playing on a historical legacy of Sunni–Shia enmity that was reactivated during the Iraq War.

The only response, according to Al-Zarqawi, is for Sunnis to defend themselves by emulating Muhammad's militant qualities: "Have you forgotten our example Muhammad—peace and prayers of God upon him—who went against the infidels and ruled them such that they could not execute an order without him? Who selected the path of jihad?" (86). Sunnis must adhere to Muhammad's violent path rather than participate in the political process:

He spread out the Sharia for you and the ummah turned its back on his jihad. Why do you delude the ummah when you can provide it with its truth against your political conspiracies and your peaceful initiatives? You know that there is no power for you on the seat upon which you sit (86).

In this speech, Al-Zarqawi (2004a) mediated disorder differently from before. He experiments with the formulaic structure of classical Arabic oration and constructed a militant identity by recalling shared meanings of Muhammad's status as a warrior, extending this attribute to all Sunni Muslims. Rather than persuade his audience through repeated Quranic references, he engages in persuasion by presenting social proof of what his audience knows of OMJ's attacks and the history of Iraq. He stresses contrasts with multiple out-groups to argue that Sunnis are under siege. As before, he cites Ibn Taymiyya for authority, but these citations serve to reinforce Al-Zarqawi's version of history. By equating the Mongol invasion of Baghdad with the U.S.-led invasion of Iraq, he insists that religious (Jewish, Christian, Shia) and national (American, Israeli) out-groups are conspiring to destroy the Sunnis, exploiting the fear of extinction to encourage violent actions now. Unlike his 2003 speech, Al-Zarqawi (2004a) does not emphasize the maintenance of group norms in social relationships, but this would become a focus for him.

"The Heroes of Fallujah"

During the week that Al-Zarqawi delivered his second speech, OMJ released its first video (Glasser and Coll 2005), lasting eleven minutes and eight seconds.[1] Unlike references to identity based on tribe or the ummah, the title, *"Usūd Fallujah"* (literally "The Lions of Fallujah"), emphasizes territorial belonging. This video is a case study in OMJ's use of video for the first time. Like both speeches, the video begins with the standard praise: "In the name of God, the beneficent, the merciful." The video then transitions into a recitation of the sixtieth verse of the Quran's eighth chapter, *Al-Anfāl*, the text of which appears on screen: "Make ready for them whatever force and strings of horses you can, to terrify thereby the enemy of God and your enemy, and others besides them that you know not; God knows them. And whatsoever you expend in the way of God shall be repaid you in full; you will not be wronged" (Arberry 1996, 176). This verse originally referred to the pre-Islamic practice of Arab tribes raiding each other for war booty (Kirmanj 2010). By beginning the video with this verse devoid of context, OMJ constructs a militant identity by equating the past with the present and by referencing the authority of the Quran for persuasion.

Al-Zarqawi appears in black clothing with a gun, declaring,

> My beloved ummah! Indeed, we are in Iraq, at a stone's throw from the place of the night voyage (*masrā*) of God's messenger, peace and prayers of God upon him. We fight in Iraq just as our forces are upon Jerusalem. Indeed, by the Quran alone is one guided and a sword gives victory. These alone are sufficient for your God toward victory (00:45–1:11).

The use of "I" and "we" treats viewers as part of the in-group. Again, Al-Zarqawi mentions the Quran for authority. Muslims believe that Muhammad ascended to heaven through the Dome of the Rock in Jerusalem, which is supposedly the architectural successor to the Temple of Solomon (Busse 1968). In the twelfth century, literary tropes of the ummah's unity, the conquest of Jerusalem, and emulation of the prophet Muhammad appeared in reaction to the Muslim loss of Jerusalem during the Crusades (Dajani-Shakeel 1976). Al-Zarqawi's use of these symbols invests these literary tropes with new meanings in the Iraq War.

Next, a slide appears, titled "The Spoils of War of the Media Office Presents the Heroes of Fallujah." With this move, OMJ appropriated the authority of the Quranic word al-anfāl ("spoils of war") for persuasion. At 1:20, the first nashīd begins: "We will lead the world with the spoils of war. And we will destroy disbelief through the spoils of war" (Sa-na-qūd al-dunya b'il-anfāl / Wa nuhātim al-kufra b'il-anfāl). Jihadists have debated whether nashīds are considered music and thus a sinful distraction from reciting the Quran (Said 2012). The incorporation of the word al-anfāl in this nashīd persuades audiences that the Quran permits violence against infidels and assures viewers of the group's piety, that the nashīd is not merely a worldly distraction. OMJ invests al-anfāl with new meanings by insisting that its militants fight the disbelievers today as Muhammad did in the past.

A second slide appears at 1:41, titled "Military Training and the Arts of Self-Defense," conveying the message that OMJ's militants are only protecting Muslims, not conducting an offensive battle. A narrator exhorts,

> My people, step forward before us! Set off from us as soldiers! We have worked out a plan for you to lead us toward honor and victory. So advance, Oh brother of Islam! Advance! Come forward, Oh brother of Islam, having become a soldier! Set off toward your glory! Indeed, glory comes from resolve! (1:52–1:59).

The narrator establishes kinship by referring to "my people" and "us." Against a soundtrack of marching footsteps, verbal commands to "step forward," "set off," "advance," and "come forward" mediate disorder by demanding violent actions. Al-Zarqawi summons powerful emotions such as "honor" and "glory" to justify violence. The video shows shared practices of masked militants—all men—marching in formation (2:00), aiming guns at targets in a synchronized fashion (2:11), and scaling walls (2:41). Figure 2.1 is a screenshot from the video, illustrating a still image of a militant on the left and moving footage of militants on the right, a visual manifestation of OMJ encouraging the fusion of individual and group identities. By showing individuals training with others, the video persuades viewers that militants reinforce group norms of violent thoughts, emotions, and behaviors in their relationships. The video allows audiences to experience parasocial relationships with individual militants and to feel transported into their world.

The soundtrack of the video consists entirely of nashīds. A second nashīd at 2:07 defines shared emotions of determination for the in-group: "We

FIGURE 2.1 A screenshot from "The Heroes of Fallujah." At left is a militant in civilian clothing. On the right, this person is shown training with others. He is identified moments earlier, appearing with a yellow circle in the video . By depicting both an individual portrait and shared practices of militant training, the video conveys the fusion of individual and group identities.

have resolved to fight, so prepare for combat." A third *nashīd* at 4:14 defines insiders through a militant interpretation of Islam by drawing contrasts with others: "Indeed, the armies of the Muslims—who is like them in the world?" A fourth hymn at 6:18 extols suicide bombers: "I will be coming, tall, patient, and stern. Upon us is a belt, and the straight path . . ." (*sa-ā-tī shu-mū-khan sa-bū-ran ʿa-nīf / a-lei-nā ha-qī-ban wa dar-bun la-tīf*). The meter, known as *mutaqārib*, consists of three poetic feet in which an unstressed syllable is followed by two stressed syllables: In the first foot, *sa* is short, whereas *ā* and *tī* are stressed. An audio loop of footsteps plays, with the *nashīd* acting as a soldier's marching song.

From 5:00 to 7:11, the video shows unmasked militants at leisure wearing casual clothes, somersaulting from the roofs of trucks, swimming in the Euphrates River, and laughing with each other. The switch from combat training to a relaxed environment communicates the group's emotional cohesion, that members like each other and are committed to the group's identity at work, play, and leisure. This depiction of positive emotion is a shift from Al-Zarqawi's speeches, which underscored fear of God's retribution, obedience to God's commands, shame at abandoning manliness, and warnings about the future extinction of Iraq's Sunnis. Figure 2.2 is a screenshot from the video of militants challenging each other to a diving contest on the banks of the Euphrates River.

FIGURE 2.2 A screenshot from "The Heroes of Fallujah." At left is a still portrait of Al-Zarqawi looking downward in piety. At right, the militants are shown swimming together. In contrast to Al-Zarqawi's speeches, this OMJ video showcases affection among group members to reinforce violent thoughts, emotions, and behaviors within the group's relationships.

From 7:11 to 7:46, Al-Zarqawi fires a machine gun in the company of others, as shown in figure 2.3. For the rest of the video, a militant (shown in figure 2.2) speaks into the camera smiling, but we do not hear his voice. We only hear nashīds and the narrator's voice. "Undertake a rebellion" (7:29), Al-Zarqawi commands as he drives off with other militants. No scenes of combat or victims are shown.

The video closes with a poem recited at 9:39:

Oh Lord of Martyrs, we believe passionately.
Thousands promise [their] love, carrying forth the banner of monotheism.
The earthquakes of Islam are close to approaching from distance.
"Allahu Akbar" ["God is great"] lives up to the promise of belief.
Oh ummah of Islam! Respond to threats with threats.
Oh Islamic State (yā dawlat-ul-Islām)! Come forth again!

FIGURE 2.3 This screenshot, from "The Heroes of Fallujah," shows Al-Zarqawi with three militants. Only Al-Zarqawi is unmasked, calling attention to his leadership. By masking all other militants, the video reinforces the message that individuals submit completely to the group's identity.

Oh ummah of Islam! Swear by God!
Don't forsake Sa'ad; don't forsake Ibn Al-Walid!
Striking necks is our calling (*harfatu-nā*), striking vein to vein.
Oh ummah of Islam! Don't waiver!
Victory approaches. Slaughter approaches. The Army of Muhammad approaches. Greatness (*tūba*) comes from supporting armies through slaughter. With your slaughter is your prayer.

This poem constructs God as the lord of martyrs, commanding an in-group of believers, emphasized by the word "we." The poem contrasts OMJ's militants, committed to monotheism, against enemy infidels. As in the first speech described in this chapter, Al-Zarqawi represents Islam through a lexicon of disaster: a series of imminent earthquakes, a response to threats with threats, "us" striking necks and veins, an Army of Islam. He commands the ummah to emulate two historical prototypes: (1) Sa'ad ibn Abi Waqqas (595–674 CE), reportedly the first Muslim to shed blood for Islam during the Battle of Badr in 624 CE, in which the fledgling, outnumbered Muslims defeated the disbelieving Meccans through divine intervention; and (2) Ibn Al-Walid, the "Abu Sulaiman" whom Al-Zarqawi referenced in his second speech. In this first OMJ video, Al-Zarqawi sets a precedent of addressing the Muslim community as a state (*dawla*) whose prayers are slaughter, thus communicating a martial group identity.

"The Heroes of Fallujah" mediates disorder by creating a multimodal experience, different from just a speech, that valorizes violence. OMJ mixes elements of classical Arabic oration such as praise to God with the citation of a verse from the Quran for authority. The video showcases militants in training and at leisure to suggest that violent group norms are maintained in positive relationships with others, by upholding the fusion of the individual's identity with that of the group. Compared with written texts, images persuade audiences by constructing a reality that provides proof of the message being delivered (Messaris 1997; Borchers 2013), through which audiences can establish parasocial relationships with individuals. From this perspective, "The Heroes of Fallujah" offers details that speeches cannot, primarily that its militants receive disciplined training and that they like each other. *Nashīds* and the final poem contrast an in-group of believers against an out-group of non-Muslim infidels. Within the poem, OMJ calls on Sunnis to emulate historical prototypes who have shed blood against non-Muslim infidels to defend the faith.

"The Winds of Victory"

In August 2004, OMJ released "The Winds of Victory." At an ambitious one hour, four minutes, and twenty-six seconds,[2] the video was praised by jihadists in online forums for depicting the religious rituals that prepare "martyrs" for suicide attacks (Shane 2006; Cataldo 2009). It is an exemplary case study in persuasion since it has been implicated in numerous American and European court cases for radicalizing militants (Stenersen 2014). Unlike "The Heroes of Fallujah," which did not construct a causal sequence of events to form a narrative, this video helps the viewer draw inferences through distinct sequences. It begins with footage of bombed buildings over which the words "democracy," "freedom," and "reform" appear. This visual effect adopts social proof as a mechanism of persuasion, insinuating a contradiction between the U.S.-led coalition's statements and actions.

Sequence 1

From 1:22 to 2:14, American soldiers kick in gates and enter houses as a child says, "My father, my father, where are you? Can't you see?" A father peers out from his doorway, and a family exits their house with hands raised in surrender before a group of American soldiers pointing guns, as shown in figure 2.4. A child laments, "Monkeys search the house and rip apart the drapes (*qad jāsat qurūd al-dayār / wa hatakū al-astār*). Father, can you hear me? My little sister is crying." The scene incorporates several mechanisms of persuasion. First, it contrasts Sunnis with American soldiers, viewed as invaders, setting up an analogy between individual American soldiers invading an Iraqi home and the U.S. Army invading Iraq. The word "monkeys" dehumanizes Americans, whereas the image of an innocent family evacuating its home at gunpoint provides a group of people with whom viewers can establish a parasocial relationship based on shared emotions of vulnerability. Second, the video offers visual proof of how the war in Iraq has affected the everyday lives of families. Finally, the sentence beginning with "Monkeys search the house" employs *saja'* for persuasion with the rhyme of *dayār* with *astār*. Through careful composition, the video mediates disorder by disrupting the viewer's thoughts and emotions, encouraging

FIGURE 2.4 A screenshot from "The Winds of Victory." At left is the barrel of a soldier's gun. Next to this is the Arabic for "My father." At right, a man opens the door to his house. The scene portrays American soldiers as foreign occupiers committing atrocities against innocent Iraqis.

them to move from a state of complacency into action. The child's call to his father recalls Al-Zarqawi's attempt to shame men into action during his first speech.

At 2:16, the first *nashīd* begins: "One day, the whole ummah groped around in the darkness of pain. Have I responded to my important dilemma with principles (*usūl*)?" By switching from the "whole ummah" to "I," the *nashīd* tries to persuade viewers by imposing an obligation to respond, forcing individuals to reflect on their responsibilities to the Muslim community. Multiple images of dead bodies, mourners, explosions, bandaged children, and injured elderly men appear, each a few seconds long. The number of such images offers social proof of numerous atrocities to enrage viewers. Overlaid on these images are various Arabic phrases: "Oh ummah! How much longer of this silence? How much longer will this bleeding continue? How many mouths of the occupier will you cover up? How much longer will you grant [them] permission to enter your sacred home?" This sequence mediates disorder by demanding violent behaviors.

The call to jihad begins at 3:54 in the following *nashīd*: "One day, we saw you crying. Where is the life of jihad? One day, the crier kept it company. I said, 'Where is the ummah?' " Brief clips of dead bodies appear, offering more social proof of the war's casualties. Figure 2.5 is a screenshot of an

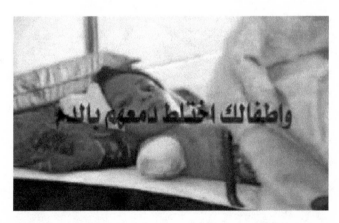

FIGURE 2.5 OMJ's early videos featured images of injured children to anger viewers. This screenshot, from the video "The Winds of Victory," shows a child convalescing after the amputation of his right arm. The Arabic text translates to "And your children mix their tears with blood."

injured child who would become a symbol of American injustice. The *nashīd* is the soundtrack for montages of the dead and injured.

At 4:56, a phrase appears: "They stare at you with eyes of hope." More injured children are shown. At 5:12: "They are [a]waiting a response from you." These phrases mediate disorder by obliging viewers to respond with violent behaviors. At 5:24, a narrator exclaims, "Everything that my noble sisters mentioned in the prisons of the Crusaders, and everything that I saw before me was a picture of this 'oppressive' freedom." The narrator contrasts the word "freedom," which flashed on screen at the beginning, with a picture of the Abu Ghraib prison, shown in figure 2.6. The image seeks to persuade viewers by marshaling social proof of prison abuses. The narrator also contrasts an American Christian out-group ("prisons of the Crusaders") with an innocent Muslim in-group for persuasion.

At 6:06, the narrator addresses Iraqis collaborating with Americans: "How does one raised to be a free Muslim remain faithful, seeing this disgrace as a soldier among the Crusaders or an officer among the infidels? Has he lost his senses? They are deprived of their religion." In contrast to the purely religious jihad presented in "The Heroes of Fallujah," this video disorders thoughts and emotions by appealing to religion *and* nationalism against

FIGURE 2.6 A screenshot from "The Winds of Victory." The phrase "The Abu Ghraib prison" appears below an image of a tortured prisoner forced to stand hooded. In its videos, OMJ exploited images of abused detainees at Abu Ghraib and Guantánamo as symbols of American tyranny.

tyrannical, American, Christian outsiders and shames their Iraqi collaborators by stripping them of a religious identity.

Sequence 2

At 6:48, a prayer appears: "I seek refuge through God from the evil Satan. In the name of God, the Beneficent, the Merciful." The narrator persuades his audience to embrace violent behaviors by citing five religious texts in succession for authority. Together, the texts convey the message that God is to be feared and obeyed in order for Muslims to triumph: (1) The 102nd verse of the Quran's third chapter, *Al-Imrān*: "O Believers, fear God as He should be feared, and see you do not die, save in surrender" (Arberry 1996, 58); (2) the first verse of the Quran's fourth chapter, *Al-Nisā*: "Mankind, fear your Lord, who created you of a single soul, and from it created its mate, and from the pair of them scattered abroad many men and women; and fear God by whom you demand one of another, and the wombs; surely God ever watches over you" (Arberry 1996, 72); (3) the seventieth verse of the Quran's thirty-third chapter, *Al-Ahzāb*: "O believers, fear God, and speak words hitting the mark, and He will set right your deeds for you and will forgive you your sins. Whosoever obeys God and His Messenger has won a mighty triumph" (Arberry 1996, 435); (4) a Hadith attributed to Muhammad: "Allah gathered the earth for me, and I have seen its east and west; indeed, my ummah will reach its dominion through what is gathered for me" [my translation]; and (5) the fifty-fifth verse of the Quran's twenty-fourth chapter, *Al-Nūr*: "God has promised those of you who believe and do righteous deeds that He will surely make you successors in the land, even as He made those who were before them successors, and that He will surely establish their religion for them that He has approved for them, and will give them in exchange, after their fear, security: 'They shall serve Me, not associating with Me anything.' Whoso disbelieves after that, those—they are the ungodly" (Arberry 1996, 359). This style of argumentation is common among Islamists who treat the Quran as the self-evident word of God, which should not be sullied with the imperfections of any human's historical, linguistic, or literary analysis (Duderija 2011). By citing all these texts up front, the narrator infers that the religious evidence to support jihad is overwhelming.

Sequence 3

At 13:54, the narrator delineates OMJ's core values of the group's identity: "We are the Organization of Monotheism and Jihad. We attack the enemy (*nusāwilu al-'adw*), and we lengthen (*nutāwilu al-baghī*) the rebellion, attempting to bring the caliphate on earth, implement the Sharia, and orient the nation toward it. We fight here, and our sights are on Jerusalem. We fight them here, and our purpose is Rome." The strategy of delineating the group's core values right after citing religious texts underpins the group's claims of behaving in conformity with God's word in the Quran and the prophet's example as narrated in Hadith texts.

At 15:00, the narrator draws another contrast between Muslims and infidels: "The only thing between us and the infidels is the sword of Islam, which we will bear until God rules among us and the nation of infidels. God is victorious over his affairs." This sentence evokes emotions of perseverance and determination to implement God's plan. As in "The Heroes of Fallujah," this video depicts shared practices of militants marching, aiming guns, and crawling in formation. Figure 2.7 shows OMJ's militants at prayer, reinforcing a group identity centered on devotion and violence.

FIGURE 2.7 Militants pray behind their leader with their weapons arrayed in front of them in "The Winds of Victory." The text that appears is the title of the video, in Arabic.

Sequence 4

The rest of the video highlights suicide missions (*al-'amalīyya al-istishhādīyya*). Unlike "The Heroes of Fallujah," which shows only militants training, "The Winds of Victory" portrays suicide attacks against the targets that Al-Zarqawi mentioned in his second speech, offering visual proof of the group's successes for persuasion: (1) the Al-Khalidiya bridge, and (2) the police force in Al-Khalidiya; (3) a military base used by the Polish government; (4) the headquarters of the U.S.-led coalition; (5) an Iraqi provincial secretariat in Karbala; (6) Italian military forces in the city of Al-Nasiriyah; (7) the leader of the interim Iraqi government; (8) the United Nations headquarters in Baghdad; and (9) a CIA post in Baghdad. Suicide bombers recite last wills and testaments, with some missions portraying multiple attackers against the same target.

All attacks begin with suicide bombers praising God and Muhammad, expressing love for their families, and justifying jihad through Quranic verses. Since all missions in this video adopt the same format, I analyze only the first attack, against the Al-Khalidiya bridge. A man with the nom de guerre Abu Harith ("the father of Harith") reads into the camera, as shown in figure 2.8. In filming suicide attackers reading last wills and testaments into the camera in the company of others, OMJ mediates disorder by communicating that thoughts, emotions, and behaviors of martyrdom are normalized and maintained within the group's relationships. The image depicts suicide bombers through night-vision filters, also shown in figure 2.8, transporting viewers into a covert world of jihad, allowing them to establish parasocial relationships and to identify with the thoughts and emotions of suicide bombers.

Abu Harith praises God and Muhammad; expresses love for his mother, father, wife, and child; and demands that others follow him on the path of jihad, making contrasts with an enemy out-group. "How can we live while our holy places are violated, the country is assaulted, and the infidels take our homes? We are all responsible before God," he fumes. Militants take turns embracing him. The militants embrace is captioned as "the procession of the lovers of angels" (*zaffa 'ushhāq al-hūr*). A *zaffa* is a bridegroom's wedding procession; the use of this term thus implies that the attacker will make love to angels after his death. Odes to jihadists emerged by the

FIGURE 2.8 An unmasked suicide bomber reads his last will and testament with militants standing behind him. The only time individuals are unmasked in "The Winds of Victory" is when they pledge themselves to a suicide mission. A masked militant holds up his right index finger, a gesture that IS uses to signify group unity and monotheism.

eighth century as the Umayyad (661–750) and Abbasid Empires (750–1258) expanded into Europe and promised the virgins of Paradise to militants through the wedding of martyrdom (Jarrar 2004). OMJ mediates disorder by reactivating this historical trope to normalize violent thoughts and behaviors in present times. Abu Harith climbs into a truck that explodes at the Al-Khalidiya bridge, as shown in figure 2.9.

The narrator praises Abu Harith effusively with phrases including "You are presently alive, and your body is preserved," "God preserves your holy body," and "His example is like that of the predecessors." This praise reinforces the shared meaning that although OMJ's militants may no longer have a physical existence following death, their souls endure. This conception of selfhood differs from that of the field of mental health, which does not require belief in a soul and links existence to the physical body's functioning (Kirmayer 2007a). The narrator's praise normalizes martyrdom for viewers by implying that they, too, can be commemorated through video.

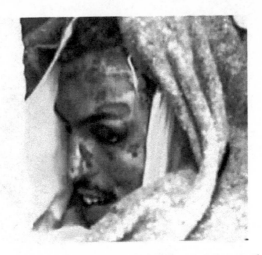

FIGURE 2.9 A screenshot of a deceased suicide bomber in "The Winds of Victory." His smile is intended to inspire other militants to become martyrs on a path of violence committed out of unconditional love for God.

Sequence 5

The video ends with two phrases that glorify martyrdom overlying an image of a staircase. The top phrase translates to "I was victorious by the Lord of the Ka'aba." The Ka'aba is the edifice around which Muslims circumambulate during the pilgrimage to Mecca. This phrase salutes militants who have died in battle against infidels and is attributed to one of Muhammad's companions who was stabbed with a spear (Combating Terrorism Center at West Point 2015a). The bottom phrase translates to "The Generous One [God] is pleased with the daily caravans of martyrs' souls." The staircase provides a visual representation of the martyr's illumined path to God and normalizes violence against infidels.

Like "The Heroes of Fallujah," "The Winds of Victory" mediates disorder by creating a multimodal experience, but through different mechanisms of persuasion. Rather than beginning the video with praises to God or citations of religious text, the video presents extensive footage of attacks on buildings and civilians as visual proof. Instead of a tribal, ethnic, or geographical identity, the video features families who have been dishonored and children demanding action from fathers. Unlike "The Heroes of Fallujah," men are depicted in rigorous training, not at leisure. They recite last wills and testaments that express love for their families and rationalize their behaviors as revenge. Shared meanings within the in-group include establishing a caliphate and Sharia; shared symbols include visual representations of injustices at Abu Ghraib and the martyr's marital procession. Emotions of familial vulnerability and dishonor forge an in-group identity based on determination to implement God's plan. By featuring militants responsible for nine attacks, audiences can establish parasocial relationships and identify with protagonists, unlike the militants (apart from Al-Zarqawi) in "The Heroes of Fallujah," who never spoke. Mechanisms of persuasion include drawing contrasts with Americans as infidel occupiers, imposing the obligation to act violently on viewers, and citing religious texts, with the inclusion of footage of atrocities as the main mechanism of persuasion. The video mediates disorder by normalizing violent thoughts, emotions, and behaviors among militants who pray together, embrace each other before attacks, and commemorate each other's martyrdom.

OMJ's Mediated Disorder

OMJ mediated disorder through different mechanisms of psychological persuasion based on the medium it used for its messaging. Extant histories of IS have described Al-Zarqawi as "an unpromising student who wrote Arabic at a semiliterate level" (Weiss and Hassan 2015, 2) and "a mediocre student who dropped out of school after ninth grade" (Stern and Berger 2015, 113). Such assessments raise the question of how he came to persuade others. I believe the answer partly lies in his skilled use of language. As languages develop self-conscious literary cultures, linguistic styles and practices crystallize into canonical forms of expression (Pollock 2009). Medieval Arabic oration formalized key characteristics such as praising God and his prophet, *saja'*, directly addressing the audience, using symbols such as lions and knights to concretize abstract ideas, and citing the Quran for persuasion (Qutbuddin 2008). In cultural psychiatry, we've recognized that culture influences the style of communication in addition to its content (Kirmayer 2006), and all mental health professionals examine speech patterns, thought patterns, and thought content during the mental status examination (Barnill 2014). I've continued this emphasis on analyzing the style as well as the substance of a text to bring out this interaction between linguistic sound and meaning (Jakobson 1937). To maximize persuasion, Al-Zarqawi positioned his speeches within the tradition of classical Arabic oration, making references to the authority of scholars and appeals to historical prototypes. This skilled use of linguistic practices adds a distinctly cultural mechanism of persuasion to Cialdini's (1993) mechanisms by focusing on language use in practice rather than only on the ideas that it communicates, what cultural psychiatrists have termed "sociolinguistic representations" to expand on the theory of social representations by closely reading texts through discourse analysis (Aggarwal 2016).

OMJ's videos feature similar mechanisms of persuasion, but they rely more on visual proof. For example, "The Heroes of Fallujah" offers visual proof about training the mujahideen that Al-Zarqawi referenced in his speeches. In "The Winds of Victory," OMJ used footage of innocent casualties as visual proof of American atrocities and filmed its militants attacking known targets to inspire others. This kind of visual proof, of militants becoming martyrs, goes beyond the mechanisms of persuasion possible with speech. Verbal statements intended to elicit altruistic acts—defined as people elevating the needs of others over their own—produce few behavioral changes compared with portrayals of individuals who actually model altruism in their lives (Henrich 2009); OMJ's videos not only signal that the martyr is altruistic, but reinforce the transmission of violent thoughts, emotions, and behaviors. The multimodality of both videos described in this chapter also introduces audiences to *nashīd*s that are composed in strict meter and reinforce violent emotions and behaviors aurally. OMJ takes advantage of each media platform to mediate disorder with different emphases on social persuasion.

Al-Zarqawi exploited social representations from Arabic literature to create a novel cultural identity, one through which OMJ's militants could commonly interpret the world and its violence. Praises to the prophet Muhammad may be formulaic in Arabic oration, but Al-Zarqawi's take on him as the ideal warrior, worthy of emulation, promoted core in-group values of heroism and sacrifice through shared practices of violent jihad. Sunni Muslims who wish to live their lives in conformity with religious texts treat the Quran as the revealed word of God and descriptions of the life of Muhammad as examples of how Muslims should behave in their own daily lives (Hallaq 1997). Al-Zarqawi mediated disorder by calling on his audience to behave violently, as Muhammad did, as a manifestation of their piety. Here we see the dynamic interplay between culture and psychology: Shared meanings, practices, and symbols based on the life of Muhammad justify violent thoughts, emotions, and behaviors for the OMJ in-group, which become further reinforced through textual references to the Quran and influential scholars for authority.

OMJ's texts also reveal a distinct evolution of collective identity over time. Shared meanings of adopting a defensive path of jihad against the U.S.-led coalition in Al-Zarqawi's speeches expanded to justify the implementation of a caliphate and a system of Sharia for all Muslims in "The Winds of Victory." In the process, OMJ mediated disorder by intervening between individuals and society to persuade people of the need for violence against the international state system. In making repeated contrasts between an in-group of devout Muslims against an out-group of nonbelieving infidels through frequent citations of the Quran and the words of Ibn Taymiyya, he expressed linguistic power by investing classical terms such as *anfāl*, *muhājirūn*, and *ansār* with new meanings in the Iraq War. All these citations elevate Sunni Muslims as a distinct and favored community that must follow God's path. The terms *muhājirūn* and *ansār* also act as local knowledge categories, which OMJ uses to separate in-groups from out-groups. Through discourse analysis, we see how the term *anfāl* is transformed from a reference in "A Message to the Tribes of the Banu Hasan" into a justification for militant behaviors in "The Heroes of Fallujah."

In cultural psychiatry, we differentiate between identities that are chosen and ascribed, with ascribed identities often emerging from power differences between groups (Kirmayer et al. 2008). By making contrasts with multiple groups—even through dehumanization— Al-Zarqawi constructed what we could term an "i-dentity" (*my* conception of the world) and a "we-dentity" (*our* conception of the world) for Muslims through violent interpretations of religious texts, as well as a "you-dentity" (*your* conception of the world) for multiple out-groups by ascribing vices such as disbelief and treachery to Americans, Christians, Israelis, Jews, Kurds, and Shia, polarizing in-group–out-group differences. OMJ's in-group–out-group contrasts set the stage for IS's state-building exercises in Syria, which have promoted in-group solidarity among Sunnis as a form of citizenship by "securitizing the Shia threat" (Mabon 2017), a theme we shall see in each chapter.

Finally, analyzing the texts in chronological order reveals evolutions in culturally shared emotions and the maintenance of in-group norms within relationships. In his first speech, Al-Zarqawi emphasized the fear of God's retribution if Muslims disobeyed the Quran; in the second, he exaggerated the fear of Sunni extinction. In contrast, "The Heroes of Fallujah" stressed masculine honor and glory, and the "Winds of Victory" appealed to multiple emotions such as vulnerability, the dishonor of Iraqis colluding with Americans, fear of God's retribution, and perseverance and determination in following His path. Although the initial propositions differ—such as the religious uniqueness of Muslims, historical wrongs committed against Sunnis, and the calamities visited upon innocent families after the Iraq War—each text disorders the emotions of its audience by demanding violent behaviors as revenge for current injustices. In his first speech, Al-Zarqawi used his position as a sympathetic guide, recalling the valor of Muslim forefathers to maintain violent group norms. In contrast, both videos depict a fusion of individual and group identities. Militants are shown at leisure, praying together in lines behind weapons, and hugging each other before attacks. OMJ promises a brotherhood of Sunni Muslims in the worldly present *and* in a heavenly future. The message is straightforward: Join us in jihad because we play together, pray together, and slay together. Isolating OMJ's unique culture and psychology allows us to observe how aspects of group identity stay the same, transform, and spread to others over time.

THREE

Al Qaeda in Iraq

OMJ, Al Qaeda, and Militant Acculturation

AS AL-ZARQAWI was constructing OMJ's cultural and psychological identity, Al Qaeda's militants were focusing on different priorities. In the Al Qaeda periodical *Saut Al-Jihad* (Hegghammer 2008; Ryan 2013), an article from the December 2003–January 2004 issue featured the last will and testament (*wasīya*) of a would-be martyr who dissuaded jihadists from fighting in Iraq:

> The people of the Arabian Peninsula should not go to Iraq because the fighting there is discord and there is not a clear banner [of jihad] at all, because the fighting there is a hand's throw to ruin, because the American military only subjects people to its fighting, because the Americans have arrested Saddam, and whoever stays is on the path to becoming a prisoner, because the matter has been settled and only a few of the mujahideen remain there (Al-Salim 2004, 23).

Recalling our conception of cultural identity from chapter 1 as one's place in the world, we can see that Al-Salim is describing an identity through religion and territorial affiliation, which manifests as a preference for jihad in the Arabian Peninsula. This differs from Al-Zarqawi's consistent message: the world's Sunnis must unite through jihad in Iraq.

We now know about the precarious contacts between Al-Zarqawi and Al Qaeda's leadership. After the U.S.-led invasion of Afghanistan in 2001, Ayman Al-Zawahiri negotiated safe passage through Iran for some of Al Qaeda's key personnel, who then met Al-Zarqawi (Finn and Schmidt 2003).

Al-Zarqawi wanted access to Al Qaeda's financing and alumni network (Zelin 2014), whereas Al Qaeda wanted to co-opt Al-Zarqawi's rising international profile (Farrall 2011). There were thorny differences. Al-Zarqawi refused to pledge allegiance to Al Qaeda's leader, Osama bin Laden, five times before October 2004 (Corera 2005). Some have interpreted the feud as a battle of personalities: "Bin Laden and his early followers were mostly members of an intellectual, educated elite, while Zarqawi was a barely educated ruffian with an attitude. . . . Zarqawi was arrogant and disrespectful of bin Laden" (Stern and Berger 2015, 16). Others point to differences in beliefs:

> In contrast to Zarqawi, although intrinsically hostile to the Shia, bin Laden and Zawahiri prioritized the struggle against the far enemy (the United States). It is worth noting that the two Al Qaeda leaders did not publicly condemn Iran and they never attacked Iranian Shias in Afghanistan or the Shias in Saudi Arabia (Gerges 2016, 74).

Others considered it an intergenerational conflict: "We can trace the roots of this ideological conflict back to the standoff between Abu Musab al-Zarqawi, al-Qa'ida's *emir* in Iraq until 2006, and the 'old guard,' Osama bin Laden and Zawahiri. Zarqawi was younger (born in 1966 as against Zawahiri's 1951)" (Atwan 2015, 61). But organizations—even terrorist groups—are more than just their leaders. What interests me as a cultural psychiatrist is the creation of a collective cultural and psychological identity as the two organizations interact: How do we analyze the OMJ–Al Qaeda merger as an interaction of cultural systems, each with its own meanings, practices, and symbols? How does examining this yield insights into IS's cultural diffusion? How can discourse analysis help us understand the overarching culture that comes from militant mergers and acquisitions (Horowitz and Potter 2014; Phillips 2014)?

In this chapter, I analyze the culture and psychology of OMJ and Al Qaeda texts before and after the formation of Al Qaeda in Iraq (AQI). A critical component of cultural diffusion is the process of *acculturation*, classically defined in mental health as "those phenomena which result when groups of individuals having different cultures come into continuous first-hand contact with subsequent changes in the original cultural patterns of either or both groups" (Redfield, Linton, and Herskovits 1936, 149). Cultural diffusion does not occur in a vacuum, since everyone has some form of culture as a social being; accordingly, studying acculturation is a priority in mental health because individuals generally act within cultural norms (Berry et al. 1992). Four types of acculturation strategy may be used when individuals from different cultural backgrounds interact (Berry 1997): (1) *assimilation*: individuals favor their new identity over the old; (2) *separation*: individuals maintain their original identity and avoid interacting with others; (3) *integration*: individuals maintain elements of their original identity and incorporate elements of their new identity; and (4) *marginalization*: they abandon both cultural identities.

Acculturation produces "behavioral shifts" at the group level that can be empirically detected, such as shifts in language use or systems of shared meanings, practices, and symbols (Berry 1980). To determine behavior shifts before and after AQI's formation, I analyze five texts: Al-Zarqawi's pledge of allegiance to bin Laden to form AQI; Al-Zarqawi's speech to the mujahideen in Fallujah; two Al Qaeda texts on Fallujah from before and after AQI's formation; and an AQI video on jihad. The Outline for Cultural Formulation (OCF) furnishes us with core variables for discourse analysis to observe behavioral shifts (Kleinman and Benson 1996) during the OMJ–Al Qaeda acculturation process.

"The Pledge to the Al Qaeda Organization Under the Leadership of Osama bin Laden"

On October 17, 2004, Al-Zarqawi (2004b) announced "the pledge of the commander Abu Musab Al-Zarqawi to the chief of the mujahideen Osama bin Laden, an announcement of good news on the rally of the Organization of Monotheism and Jihad under the banner of Al Qaeda" (173). This speech is a case study in how Al-Zarqawi viewed the process of acculturation. He begins by labeling the merger "an anger for the enemies of God and a delight for every Muslim" (173). He is using two forms of social persuasion here: drawing contrasts between in-groups and out-groups and claiming that he speaks for "every Muslim." As with "My Beloved Ummah" (discussed in chapter 2), he endows his *tahmīd* to God with military themes, now of unifying Muslims: "Praise be to God who united the ranks of the mujahideen (*wahhada sufūf al-mujāhidīn*) and who severed the unity of the infidels (*farraqa shaml al-kāfirīn*)" (173–74). Al-Zarqawi uses *saja'* for linguistic persuasion. He cites the 103rd verse of the Quran's third chapter, Āl- ʾImrān, for authority: "And hold you fast to God's bond, together, and do not scatter" (Arberry 1996, 87). By citing a reference with a verbal command—"hold you fast"—Al-Zarqawi mediates disorder by imposing a "we-dentity" upon Muslims to behave in conformity with God's orders, as he did in "A Message to the Tribes of the Banu Hasan." From the outset, Al-Zarqawi situates the OMJ– Al Qaeda merger in shared meanings of Muslim unity through belief in God against nonbelievers.

Similarly, Al-Zarqawi (2004b) praised the prophet Muhammad by drawing contrasts between a Muslim in-group and non-Muslim out-group:

> Peace and prayers upon the one whom God created in the hearts of the believers, who were like a solid foundation in the face of the enemies of religion, who were violent against the infidels but compassionate among themselves. And peace and prayers upon his family and his companions who raised the sword of truth through a single hand and destroyed the heads of the worthless (bātil)" (174).

The phrase "a single hand" (yadd wāhida) again stresses Muslim unity and draws upon the same etymological root, in which God united (wahhada) the mujahideen. Across cultures, groups that perceive themselves under threat regulate in-group norms by invoking metaphors of a collective body that exercises tight social control through rituals of purity (Scheper-Hughes and Lock 1987). References to "a single hand" of the Muslim ummah exemplify in-group identity consolidation through contrasts with "worthless" outsiders. In basing identity on religion, Al-Zarqawi attempts to instill amity toward fellow Sunnis and enmity toward non-Sunnis, mediating disorder by polarizing emotions. The Arabic word bātil carries connotations of worthlessness, lying, and falsehood (Wehr 1976, 78), and Al-Zarqawi dehumanizes non-Muslims by implying that their lives have no value.

Al-Zarqawi (2004b) invokes the authority of God to explain the circumstances behind OMJ's merger with Al Qaeda:

> Communications lasted for eight months between Shaykh "Abu Musab," May God protect him, and the brothers in Al Qaeda. An exchange of [their] points of view was concluded. Then a potent interruption occurred. It did not take long before God ennobled us with the resumption of communications. Our noble brothers in Al Qaeda understood the strategy of Jamā'at Al-Tawhīd Wa-l-Jihād [OMJ] in the

Land of the Two Rivers, the Land of the Caliphs. Their hearts were happy from its [the OMJ's] methodology in it [Iraq] (174).[1]

Al-Zarqawi leads his audience to believe that God's intervention protected him, just as God is responsible for "ennobling" both groups by resuming their communications. "Our noble brothers" treats Al Qaeda's militants as members of the OMJ in-group through bonds of kinship. The reference to Iraq as the "Land of the Caliphs" recalls the Abbasid Caliphate (750–1258), which had a capital in Baghdad before its sacking by the Mongols, reminding listeners of OMJ's goal to implement the caliphate from "The Winds of Victory." William McCants (2015) notes that IS draws upon apocalyptic symbols and practices from the Abbasid Caliphate to foment revolution against the nation-state. Al-Zarqawi's speech indicates that the Abbasid Caliphate inspired a militant identity at least a decade beforehand, the ideas of which have diffused successfully to inform IS's self-conception.

Al-Zarqawi (2004b) then announces the merger:

We inform it [the ummah] [of] news of the pledge of *Jamā'at Al-Tawhīd Wa'l-Jihād*, from top to bottom [*amīran wa junūdan*; literally "its leader and soldiers"], to the chief of the mujahideen "Osama bin Laden" based on listening to and obeying [him] in pleasant and unpleasant situations [*al-manshat wa'l-makrah*] for jihad on the path of God until there is no disunity (*fitna*) and the religion of all is God's (174).

Here, Al-Zarqawi disorders the thoughts of his audience through a clear chain of logic: God united the ranks of the mujahideen → Muhammad and his companions acted as the original mujahideen by fighting infidels → Muslims were compassionate to each other and violent toward everyone else → we emulate the prophet's example by obeying Osama bin Laden on God's path of jihad. Al-Zarqawi's phrase "from top to bottom" underscores his expectation that AQI will maintain group norms of violent thoughts, emotions, and behaviors against infidels throughout all relationships in the new organization. The Arabic word *fitna* draws upon shared meanings of a civil war or schism that could endanger the unity of the Muslim community, as occurred during the First Fitna (656–661 CE) over who would become the caliph (Gardet 1991). By using *fitna* here, Al-Zarqawi invests the word with new meanings in the Iraq War, meanings that denote schisms among competing mujahideen groups that could fracture the unity of the over-arching militant identity.

Al-Zarqawi (2004b) closes his speech with an exhortation for others to join him:

> Come, Oh youth of the ummah, under the banner of the chief of the mujahideen! Together, we will raise the profession of faith, "There is no God but God" beating high, as our heroic forefathers raised it. We will purify the lands (*dayār*) of Islam from every infidel and sinful apostate until Islam enters the dwelling of every nomad and city dweller (*kulli madarin wa wabarin*).

The word "we" urges the audience to behave heroically like their forefathers from Islam's revelation, ascribing a "we-dentity" upon all Muslims based on an exclusivist refusal to accommodate non-Muslims. As in earlier speeches, Al-Zarqawi recalls early military conflicts between Muslims and non-Muslims to equate past with present circumstances. Despite his commitment to violent jihad, Al-Zarqawi's construction of shared meanings to establish OMJ's cultural identity has shifted: His earlier speeches rallied Sunnis to defend themselves against Jews and Christians, but this speech demands that Sunnis "purify" all people through conversion offensively. In the last sentence, Al-Zarqawi uses *saja'* with words from the classical lexicon. Nomads (*ahl al-wabar*) and city dwellers (*ahl al-madar*) constituted separate bases of social authority before the spread of Islam led to sedentary, permanent dwellings in the Arabian Peninsula (Eickelman 1967; Suleiman 1995). Al-Zarqawi proposes that Islam can, once again, unite all segments of society.

Al-Zarqawi's (2004b) speech mediates disorder by disrupting the audience's thoughts and emotions to incite violence, but differently from the speeches described in chapter 2. Al-Zarqawi continues to experiment with Arabic rhetoric for persuasion, infusing the *tahmīd* to God, praise for his prophet, and *saja'* with meanings that his audience would share, tailored to his message. He contends that OMJ and Al Qaeda shared common meanings around collective Muslim unity that requires jihad against infidels. He employs three key mechanisms of psychological persuasion: stipulating propositions for his audience to accept, invoking the authority of the Quran, and drawing contrasts with enemy infidels. Notably, he does *not* cite religious scholars or historical prototypes other than Muhammad and his companions for authority. Nor does he claim that members of both militant groups liked each other and decided to merge. Instead, the merger occurred based on agreement over the correct methodology of jihad. Nonetheless, he cultivates emotions of solidarity among Sunnis and animosity toward non-Muslims, which he hopes will survive in the newly formed AQI's organizational relationships.

For the first time, Al-Zarqawi articulates an awareness of hierarchy. He repeatedly refers to Osama bin Laden as "chief of the mujahideen" and stresses that OMJ's militants will obey Al Qaeda "from the top to the bottom" to avoid disunity within the Muslim ranks. In receiving Al-Zarqawi's pledge, bin Laden (2005) publicized AQI's new leadership structure: "The warrior brother Abu Musab Al-Zarqawi is the commander of the organization AQI. It is incumbent upon the brothers in the organization there to listen to and obey him" (5). Even though Al-Zarqawi and bin Laden, as leaders of their respective organizations, tried to expedite the acculturation process, we will see that some in Al Qaeda resisted this.

"A Message to the Ummah and the Mujahideen in Fallujah"

On November 12, 2004, Al-Zarqawi (2004c) delivered his first speech after OMJ and Al Qaeda merged into AQI. The speech is a case study in how Al-Zarqawi constructed a militant cultural and psychology identity after AQI's formation. A militarized *tahmīd* to God, praise for his prophet, and *saja'* had become standard in his speeches, but this text also exhibits parallel grammatical phrases (*izdiwāj*):

> Praise be to God, the fortifier of Islam with his assistance (*bi-nasri-hi*), the vanquisher of polytheism with his subjugation (*bi-qahri-hi*), the expediter of his affairs with his order (*bi-amri-hi*), the tempter of the infidels with his hatred (*bi-makri-hi*), who appointed the days of fortune with his justice (*bi-'adli-hi*). And peace and prayers upon the one whom God raised as the lighthouse of Islam with his sword (*bi-saifi-hi*) (176).

Classical Arabic rhetoric encourages parallel sentence structure and grammatical repetition, a mode of linguistic persuasion (Koch 1983). Al-Zarqawi also begins each clause with a praiseworthy attribute ("fortifier of Islam"), followed by a prepositional phrase ("with his assistance"). He contrasts victorious Muslims with defeated infidels. More so than in his earlier speeches, Al-Zarqawi tries to persuade his audience with linguistic tropes from classical Arabic rhetoric.

For authority, Al-Zarqawi (2004c) cites the twenty-second verse of the Quran's thirty-third chapter, *Al-Ahzāb*: "When the believers saw the Confederates they said, 'This is what God and His Messenger promised us, and God and His Messenger have spoken truly.' And it only increased them in faith and surrender" (Arberry 1996, 123). The citation of this verse is strategic; biographies of Muhammad suggest that this entire chapter of the Quran was revealed when the nascent Muslim community confronted a conspiracy from polytheists and their collaborators within the Muslim community (Ünsal 2016). By beginning his speech with this reference, Al-Zarqawi deploys shared meanings of piety and steadfastness to contrast Muslims with non-Muslims.

Al-Zarqawi (2004c) then extends this in-group–out-group contrast to the present:

> With it [jihad], the darkness of humiliation which had covered the chest of the ummah for a long period of time at the hands of the Jews, Crusaders, and their followers from among our apostate leaders has dispersed. This is the truth that America, and those with it, understands. It spreads throughout the earth with them since they feel that the winds of jihad will shake their thrones and rock their foundations (177).

Here, he mediates disorder by disrupting the emotions of listeners, asking them to recall their collective "humiliation" at the hands of the Jews, Christians (referred to as "Crusaders"), and their Sunni quislings. Al-Zarqawi draws contrasts not just linguistically but also thematically, pitting Muhammad as "the lighthouse of Islam" against "the darkness of humiliation." He represents America and its enemies as afraid, especially so of Islam's revolutionary potential, employing verbs such as "shake" and "rock" to convey the violent effects of jihad.

Al-Zarqawi (2004c) then turns to his audience:

> I address you, Oh ummah! The blood of your sons flows in Iraq generally, and Fallujah specifically, after which the slaves of the Crusaders—and those among them from our countrymen sons—engaged them, those who sold their religion

for this world. And they, such as the [Kurdish] peshmarga forces and the rejectionists [the Shia], have betrayed God and his prophet (177).

In "My Beloved Ummah" (described in chapter 2), Al-Zarqawi drew contrasts with multiple outgroups like Christians, Jews, Kurds, and the Shia to persuade Sunnis of their uniqueness throughout history. Here, he personalizes this eternal conflict by demanding that his audience recognize Sunni casualties as "your sons," accusing Iraqis who cooperate with Americans of treachery. In a rhetorical power move, he imposes the proposition that this "selling of religion" occurs not just against fellow Sunnis but also against God and Muhammad, in this world and the next. He further dehumanizes these outgroups with the sentence, "They are like the dog of a hunter who follows his master" (177).

Instead, Al-Zarqawi (2004c) declares that the ummah will triumph:

> Now is a time for patience; then the outcome will be yours by the permission of God. Remember the Battle of the Confederates, the Battle of the Trench, when the prophet—peace and prayers upon him—informed his companions of the rulers' treasures. With calamities come charms through God's cooperation. Help and assistance have come to you (178).

The Battle of the Confederates (*Al-Ahzāb*), also known as the Battle of the Trench, lasted twenty-seven days in the year 627 CE, when Muhammad's outnumbered army defeated a confederacy of Arab and Jewish tribes in Medina (Serjeant 1964; Faizer 1996). For authority, Al-Zarqawi cites the Quran, equating Muhammad's triumph with the conflict in Iraq, appealing to shared meanings of divine intervention and a shared emotion of steadfastness. He proclaims that the war in Iraq has cosmic consequences: "This is among the most distinguished battles in the history of Islam and disbelief, so stand as a nation, as a single man. Burn the land under the footsteps of the attack" (178). Aside from contrasting Islam and disbelief, he makes contrasts within the Muslim community based on participation in jihad: "What are you doing, ummah of Islam? What are you saying, scholars of Islam?" (178). These two sentences provoke violence and subvert the authority of intellectuals who have failed to defend AQI's ingroup norms for violent thoughts, emotions, and behaviors to the broader Muslim community.

Al-Zarqawi's (2004c) speech to the mujahideen in Fallujah mediates disorder in a number of ways. He uses all the major elements of classical Arabic rhetoric: the *tahmīd* to God, praise for his prophet, *saja'*, and parallel constructions. He claims that Sunni humiliation is the result of enemy conspiracies and has finally ended only through violent jihad. As in "The Pledge to the Al Qaeda Organization Under the Leadership of Osama bin Laden," he employs three mechanisms of persuasion: stipulating propositions for his audience to accept, invoking the Quran's authority, and drawing contrasts with enemy infidels. By recollecting shared meanings of Islamic history, he equates the triumph of Muhammad's outnumbered army with the present Iraq War, investing the term *Al-Ahzāb* with new meanings to encompass all groups who oppose the Sunni mujahideen. The speech advises collective patience and determination. Al-Zarqawi stirs the audience to violent action by challenging Muslim scholars who have interpreted the Quran's message nonviolently. In the process, he plays an intermediary role between the public and educated elites by using the internet to position himself as an authoritative interpreter of religious texts. We do not hear about Al Qaeda in this speech, though Al-Zarqawi insinuates an expectation of cooperation from other Sunni mujahideen groups by exclaiming that "help and assistance have come."

The Arabic Periodical *Mu'askar Al-Battār*

From the start of the Iraq War, Al-Zarqawi insisted on treating Fallujah as a major arena of insurgency. This is evident in his speeches "The Heroes of Fallujah" and "A Message to the Ummah and the Mujahideen in Fallujah." In contrast, Al Qaeda's writers did not prioritize jihad in Iraq. Let's examine shared meanings, practices, and symbols in two texts from an Al Qaeda periodical, one from before and one following the formation of AQI. These texts are case studies in how Al Qaeda's members viewed the acculturation process in merging with OMJ. Beforehand, *Mu'askar Al-Battār*[2] (*Camp of the Sword*)—an Al Qaeda periodical that ran from January until November 2004 with essays on politics and military training (Hegghammer 2006a, 2008; Stenersen 2008)—included Fallujah in the title of just a single article. In the twelfth issue, from May–June 2004, an article titled "The Twelfth News

Statement on the Topic of a Secret Ambush in Fallujah," begins with a single verse from the Quran:

> When the sacred months are drawn away, slay the idolaters wherever you find them, and take them, and confine them, and lie in wait for them at every place of ambush. But if they repent, and perform the prayer, and pay the alms, then let them go [on] their way; God is All-forgiving, All-compassionate (Arberry 1996, 207).

Like OMJ, Al Qaeda cited the Quran to persuade audiences that violence against enemies is justified, even commanded. The article then lays out facts of one particular ambush in prose that is bare compared with Al-Zarqawi's ornate style:

> On the morning of the fourteenth day of the month *Rabi' Al-Awwal* of the *hijrī* year 1425 in the city Riyadh, specifically at a seaside dwelling on Al-Kharj road near the first industrial city, and by the grace of God alone, several mujahideen from Fallujah undertook a secret ambush of a group of American officers who were traveling in three civilian cars (GMC—Yukon). They were officers of the base at Sultan al-Kharj, which includes the command and control center of the aggressing U.S. forces. The attack resulted in two direct deaths and a third who was seriously injured. The mujahideen managed to escape (4).

This text mentions Fallujah only as a deployment location of militants who completed an attack in Saudi Arabia, not as a destination for jihad. The writer praised Al Qaeda's efforts in the Arabian Peninsula: "On this occasion, we remind our Muslim brothers everywhere (in Palestine, Afghanistan, Iraq, and elsewhere) that our hearts are with them. We will not fail them. The government of the Al Saud family does not represent our noble Muslim people" ("The Twelfth News Statement on the Topic of a Secret Ambush in Fallujah" 2004, 4). The article presents Al Qaeda's abiding interest in overthrowing the Saudi government. It also uses three evident mechanisms of persuasion: references to the authority of the Quran, contrasts between Muslims and non-Muslims as well as ignoble Muslim rulers and their "noble" subjects, and an attempt to instill affection in readers with the phrase "our hearts are with them."

The formation of AQI expanded Al Qaeda's focus to include Iraq, and specifically Fallujah, but in ways that subtly differ from Al-Zarqawi's messaging. In an article titled "God Is with You, Oh Fallujah," published in *Mu'askar Al-Battār* after AQI's formation, Al-Faruq Al-'Amari (2004) laments the deteriorating situation in Iraq. He begins with a brief *tahmīd* and praise to the prophet: "Praise be to God, Lord of the worlds, and may there be no aggression except against the oppressors. Peace and prayers upon our prophet, the one who is our beloved and our master, Muhammad bin Abdullah, and upon his family and companions" (3). Al-Zarqawi's embellished style of oration yields to the brevity of Al-'Amari's written text. Al-'Amari (2004) contrasts a Muslim in-group with a Christian out-group by referring to the Iraq War as a Crusade,

> which the American Army has launched against the people of Islam, particularly against the Sunnis in Fallujah and more generally in those areas neighboring the cities of Anbar province. The attack started, as is the custom of the cowardly Americans, with intense airstrikes by F-16 aircrafts against the steadfast city (3).

Besides religious contrasts, Al-'Amari contrasts shared emotions of Muslim steadfastness against Christian cowardice to the extent of dehumanization: "The people there have pledged their determination to defend the essence of Islam from being plundered by human pigs" (3).

Al-'Amari (2004) then mediates disorder by disrupting the thoughts and emotions of readers in accusing them of complacency: "What fills the heart with grief and the eye with blood is that the youth of Islam were content with observing the situation from a distance in Iraq" (3). He goads his readers to action: "For how long, Oh youth of Islam? For how long will we be in this miserable situation?" (3). This sentence ascribes a "we-dentity" to the audience by forcing an attachment of personal responsibility to the Iraq War. For persuasion, the author references a leading jihadist: "Proceed according to what Shaikh Saud Al-'Utaybi said in his last statement: 'You are embarking on jihad in the Arabian Peninsula, so where is Iraq?' " (3). Saud Al-'Utaybi belonged to a generation of Arab jihadists who fought abroad during the 1980s and 1990s, returned to Saudi Arabia, and propagated an Islamist worldview upon joining Al Qaeda in the Arabian Peninsula (Hegghammer 2006b). Al-'Utaybi insisted that Arabs should wage jihad in Afghanistan, Chechnya, or Iraq *only if* they could not undertake jihad in Saudi Arabia (Hafez 2007).

Based on this reasoning, Al-'Amari (2004) stops short of convincing readers to travel to Iraq: "Oh people of Fallujah! Indeed, your brothers on the Arabian Peninsula will do what they can, God willing, to support you. We ask God that the mujahideen remain on His path and that He assist the people of Islam and jihad" (3). Like Al-'Utaybi and Al-Salim's last will and testament, quoted at the beginning of this chapter, Al-'Amari prioritizes territorial affiliation over religion as he addresses Sunnis in the Gulf.

Mu'askar Al-Battār's texts demonstrate that even though OMJ and Al Qaeda shared meanings of collective Sunni subjugation throughout history and practices of violent jihad, members of Al Qaeda did not prioritize jihad in Iraq upon AQI's formation. Instead of full assimilation, some integrated Al Qaeda's active support for jihad in the Arabian Peninsula with passive support for OMJ's focus on Iraq. For assimilation or integration processes to be successful, individuals must shed some elements of their original cultural identity before they can incorporate elements of a new identity. Otherwise, cultural conflict will occur, risking separation or marginalization as alternative acculturation processes (Berry 1992). Power dynamics can also influence acculturation: Group leaders may try to force assimilation, but individuals can exert agency to resist these pressures (Bowskill, Lyons, and Coyle 2007; Guarnaccia and Hausmann-Stabile 2016). From this perspective, Al-'Amari exhibits clear agency in refusing to shed Al Qaeda's original priority of jihad in the Arabian Peninsula. Contrary to bin Laden's order, not all the brothers in AQI listened and obeyed Al-Zarqawi "from top to bottom."

The OCF framework also reveals differences between OMJ and Al Qaeda in the mechanisms of persuasion used in their media. Like Al-Zarqawi, writers in *Mu'askar Al-Battār* cited the authority of the Quran and emphasized contrasts between Muslims and non-Muslims. Unlike Al-Zarqawi, however, Al Qaeda's writers tried to persuade readers to like them through empathy ("our hearts are with them") and encouragement ("God is with you"), not by highlighting the risk of retribution for deviating from God's path, as in "A Message to the Tribes of the Banu Hasan," or magnifying the fear of Sunni extinction to instigate violent behaviors in the present, as in "My Beloved Ummah." Moreover, Al Qaeda's writers cited contemporary scholars like Saud Al-'Utaybi, not just medieval scholars such as Ibn Taymiyya, whom Al-Zarqawi routinely invoked. The language in Al Qaeda's texts is also softer; texts request God to help the mujahideen rather than incite readers to act violently through direct address and verbal commands. Al Qaeda's writers may have theoretically supported the jihad in Iraq, but they did not uniformly support it as an in-group norm within AQI's organizational relationships.

"All Religion Will Be God's"

At forty-six minutes, thirty seconds, "All Religion Will Be God's"[3] marks a shift in online jihadist activities. AQI released the video on June 29, 2005, with a dedicated web page and different download links based on connectivity speed. The video is a case study of the first known instance of a militant organization integrating physical and digital war in real time with full awareness of media's capacity to instigate violence (Glasser and Coll 2005). The video begins with a recitation of the fifty-first verse of the Quran's fifth chapter, Al-Māida: "O believers, take not Jews and Christians as friends; they are friends of each other. Whoso of you makes them his friends is one of them. God guides not the people of the evildoers" (Arberry 1996, 108). With this beginning, AQI exploits two mechanisms of persuasion: drawing contrasts between a Muslim in-group and non-Muslim out-groups and appropriating the Quran's authority. A graying Osama bin Laden walks down a hill with a cane—presumably in Afghanistan, judging by his style of dress—warning Muslims against befriending Jews and Christians, whom he calls "the greatest among the infidels," another expression of in-group–out-group contrasts. Unlike in "The Heroes of Fallujah," Al-Zarqawi does not appear in the beginning, which signals bin Laden's overall leadership of AQI.

From 2:12 to 4:00, footage from four films is aggregated: a man kneeling before a masked executioner (figure 3.1), an ambulance being searched, a veiled woman wailing, and soldiers from the Iraqi Army dancing. The audio from each clip is inaudible, overshadowed by a nashīd whose refrain repeats: "Will they deny what they are going to hear?" Like "The Winds of Victory," this video mediates disorder through several mechanisms of persuasion that engage the senses of sight and sound simultaneously. The montage of four films offers visual proof of the war's consequences: The mujahideen conduct operations against others, government officials torment civilians by searching ambulances, women wail over the deaths of their sons and husbands, and Iraqis co-conspire with the Americans. The nashīd aims for psychological persuasion by demanding that viewers acknowledge the truth of what they are witnessing. Unlike OMJ's videos and Al-Zarqawi's

FIGURE 3.1 A screenshot from AQI's video "All Religion Will Be God's." An unmasked man crouches before a masked militant. From 20:35 to 23:26, the video explains that the man used to be an employee of the Iraqi Ministry of Interior. For this reason, AQI labels him an "apostate" even though he is a Sunni Muslim (*murtadd*). The flag's top line of text is a phrase from the Muslim profession of faith: "There is only one God and Muhammad is the prophet of God." The second and third lines identify the group to which the militant belongs as AQI: "The Base [*Qāida*] of the Organization of Jihad in the Country of the Two Rivers."

speeches, which drew upon the repertoire of classical Arabic oration for linguistic persuasion, the video does not feature elaborate *tahmīds*, praises to the prophet, or *saja'*.

The film mediates disorder differently from the videos described in chapter 2. "The Heroes of Fallujah" featured OMJ's in-house content. In "The Winds of Victory," the first six minutes consisted of the narrator's commentary playing over news footage. In contrast, the first twenty minutes of "All Religion Will Be God's" are docudrama, the blending of identifiable people and events with dramatic narrative structures. This is meant to persuade viewers by offering undeniable visual proof of a distinct worldview (Lipkin 2002). Apart from showcasing real people whom audiences recognize, docudramas persuade viewers through sequences that "establish legitimating strategies because the varying proximities they provide allow pictorial and spatial inferences to be made" (Lipkin 1999, 69). AQI sequences this video to induce specific inferences, with each sequence contrasting an in-group of Sunnis who believe in jihad against all others.

Sequence 1

At 4:02, a caption appears: "Baghdad. *Azār* [March 2003]." A narrator exclaims, "A tyrannical war. Another round in the series of Crusader Wars whose leader is the head of disbelief (*kufr*), America. The war has not proceeded according to what it planned and expected." The video shows aerial bombings of buildings and American tanks racing across a desert. The narrator continues: "Its convoys have entered the land of Iraq, as the most insane Rome began spreading its deceitful joy over the announcement of the end of military operations." "Rome" recalls the role of the Catholic Church during the Crusades and is a word that bin Laden used generically to refer to Western Europe, reminding audiences of the historical animosity between Christians and Muslims (bin Laden 2004). President George Bush appears, delivering his "Mission Accomplished" speech. The film, which ascribes a uniform Christian identity to all Americans, disorders the emotions of viewers by arousing distrust in Christians.

Sequence 2

At 4:54, the narrator counters: "The fool does not know. In fact, the war has not ended. Instead, it has only begun now." Footage of attacks appears with captions identifying their locations and body counts. All attacks in this video are listed in the following box in order of appearance. The soundtrack consists either of audio from the attacks, *nashīd*s, or brief narrations. The *nashīd*s mediate disorder by pressing for violent behaviors. The first *nashīd*'s refrain is "Blow them up, blow them up, wherever you find them." The verbal command ascribes a militant "you-dentity" to the audience. The second refrain valorizes shared respect, restored through violent confrontation: "The passages of blood, the passages of blood. We march on the path of God. Glory returns to religion; honor returns to religion." The narrator not only draws contrasts with non-Muslims but calls for their total annihilation.

Unlike OMJ's videos featuring parasocial characters, the video films attackers from afar, who do not address the audience.

All targets listed in the preceding box are symbols of the American or Iraqi government: American tanks, military convoys, Iraqi installations, and locations with a police presence. Through this sequencing, AQI attempts

Suicide Attacks in "All Religion Will Be God's"		
Target of the Attack	Geographical Location	Number of Casualties
American tank	Ramadi	20 American soldiers
American tank	Saqlawiyah	—
American tank	Youssoufia	—
United Nations headquarters	Baghdad	—
American military convoy	Abu Ghraib	14 American soldiers
Armed clashes (*ishtibākāt*)	Tel Afar	—
American tank	Mansour	12 American soldiers
American armed convoy	Al-Dawra highway to Baghdad	25 American soldiers
American tank	Ramadi	—
Iraqi "spy"	Baghdad	1 Iraqi
Iraqi military recruitment center	Baghdad	45 Iraqis
Police intersections	Baquba	12 Iraqis
Police station	Baghdad	20 Iraqis
Directorate of police	Baquba	28 Iraqis
American military convoy	Tal Afar	—
Police station	Baquba	7 Iraqis
Militia headquarters	Ramadi	—
Police checkpoints	Tal Afar	—
Police station	Tal Afar	—
Car bombings	Mosul	—
Attempted assassination of the interim prime minister, Ayad Allawi (b. 1944)	Baghdad	—
Assassination of the former interim prime minister, Ezzedine Salim (1943–2004)	Baghdad	1 Iraqi
Assassination of a police chief	Baghdad	—

Note: – indicates that the number of casualties from the attack was not provided.

FIGURE 3.2 A screenshot from "All Religion Will Be God's." Militants battle American-led coalition forces in direct combat rather than conduct only suicide attacks, as was depicted in OMJ's videos.

to elicit inferences that the war has *not* gone according to America's plan and that combat operations are continuing. To promote a transnational religious identity, the narrator states, "Our jihad in Iraq is like how it is in Afghanistan, Kashmir, Chechnya, and Bosnia: a pure, legal jihad. We come from the lands of different countries" (8:53). The text mediates disorder by stipulating the proposition that AQI's violent actions against the nation-state are "pure" and "legal". The video shows AQI militants battling American forces, as shown in figure 3.2. Unlike "The Heroes of Fallujah," which showed militants training or relaxing together, and unlike "The Winds of Victory," which showed militants embracing before attacks, the only time that AQI depicts relationships is when men commit attacks together.

Sequence 3

The narrator names multiple outgroups. At 9:58, the narrator announces, "This ummah will not be subjugated. It is used to the style of cunning and deceit." Images appear of American officials meeting with Arab rulers to persuade viewers that Muslim rulers are colluding with disbelievers. The narrator labels Arab rulers "hypocrites" (*munāfiqīn*) and "clients" ('*umalā*) of "our nation." In the Quran, *munāfiqīn* refers to those who claim to be Muslims but betray the community (Penrice 2004). Here, the narrator evokes shared meanings from the Quran of sincerity and duplicity, all the while investing *munāfiqīn* with a new connotation: Arab rulers betraying their Muslim citizenries. Here, culture reinforces social psychology by providing AQI with a religious term to designate Muslim rulers as an out-group.

Apart from rulers, the narrator names two other out-groups as co-conspirators: "The first category: various groups of cargo drivers, contractors, and interpreters. They have tied themselves to becoming treacherous slaves while lowly serving the Jews and Crusaders" (until 12:31). Interpreters and contractors appear, wearing combat fatigues, smiling, and taking pictures with American soldiers. The narrator continues: "The second category: they are represented by those who are called 'the security apparatuses' from among the police and the army who have distanced themselves from the land" (12:50–13:00). Iraqi soldiers dance in the streets, searching vehicles such as ambulances and shooting civilians in the street. In both cases, the video tries to persuade viewers by producing visual proof of Iraqis serving the interests of non-Muslims rather than those of the Muslim population.

Sequence 4

The narrator discusses casualties:

> The occupation of America has led to an ugly result. The truth of it is not hidden except for those whose hearts are sickened. It has forced the bombing of cities, the destruction of places, especially those that are inhabited, the killing of children, and raids and attacks in which only the elderly and children are available to surrender, in addition to the issue of imprisoning women (13:43).

The video disrupts the thoughts and emotions of viewers through the visual proof of images that are even more graphic than those of "The Winds of Victory": Men dig for the corpses of children in the rubble of destroyed buildings, and severely maimed and bloodied children are shown. The narrator describes Abu Ghraib as "the underpinning of the tragedy," (14:07) as the same image of a man standing hooded in "The Winds of Victory" is shown. The sequence mediates disorder by contending that viewers who feel no anger must have "sickened" hearts.

The video transitions to a report on war atrocities at 18:04. The narrator exclaims,

> The organization Human Rights Watch—an American organization that cannot be labeled as sympathetic to what the mujahideen says since it is based on disbelief— has said in its ninety-six-page report about the situation in Iraq after the invasion that the gathering of people in Iraqi prisons and what has transpired according to official Iraqi plans exceed what took place during the time of Saddam.

This segment exploits many mechanisms of psychological persuasion: citing the authority of Human Rights Watch, heightening the organization's credibility by contrasting its secular perspective with the religious world-view of the mujahideen, and invoking social proof of what the audience knows to be true pertaining to Saddam Hussein's despotism. As visual proof, the video shows examples of torture while the narrator reads the report's conclusions, shown in figure 3.3.

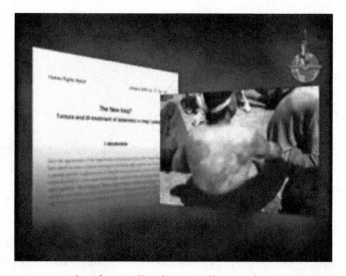

FIGURE 3.3 A screenshot from "All Religion Will Be God's." The video persuades viewers by continuously offering visual proof of the narrator's statements.

The image in this figure exemplifies how AQI mediates disorder differently depending on the media platform. The video disrupts the thoughts and emotions of viewers by *visually* juxtaposing images to build the association between the contemporary Iraq War and civilian atrocities and *aurally* reinforcing this association by reading out Human Rights Watch's findings. This multimodal disruption would not be possible with platforms that rely on only one sense for persuasion such as sound for speeches or sight for photographs.

Sequence 5

At 24:24, the narrator extols AQI's response: "The Muslims know who has adopted the path of God. They know that the mujahideen are the ones who expend their souls for their positions. A path that requires the expenditure of people, money, and children." This last sentence commemorates AQI's militants, who sacrifice everything, including their families, to defeat non-Muslim disbelievers. At 25:07, the narrator mediates disorder by imposing an obligation upon viewers to respond with violence in kind: "It is incumbent upon us to reply to words with words and reply to blood with blood." From 25:20 until 45:45, the video shows footage of the attacks in listed in the preceding box as *nashīd*s play in the background. At 45:45, the narrator congratulates Muslims for initiating jihad, suggesting that AQI's militants will maintain violent in-group norms through interpersonal bonds of affection: "I bring good news to the Muslim ummah of what has happened with God's cooperation. Affection has begun among the heroes. And it will be there with us against the infidels and the apostates in battles. God is victorious over his command, but most people do not know."

"All Religion Will Be God's" mediates disorder as a docudrama that reflects AQI's emergent cultural identity. Unlike the effusive style reminiscent of classical Arabic oration in OMJ's texts, this video relies on news footage to present indisputable proof of the Iraq War's devastation, forcing the audience to accept AQI's claims of accurately representing the situation on the ground. A verse from the Quran frames recurrent contrasts drawn with non-Muslims. Through calculated sequences, the narrator advances shared in-group meanings that disrupt the thoughts and emotions of viewers by contrasting multiple outgroups to induce specific inferences: America's tyrannical war has not proceeded according to the plans of the inimical Christians and Jews → the war has only now begun with the mujahideen committing attacks → Iraqi rulers, civilians, and security forces who collaborate with the U.S.-led coalition are hypocrites who must be targeted → foreigners conspire with local collaborators to inflict horror on the Muslim population → only the mujahideen can defend the population. By asserting that its jihad is "legal," AQI positions itself between individuals and the Iraqi state in urging violence. *Nashīds* provoke the audience to kill enemies wherever they are found. Unlike the depictions of militants training, relaxing, or congratulating each other before attacks in OMJ's videos, "All Religion Will Be God's" does *not* depict relationships within the organization as a mechanism to maintain social norms for violent thoughts, emotions, and behaviors.

AQI's Mediated Disorder

By applying the Outline for Cultural Formulation through a discourse analysis of militant media before and after the OMJ–Al Qaeda merger, we can observe the acculturation process in the formation of AQI by tracing shifts in language use, meanings, practices, and symbols. Before the merger, OMJ and Al Qaeda demonstrated certain commonalities: a worldview that pitted Muslims against non-Muslims and shared practices of violent jihad against enemy out-groups. Both organizations took advantage of the symbolism in the prophet Muhammad's triumphs to draw an analogy between past battles and the contemporary Iraq War. Both groups maintained that only patience and steadfastness in jihad could redress collective grief and historical humiliation. The mechanisms of psychological persuasion used in each group's media are similar: citing the Quran consistently for authority, drawing frequent contrasts between Muslims and non-Muslims, and forcing audiences to accept initial propositions in the course of developing arguments. Like OMJ's "The Winds of Victory," AQI's "All Religion Will Be God's" used extensive footage of innocent casualties as visual proof of American atrocities and footage of its militants attacking official institutions of the state in order to inspire others. Its *nashīds* were composed in strict meter to reinforce this visual proof, mediating disorder by stirring audiences to kill enemies everywhere.

[72]

To promote a unified identity during situations of high competition, cultural groups promote behavioral shifts in three ways: encouraging people to copy high-frequency behaviors, promoting the imitation of successful individuals, and punishing nonconformists (Henrich 2004). The depiction of militants successfully attacking enemies in "The Winds of Victory" and "All Religion Will Be God's" crystallizes a militant group identity by promoting the imitation of individuals whom the group considers successful. Throughout these texts, historical terms from the Quran such as *fitna*, *ahzāb*, *murtadd*, and *munafiqīn* acquired new connotations in the Iraq War, which AQI uses to categorize in-groups and out-groups. In "All Religion Will Be God's," AQI mediates between individuals and society by insisting that its actions against the nation-state are "a pure, legal jihad."

Despite these similarities, there are plain differences. Unlike Al-Zarqawi, Al Qaeda's writers dispense with the extravagant style of classical Arabic oration. While a *tahmīd* to God and praise to the prophet are present, little effort is expended on *saja'* or parallel grammatical structures for linguistic persuasion. One could counter that the Al Qaeda texts I analyzed are from written periodicals, as compared to Al-Zarqawi's speeches, and that the media platform influences the types of linguistic practice that both groups used to spread their violent messages. However, that argument would not account for why both videos described in chapter 2 used forms of linguistic persuasion from classical Arabic oration absent from AQI's "All Religion Will Be God's." Perhaps a group-level behavioral shift in language use occurred. Classical Arabic rhetoric developed *saja'* and *izdiwāj* in an oral society in which speakers drew on personal charisma to persuade audiences (Halldén 2005). At the start of the Iraq War, Al-Zarqawi may have been drawing on his charisma as a motivational speaker to persuade audiences by posting speeches online to construct a new identity for OMJ. This may have not been necessary with "All Religion Will Be God's," since enough time had elapsed after the start of the Iraq War for AQI to acquire news footage that offered visual proof of the war's consequences. The messenger did not need to be persuasive because the message itself was. We will see in chapter 4 that Al-Zarqawi's use of classical Arabic linguistic practices reappears, suggesting that the full armamentarium of psychological persuasion is differentially deployed depending on who runs the group's media. We will also see in chapter 6 that IS's so-called caliph, Abu Bakr Al-Baghdadi, lifts Al-Zarqawi's entire introduction from "A Message to the Ummah and the Mujahideen in

Fallujah." These trends are observable through the OCF framework because of discourse analysis's close attention to the meanings, practices, and symbols that compose a group's identity.

Behavioral shifts also exist in the depiction of in-groups and out-groups during the AQI acculturation process. Unlike OMJ's videos, which showed militants at leisure, praying together, and preparing each other for attacks, "All Religion Will Be God's" does not focus on the interpersonal bonds of its members. This may reflect challenges during the acculturation process of militants knowing exactly how to relate to each other. Al-Zarqawi's authoritarian style of leadership is on display in "The Pledge to the Al Qaeda Organization Under the Leadership of Osama bin Laden," in which he insists that OMJ's militants would obey Osama bin Laden "from top to bottom." This leadership style differs from that of the writers in Al Qaeda's *Mu'askar Al-Battār*, who tried to foster likeability among readers as a mechanism of persuasion. Another shift is apparent in depictions of enemy out-groups: While both groups despised Jews, Christians, and Arab collaborators, Al-Zarqawi also targets the Shia and Kurds in "A Message to the Ummah and the Mujahideen in Fallujah," as he did in the speeches described in chapter 2. Drawing contrasts with Shia and Kurds was not a priority for Al Qaeda's writers or in AQI's "All Religion Will Be God's."

These negotiations over AQI's group identity—which I have demonstrated in OMJ's and Al Qaeda's media before and after the merger by using the OCF framework—reflect themes in written correspondence between Al-Zarqawi and Al Qaeda leaders apprehended by American forces in Iraq. In a letter to Al-Zarqawi from July 2005—the month "All Religion Will Be God's" was released—Al-Zawahiri (2005) acknowledges that Iraq was not his priority:

> It has always been my belief that the victory of Islam in this era will not be realized until a Muslim state is established upon the prophetic methodology in the heart of the Islamic world, and with delimiting (*tahdīd*) the region of the Levant, Egypt, and its borders around the Peninsula and Iraq, but whose center would be the Levant and Egypt.

We see this sentiment prevail among the writers of *Mu'askar Al-Battār*. Al-Zawahiri (2005) rebukes Al-Zarqawi for targeting the Shia: "Will it be possible for the mujahideen to kill all of the Shia in Iraq? Has any Islamic state in history tried this? Why do they kill the Shia masses even though they [the Shia] are pardoned for [their] ignorance? What loss would be inflicted upon us if we did not attack the Shia?" *Mu'askar Al-Battār*'s writers also did not call on Al Qaeda's militants to attack the Shia. This clearly indicates an intractable difference over defining hostile out-groups, with Al Qaeda's members resisting OMJ's definition of the Shia as a group meriting attack after AQI's formation. This difference indicates that applying the OCF framework to study the media of two militant groups before and after their merger through discourse analysis can empirically disclose the acculturation process in real time, and potentially exploit intergroup differences to inform counter-messaging.

From this perspective, we can trace IS's inheritance of Al-Zarqawi's legacy. In its sixth issue of *Dabiq*, published almost a decade later, IS mocked Al-Zawahiri for refusing to kill the Shia despite their collaboration with the U.S. government: "If adh-Dhawārī were to consider making *takfīr* of them [calling them infidels], he wouldn't 'make *takfīr*' of them except for one justification: supporting America in their aggression towards the Muslims" (ash-Shāmī 2014–2015, 19). IS's argument matches Al-Zarqawi's messages described in the chapters 1 and 2: In "My Beloved Ummah," he alleges that the Shia supported the Mongols over Sunni Arab rulers, and in "A Message to the Ummah and the Mujahideen in Fallujah," he condemns the Shia for supporting the U.S.-led coalition. Now, IS was delegitimizing Al Qaeda by ascribing the group a "you-dentity" that it indirectly supports America by refusing to label the Shia as blasphemers, revealing a consistency in media messaging despite the group's evolution.

Another letter from Al Qaeda's Atiyah Abd Al-Rahman (1969–2011) at the end of 2005 admonishes Al-Zarqawi for mediating disorder by subverting the authority of religious scholars: "Take care of the class of religious scholars and elders, especially in Iraq and in the whole world, and respect them entirely. Do not confront any one of them no matter what, no matter what errors they commit in shaping the hearts of the public until God is victorious" (Al-Rahman 2005). This letter also illustrates the contested acculturation process between OMJ and Al Qaeda to determine which meanings should be central to AQI's identity. Intergroup polarization occurs when groups define their norms for thoughts, emotions, and behaviors in complete opposition to those of other groups (Hogg, Turner, and Davidson 1990). Al-Rahman's letter shows that Al Qaeda's core leadership was frustrated with Al-Zarqawi defining his in-group's identity in complete opposition to multiple out-groups, including Sunni religious scholars who did not support his violent positions on jihad—and whom Al Qaeda's leadership was not prepared to estrange.

Let us now revisit fundamental assumptions about the general acculturation process, keeping in mind these contests over cultural identity. The psychologist John Berry, who classically described the four processes of acculturation, writes,

> Cultural identity involves, at its core, a sense of attachment or commitment to a cultural group, and is thus a cultural as well as a psychological phenomenon. In this sense, it requires the existence of a cultural group, which can be actual and viable at present, remembered from one's past, or imagined in one's future (2006, 170).

Berry underscores that acculturation occurs at the level of the group as well as at the level of the individual: "The concept of acculturation is employed to refer to the cultural changes resulting from these group encounters" (1997, 6). But what if the members of a group do not act the same way because of their sense of attachment and commitment to their original cultural group, as we have seen with Al Qaeda's members? And what if their thoughts, emotions, and behaviors are not in alignment? Al-Faruq Al-ʾAmari obviously did not heed bin Laden's order to obey Al-Zarqawi, even after AQI's formation. One explanation is that individuals have varying degrees of attachment to group norms. As cultures spread into new environments, individuals may display socially acceptable behaviors without committing to in-group norms because they want their behaviors to match the majority's, not from agreement with the group but to avoid punishment upon deviating from in-group norms (Henrich 2004). In this light, Al-ʾAmari's text departs from the obedience that bin Laden and Al-Zarqawi demanded upon AQI's formation.

Instead, I suggest a new acculturation strategy that calls attention to the ambivalence of individuals when two distinct groups interact. Writing about the hybrid identity that results when cultures mix, Homi Bhabha (1996) suggests,

> Strategies of hybridization reveal an estranging movement in the 'authoritative,' even authoritarian inscription of the cultural sign. At the point at which the

precept attempts to objectify itself as a generalized knowledge or a normalizing, hegemonic practice, the hybrid strategy or discourse opens up a space of negotiation where power is unequal but its articulation may be equivocal.

Despite bin Laden's authoritative and authoritarian inscription of leadership in Al-Zarqawi, individuals like Al-'Amari expose an ambivalence; passive praise for jihad in Iraq does not lead to his actively calling on others to become foreign fighters after AQI's formation. As a relatively powerless member of Al Qaeda compared to bin Laden, his articulation of support is equivocal, in the sense of being ambiguous and indefinite. For this reason, Al-'Amari's text captures a fifth acculturation strategy that I call *equivocation*. Equivocation—from the Latin *aequus* ("equal") and *vocare* ("to call")—reminds us that individuals may publicly call out their equality, similarity, or identification with others during the process of acculturation, but think, feel, and behave in ambiguous or even noncommittal ways. A public articulation of assimilation or integration with others may be an act of performance in response to power differences, not necessarily a reflection of private commitments. We do not know about the kinds of pressures that individuals like Al-'Amari encountered, but it is doubtful that he could risk insubordination without punishment within Al Qaeda. A cultural psychiatry perspective on the diffusion of militant identities shows us that analyzing texts individually and in relation to each other reveals the work of culture through intertextuality, the construction of a cultural identity through texts based on shared meanings and practices assigned to social participants (Kristeva 2005). Cultural psychiatry reminds us that the act of constructing shared meanings, practices, and symbols to define normative thoughts, emotions, and behaviors is disruptive and unstable; and that language captures the traces of lived experiences for people—including militants—caught up in complex, threatening, and uncertain conditions in the contemporary world (Good et al. 2008) like the Iraq War.

FOUR

The Assembly of the Mujahideen Council

Common Group Identity Formation

IN JANUARY 2016, a month after Al-Rahman's letter to Al-Zarqawi, AQI and five other groups formed the *Majlis Shūra Al-Mujāhidīn* (Assembly of the Mujahideen Council [AMC]). We know little about AMC, as this aspect of IS's evolution has received scant and contradictory attention. Some have briefly discussed AMC's formation through the rise of Ibrahim Awwad Ibrahim Al-Badri (b. 1971), IS's self-styled caliph, now widely known as Abu Bakr Al-Baghdadi, in Iraq's jihadist circles: "Ibrahim didn't join al-Qaeda until 2006, when his militia enlisted in al-Qaeda's umbrella organization, Majlis Shura al-Mujahidin. When the Islamic State declared itself later that year, Ibrahim was made the head of all the Shari'a committees in the group's 'provinces'" (McCants 2015, 76). The cultural psychiatrist wants to know what exact meanings, practices, and symbols these Sharia committees advocated to propagate a Muslim identity. Al-Baghdadi appears to have participated in AMC well after its establishment: "When al-Zarqawi was killed in 2006, Baghdadi brought his group under the Majlis Shura Council (MSC) umbrella, at Abu Hamza's invitation" (Atwan 2015, 116). Why would Al-Baghdadi bring his group under this umbrella when other groups resisted, as we shall see in chapter 5?

Others consider Al-Zarqawi to have been the force behind AMC: "He needed to dispel one of the greatest liabilities to AQI's popular appeal—its perception as a foreigner's jihadist arm. He thus needed to 'Iraqize' his franchise. In January 2006 al-Zarqawi announced the creation of the Majlis Shura al-Mujahidin fi al-Iraq" (Weiss and Hassan 2015, 49). Al-Zarqawi may have created AMC at the request of Al Qaeda: "Zawahiri worried that the al-Qaeda brand was increasingly counterproductive in Iraq, and he urged Zarqawi to develop something more appealing to Iraqis. On January 15, 2006, al-Qaeda in Iraq's spokesman announced the establishment of the Mujahidin Shura Council" (Fishman 2016, 79). What interests me as a cultural psychiatrist is: How could the AMC ever really "Iraqize," when we've seen Al-Zarqawi appeal to foreign fighters through his use of the terms "migrants" (*muhājirūn*) and "helpers" (*ansār*) since the start of the Iraq War?

A third group of scholars has not identified any single party responsible for AMC, noting its presence only as a transitory phase between AQI and the Islamic State of Iraq (ISI). Jessica Stern and J. M. Berger (2015) write, "Within a few months, a coalition of jihadist insurgents known as the Mujahideen Shura Council announced the formation of the Islamic State of Iraq" (26). Similarly, Fawaz Gerges (2016) notes, "Despite the internal dissension, and with the support of the six Sunni Islamist groups who joined ranks with AQI in January 2006, AQI pushed forward, and, on October 13, 2006, the Mujahideen Shura Council announced the formation of the Islamic State of Iraq" (103). Instead of treating AMC as a layover between AQI and ISI, what can we learn about the group's culture and psychology, historically and currently, through its media?

We saw in chapter 3 that OMJ and Al Qaeda strongly disagreed over the extent to which the Shia represented an out-group worth targeting and whether religious scholars merited cultivation or scorn. If the acculturation process to form AQI elicited disagreement between two groups, how did six groups subsume their differences to form AMC? What group-level shifts in language or systems of shared meanings, practices, and symbols came to define AMC's identity? After groups that were formerly in competition reduce boundaries with each other to form a common overall identity, the decrease in social distance can improve relationships with former out-group members (Gaertner et al. 1989). Mere contact between groups does not ensure a common overall identity, however; conditions of cooperative interdependence and supportive social norms must also exist (Gaertner et al. 1994; Gaertner, Dovidio, and Bachman 1996).

In this chapter, I analyze the emergence of AMC's common identity through four texts: AMC's founding statement, a video that introduces the likeability of militants as a new form of psychological persuasion without referencing religious texts at all, a video that depicts militants in institutions that imitate the nation-state, and a treatise that defends the declaration of ISI and a new type of self.[1] By applying the OCF framework to AMC's media through discourse analysis, we can observe the meanings, practices, and symbols that define a common group identity (Brewer and Gardner 1996) as a culture and psychology of militancy penetrated Iraq's Sunni mujahideen groups.

AMC's Founding Statement

On January 15, 2006, AMC issued its first statement.[2] It is an exemplary case study as the first media product to articulate the cultural and psychological identity of the newly formed group. It begins with a brief *tahmīd*— "In the name of God, the beneficent, the merciful"—and cites the authority of the fourth verse of the Quran's sixty-first chapter, *Al-Saff*: "Praise be to God who ordered association (*jamā'a*) and was pleased with his people, who is the most truthful of the speakers: 'God loves those who fight in His way in ranks, as though they were a building well-compacted' " (Arberry 1996, 274).

The phrase "a building well compacted" (*bunyān marsūs*) appeared in Al-Zarqawi's pledge to Al Qaeda (discussed in chapter 3), which I translated then as "a solid foundation." The phrase historically described a building that was strongly constructed with well-cut stones (Ghabin 1998). In using this phrase, AMC was taking shared meanings from the Quran to promote a shared practice of militant jihad, investing the symbol *bunyān marsūs* with a new meaning of in-group unity among Iraq's mujahideen groups: each group is the well-cut stone for the foundation of jihad As in Al-Zarqawi's speeches, the prophet Muhammad appears as a historical prototype whose militarism is worthy of emulation: "Peace and prayers upon the leader of the mujahideen, our prophet Muhammad, and upon his family and his companions who walked upon his path, protected his tradition, and joined the community in their jihad and their call."

AMC mediates disorder by disrupting the audience's thoughts to stipulate initial propositions that equate past and present circumstances: God ordered His community to fight on His path → Muhammad, his family, and his companions followed His path of jihad → Muhammad is "our prophet," and we must protect his tradition, as did his family and companions.

The direct address using the word "our" consolidates an in-group identity based on militant Islam.

The statement also introduces the reasons for AMC's formation, drawing contrasts with multiple out-groups for persuasion: "The Crusader armies and their followers among the Rejectionists [Shia] and secularists invaded the seat of the caliphate Baghdad and struck the Muslims from a single bow, looking to support their disbelief and realize the dreams of their Jewish masters." In chapter 3, I demonstrated that Al-Zarqawi reviled the Shia as an out-group despite personal letters from Al Qaeda's leadership rebuking his stance well after AQI's creation. AMC's founding statement discloses a clear behavioral shift toward treating the Shia as outsiders after AQI's founding. AMC's representation of Baghdad as the "seat of the caliphate" ignores Iraq's entire postcolonial history after the fall of the Ottoman Empire. According to recent estimates, 99 percent of Iraq's population is Sunni or Shia Muslim, and the Shia compose roughly 60 to 65 percent of that (Central Intelligence Agency 2015). In belonging to the Sunni minority, Saddam Hussein promoted Arab nationalism, not religion, through his secular Ba'ath Party to win popular legitimacy across religious (Sunni, Shia, Christian) lines (Ahram 2002). With the phrase "looking to support their disbelief," AMC warns that Sunnis are under siege from multiple enemies.

For further persuasion, the statement draws contrasts and cites the authority of the Quran in describing the fractured response among Sunni jihadists:

> It was obligatory upon monotheists from among the Sunnis and the community, among those who chose the path of jihad and struggle against the disbelievers in all of their types and forms, to come together to assist the truth, becoming close and loving with one another, repudiating polytheism, pursuing a goal that is not neutral or retreat: "Fight them, till there is no persecution and the religion is God's entirely" (Arberry 1996, 201).

The impersonal construction "it was obligatory" conveys obligation through a perceived duty. The text contrasts monotheists and disbelievers, highlighting common emotions of affection in coming together against polytheists. Positive affect produces an inclusive common group identity by reducing bias among individuals who before may have seen each other as rivals (Dovidio et al. 1995). AMC's statement suggests that its constituent groups tried to strengthen bonds with each other through positive affect, not simply denouncing out-groups. This excerpt ends with a citation of the thirty-ninth verse of the Quran's eighth chapter, *Al-Anfāl*, whose ending is the same as the title of AQI's video "All Religion Will Be God's," thus demonstrating that AMC had adopted OMJ's and AQI's practice of interpreting the Iraq War through Quranic concepts and vocabularies invested with new meanings.

The text lists all the groups that formed AMC:

> The following jihadist groups—(1) the Organization of Al Qaeda in the Land of Two Rivers, (2) the *Al-Mansūra* Army, (3) the *Ansār Al-Tawhīd* Brigades, (4) the Islamic Jihad Brigades, (5) the *Ghuraba* Brigades, (6) the *Ahwāl* Battalions—have decided to form a council under the name *Majlis Shūra Al-Mujāhidīn Fī Iraq*.

The statement ends by citing the authority of forty-first verse of the Quran's twenty-second chapter, *Al-Hajj*, to issue a violent call for action:

> The council calls on Muslims within and outside the Land of Two Rivers to join the jihad in the Land of Two Rivers in support of their religion, defending the weak, establishing the seat of Islam, and implementing the rule of God's Sharia over his earth, as He—may He be exalted—said, "We establish them in the land, perform the prayer, and pay the alms, and bid to honour, and forbid dishonour; and unto God belongs the issue of all affairs" (Arberry 1996, 32).

In chapter 2, I mentioned that OMJ called for the establishment of Sharia to counter the nation-state system in their videos "My Beloved Ummah" and "The Winds of Victory." AMC's statement demonstrates that five other groups accepted and adopted this aspect of OMJ's identity. The phrase "Muslims within and outside the Land of Two Rivers" was meant to appeal to Sunnis everywhere, encouraging them to participate in jihad rather than to "Iraqize" AMC.

AMC's founding statement mediates disorder by disrupting the audience's thoughts and emotions. The shared meanings from the Quran regarding the need for unity among Muslims justify shared militant jihad against all non-Sunnis through the same line of reasoning that Al-Zarqawi used in his speech pledging allegiance to bin Laden (discussed in chapter 3). AMC's statement uses three mechanisms of psychological persuasion: invoking the authority of Quranic verses, stipulating propositions for the audience, and drawing contrasts with multiple out-groups, including Christians, Jews, secularists, and Shia. AMC invokes the authority of the prophet Muhammad and his companions as historical prototypes who protected God's path, which the mujahideen must follow now. Like Al-Zarqawi's call for solidarity among Sunnis during the formation of AQI, AMC's statement indicates that violent group norms will be maintained in positive relationships with other in-group members with a focus on "becoming close and loving with one another." The statement calls on Muslims everywhere to replicate the unity of AMC by establishing Sharia in Iraq through jihad.

"Fatima's Fiancé"

Unlike all other videos from this era of the group, the nine-minute video is a case study in the use of humor between protagonists. The video[3] begins with scrolling text against a red curtain, as shown in figure 4.1. The text comes from a letter written by a female inmate at Abu Ghraib named Fatima. Some Iraqis contend that she penned the letter in blood after being raped by her guards, which incited attacks against the facility once her letter was

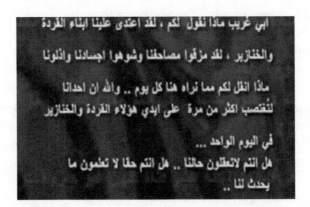

FIGURE 4.1 A screenshot from AMC's video "Fatima's Fiancé." The text reproduces a letter from an inmate at Abu Ghraib. The use of this letter at the beginning of the video is intended to persuade audiences by drawing on social proof of abuses at the facility.

smuggled out. The U.S. Department of State has denied these allegations (Awan 2007). Abu Ghraib appeared briefly in OMJ's "The Winds of Victory" and AQI's "All Religion Will Be God's"; here, it is central to the narrative.

Fatima's letter reads,

> My sister! The mujahideen are on the path of God. We say to you that we are your sisters in the Abu Ghraib prison. The sons of monkeys and pigs have attacked us. They have ripped up our texts, disfigured our bodies, and disgraced us. . . . We have been incited through multiple violations in a single day at the hands of these monkeys and pigs.

Here, Fatima is contrasting Muslims and non-Muslims for persuasion. As in OMJ's "A Message to the Tribes of the Banu Hasan" and "The Winds of Victory," AMC dehumanizes hostile out-groups by labeling them "monkeys and pigs." As a second mechanism of persuasion, similar to the "The Winds of Victory," the letter imposes an obligation upon the audience to reflect on abuses against prisoners: "Are you not aware of our situation? Do you have the right not to know what is happening to us?"

The letter mediates disorder by disrupting the thoughts and emotions of the audience through graphic details of abuse: "There are thirteen girls in prison with me, all of whom are unmarried. I have heard and seen all of their violations. They prevented us from wearing clothes and offering prayers. This drove them to commit suicide after the American dogs raped and punished them severely." Some Islamic laws and social custom in rural Arab societies have traditionally treated chastity as a virtue among unmarried women (Antoun 1968; El Saadawi 2007). Fathers and brothers have conducted honor killings against female relatives for engaging in sexual practices outside marriage and bringing dishonor to the family (Abu-Odeh 2011). Fatima's letter indicates that the women in Abu Ghraib killed themselves based on perceptions of their dishonor, exhibiting shared meanings of gender norms, shame and humiliation, and a shared practice of suicide in response to notions of impurity.

Her letter ends with a call to action: "I am Fatima, your sister in God. I say to you, 'Fear God. . . . Leave their tanks and their planes outside and pay attention to us here inside Abu Ghraib prison. Kill us with them. Destroy us with them. Don't leave us with them.'" The letter draws contrasts through religion, with Fatima extending kinship to the mujahideen as a "sister in

God." By appealing directly to the audience and using verbal commands—"fear God," "leave their tanks and their planes," "pay attention to us," "kill us," "destroy us"—the letter mediates disorder by disrupting thoughts and emotions to incite violence against Abu Ghraib as a security installation that symbolizes American tyranny in Iraq.

At 1:05, a text slide appears:

> Like all of us, Abu Muawiya Al-Shamali read a message to us from our sister inside the Abu Ghraib prison before she was blessed with martyrdom on the path of God. Abu Muawiya's eyes did not turn away nor did it cause him to wet his pants. He resolved sincerely to avenge her and every free Muslim woman. He did not find his soul pricey; he placed it cheaply on the path of God and sacrificed for the honor of his sisters, hoping that God would accept him as a martyr and marry him to this girl.

This text employs two mechanisms of persuasion. First, the phrase "like all of us" relies on social proof, that the audience is aware of the situation inside Abu Ghraib and does not need more information to assess the truth of the video's claims. Second, it accentuates the contrast between Muslims "on the path of God"—a path of violent jihad since Al-Shamali did not consider his soul "pricey"—and non-Muslims. Media narratives reinforce social norms by encouraging audiences to copy the behaviors of prototypical members, ones who conform to in-group expectations for thinking, feeling, and behaving (van Knippenberg, Lossie, and Wilke 1994; Hogg and Reid 2006). By embodying in-group meanings of martyrdom, emotions of resolution to avenge "every free Muslim woman," and behaviors of self-sacrifice, Al-Shamali becomes a parasocial character with whom audiences can establish a relationship and psychologically identify by aligning their thoughts, emotions, and behaviors. Like OMJ's "The Winds of Victory," this video uses wedding symbolism to praise martyrs as bridegrooms.

From 2:11 to 3:52, Abu Muawiya Al-Shamali speaks into the camera, flanked by the Quran atop a machine gun, as shown in figure 4.2. Unlike the other videos analyzed in this book, this video shows the protagonist stumbling over his lines repeatedly, laughing with the cameraman:

> Oh, America. . . . Oh, men of religion, who are for paradise and religion. . . . Oh, men of religion, who are for paradise and religion. . . . Oh, men of religion, who

FIGURE 4.2 The protagonist of "Fatima's Fiancé" jokes repeatedly with his cameraman as he struggles to deliver his lines.

are for paradise and religion. . . . The youth are committed to religion. . . . Oh,
men of religion. . . . Oh, youth of religion. . . . Oh, Lord of the universe. . . . Oh,
Lord of this book. [He points to the Quran.] Oh, revealer of this book. . . . Fatima,
who was killed at Abu Ghraib.

Humorous messages can persuade audiences by fostering likeability and
trust in characters, reducing the likelihood of resistance to a message or to
counter-argumentation (Sternthal and Craig 1973; Eisend 2009). This style
of participatory documentary, in which filmmaking is the product of a collaboration between participants, rather than an objective observation of
characters (Rabiger 2015), conveys to viewers that AMC's members maintain in-group norms for violence throughout their positive relationships
with each other. The video manifests affection between protagonist and
cameraman. By showcasing Al-Shamali mistaking his lines, the video also
communicates that its militants can laugh and joke with each other, normalizing expectations that making mistakes is acceptable on the path of
violent jihad. Figure 4.2 shows him struggling to remember his lines.

At 3:52, Al-Shamali gets into a car. The cameraman says, "May God
accept you," as both men laugh with each other. The cameraman films the
explosives planted in the car. Al-Shamali laughs and speaks, but his voice is
drowned out by a *nashīd* with the refrain "We do not die on the path of God,"

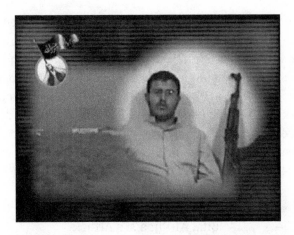

FIGURE 4.3 A screenshot from "Fatima's Fiancé." Al-Shamali was shown joking with his cameraman just moments before. At right, Al-Shamali delivers his lines angrily, as his attack unfolds on the left.

reinforcing shared practices of militancy and a shared meaning of an eternal self that exists independently of the material body. From 6:36 to 7:04, Al-Shamali delivers his speech fluently—using the phrases he could not master before—as shown in figure 4.3. The relative inaudibility of his speech conveys that his stern demeanor is more important than his message.

By juxtaposing Al-Shamali's image with the scene of his attack at a security checkpoint, the video offers visual proof of the attack's success to persuade audiences. A text slide states that the operation killed twenty American soldiers.

"Fatima's Fiancé" mediates disorder by creating a multimodal experience that portrays violence against the Abu Ghraib detention facility in response to Muslim humiliation. This video does not cite texts from the Quran or Hadith for authority or feature stylistic elements of classical Arabic oration to persuade audiences. Instead, it begins with a letter that contrasts Muslims with non-Muslims and imposes an obligation upon viewers to reflect on the abuses being committed at Abu Ghraib. By drawing upon shared meanings of gender norms, shared emotions of shame, and a shared practice of suicide as response to dishonor, the video's purpose is to enrage viewers. Instead of historical prototypes from the first generation of Islam or the Crusades, the video portrays Al-Shamali as a prototypical in-group member who conforms to norms of martyrdom, vengeance, and self-sacrifice. The use of humor elicits likeability as a mechanism of persuasion so that the audience can be transported into Al-Shamali's world and enjoy a parasocial relationship with him. The jovial bond between Al-Shamali and his cameraman suggests that violent in-group norms are maintained through affection with other members of AMC, encouraging a fusion between individual and group identities. The juxtaposition of Al-Shamali eventually delivering his message successfully as the attack transpires offers visual proof of the mission's success with a *nashīd* reminding viewers that the soul endures after the demise of the body on God's path of jihad.

"Bilal Al-Kubaisi's Attack"

This video is the first to incorporate images and vocabularies of statehood. For this reason, it is a case study of the group's identity shift. The video,[4] running twenty-one minutes and thirty seconds, begins with two text slides: a written *tahmīd* to God and AMC's logo. The Arabic word for attack, *ghazwa*, recalls the classical genre of *maghāzī* literature on the prophet Muhammad's battles, which were used to teach the first generation of Muslims that God supported the faithful against larger, better-equipped armies during battles such as that of Badr (Faizer 2014). Al-Zarqawi speaks into the camera:

> Rise up, Oh carriers of the banner! Where are the lions (*usūd*) of Anbar? Where are the lions (*luyūth*) of Salahuddin? Where are the great men (*rijālāt*) of Baghdad? Where are the knights (*fursān*) of Nineveh and the heroes (*abtāl*) of Diyala? Where are the Salahuddins of Kurdistan? You are the lions (*usūd*) of monotheism (*tawhīd*) (until 00:30).

With these words, Al-Zarqawi uses several mechanisms of persuasion to mediate disorder. First, he imposes an obligation upon his audience to behave violently by urging them to "rise up" and prove that they are "lions of monotheism." By the twelfth century, poets extolled Salahuddin's victories during the Crusades by comparing him to a lion that ruled over all the other animals, demonstrating values of dignity, bravery, courage, and valor (Al-Garrallah 2010). Classical Arabic has more than a thousand words for "lion," and poets demonstrated their linguistic prowess by using different synonyms in the same text (Stetkevych 1986); here, Al-Zarqawi uses *usūd* and *luyūth*. Al-Zarqawi's vocabulary is also replete with medieval symbols— banner men, lions, knights, and heroes—to equate victories during the Crusades with the Iraq War, similar to his use of Salahuddin as a historical prototype in "A Message to the Tribes of the Banu Hasan." As a second mechanism of persuasion, Al-Zarqawi contrasts a monotheistic in-group of Muslims against a polytheistic enemy out-group.

Al-Zarqawi deploys techniques of persuasion drawn from classical Arabic rhetoric. We saw in chapter 3 that Al Qaeda's and AQI's texts did not emphasize linguistic persuasion after the OMJ–Al Qaeda merger. In this video, however, Al-Zarqawi returns to this style, using assonance (*usūd Anbār*), consonance (*fursān Nineveh*), a narrow type of *saja'* rhyming based on word symmetry (*rijālāt Baghdād, abtāl Diyāla*), and parallel grammatical constructions that pair a symbol of masculinity with a Sunni-dominated region in Iraq ("lions of Anbar," "great men of Baghdad"). Al-Zarqawi also uses classical words that OMJ has invested with new meanings to equate past with present:

> Where are the migrants who followed Muhammad (*muhājirūn*)? Where are his helpers (*ansār*)? Where are the companions (*ashāb*) of purity and spoils of war (*anfāl*)? Where are the people of the two *sūras* [Quranic chapters] of victory (*fath*) and combat (*qitāl*)? (until 00:47).

The last sentence invokes the Quran's authority to persuade viewers of violence.

Like AQI's "All Religion Will Be God's," AMC sequences this video to induce specific inferences, but with a clear difference in messaging. Rather than first show footage of atrocities to which militants react through multiple attacks, this video conducts an in-depth examination of one militant's career in jihad. Unlike expository documentaries that depict familiar events for the audience, biographical documentaries showcase trustworthy characters with whom the audience can establish parasocial relationships for persuasion (Slater 1997; Appel and Malečkar 2012).

Sequence 1

From 2:07 to 4:13, a narrator reads aloud text, also shown on screen, that portrays Bilal Al-Kubaisi as the prototypical in-group member, as shown

FIGURE 4.4 A biography of a militant in "Bilal Al-Kubaisi's Attack." Unlike earlier videos, which showed only militants reading out last wills and testaments before committing their attacks, this video frames Al-Kubaisi as a prototypical in-group member by illustrating his trajectory in jihad.

in figure 4.4. The narrator praises him for representing the group's core values: *faith* ("He was on the path of monotheism during the days of Iraq's polytheism"), *violence* ("He began jihad from the beginning of the occupation"), *affection for in-group members* ("He was joyful, happy, optimistic with victory, and moved from hearing about the sorrows of the Muslims"), *enmity toward out-groups* ("He was among those for whom the words of God—may He be exalted—applies: 'The humblest among the believers, the noblest against the disbelievers such that he was violent against the disbelievers and the hypocrites"), and *fearlessness* ("He was bold, courageous, and participated in many battles in Ramadi"). AMC uses Al-Kubaisi to contrast monotheistic Muslim believers with polytheistic non-Muslim disbelievers.

The narrator directly addresses Iraq's tribal leaders:

This is the state of one tribe among the noble tribes of Anbar—what about the other tribes, the people in places with great trouble? Battling God's enemies, peaceful toward God's companions, battling the hypocrites. If only the people approached them, went with them, and were among them.

[90]

The video mediates disorder by valuing Al-Kubaisi as an ideal group member whom others should emulate and by drawing contrasts between Muslims and non-Muslims. Saddam Hussein incorporated Sunni tribes within bureaucratic and security institutions to guarantee loyalty (Baram 1997; Al-Mohammad 2011). Here, AMC summons these very tribes to revolt against the state.

Sequence 2

At 4:42, a slide introduces a new segment titled "Scouting the Targets." Footage appears of militants planning attacks by drawing up blueprints and discussing assaults from from various angles. The title "Scouting the Targets" and its caption "Division of Military Targets" illustrate a shift in linguistic practices as AMC adopts the vocabulary of statehood. In analyzing the breakdown of law and order in postcolonial societies, the anthropologists John Comaroff and Jean Comaroff (2006) write,

> Criminal violence does not so much repudiate the rule of law or the licit operations of the market as appropriate their forms—and recommission their substance. Its perpetrators create parallel modes of production and profiteering, sometimes even of governance and taxation, thereby establishing simulacra of social order (5).

With this shift in linguistic practice, AMC appropriates the lexicon of the law to establish simulacra of social order, trying to persuade viewers of its governance capabilities through visual proof of its operations.

Sequence 3

At 5:38, a slide introduces a segment titled "Planning the Operation." A "field leader" named Abu Dajana Al-Iraqi speaks to an unmasked Al-Kubaisi (figure 4.5). He reiterates the in-group's core values: "Oh brother, the most beloved thing in Iraq is the caliphate and jihad. Perseverance is perseverance, and patience is patience." The video appropriates the language of statehood by using the terms "field leader," "operations," and "soldiers."

FIGURE 4.5 A screenshot from "Bilal Al-Kubaisi's Attack." The caption uses the term *soldiers* (*junūd*) to refer to AMC's militants as onscreen text explains the mission.

Al-Iraqi points to a blueprint on the wall, using visual proof to persuade viewers of the meticulous planning of Al-Kubaisi's attack.

Sequence 4

At 6:41, a slide reads "The Martyr's Last Will and Testament." Al-Kubaisi speaks into the camera under a tree. His speech conforms to accepted practices of classical Arabic oration with a *tahmīd*: "In the name of God, the beneficent, the merciful." Next, he recites the *shahāda*, the profession of faith for all Muslims, to define his in-group: "I bear witness that there is no God but God and that he has no partners. And I bear witness that Muhammad is his slave and prophet, the leader of the mujahideen, the sincere, the martyrs, and the good." Al-Kubaisi treats Muhammad as an authoritative historical prototype whose model of behavior must be emulated. He cites the authority of a Hadith text narrated by Umar ibn Al-Khattab (584–644 CE), a companion of Muhammad's who was the second caliph in history, as well as the conqueror of the Byzantine and Sassanid Empires (Hourani 1991):

> The prophet of God—peace and prayers upon him—said, "Actions depend on intentions. And every person will obtain what he intends. So whoever migrated for God and his prophet, his migration is for God and his prophet. And whoever migrated for worldly benefits will receive it."

As a mechanism of psychological persuasion, this text contrasts those who pursue worldly pleasures with those who pursue God's path of jihad. Here, the pursuit of worldly benefits is incompatible with following God's path.

Al-Kubaisi expresses humility, a way to cultivate likeability:

> I ask God the greatest who entrusted me on this path: Choose me among the people as you chose the brothers who preceded me. Accept me among the martyrs and the pious. Include me among the prophets and the martyrs. Oh God, I have undertaken this action out of hatred for this world and not fearing it. Rather, I have undertaken this action wanting to meet God, mighty and majestic is He.

Rather than arrogantly express certainty that his attack will guarantee him salvation, Al-Kubaisi entreats God to "choose," "accept," and "include" him, demonstrating piety. Finally, Al-Kubaisi mediates disorder by imposing an obligation upon the audience to act violently in following God's path of jihad: "To my brothers of the mujahideen in all places around the earth. Upon us is the obligation of unity between the word of God (*kalima*) and patience (*sabr*)." Through these mechanisms of persuasion, Al-Kubaisi disrupts the thoughts of his audience by inducing specific inferences: God's prophet, Muhammad, was the leader of the mujahideen → those who forsake this world can meet God and his prophet → I have forsaken this world to meet God → the mujahideen should also forsake this world in following God's orders.

Like "The Winds of Victory," this video features Al-Kubaisi in the company of other militants to offer visual proof of AMC maintaining in-group norms for violent thoughts, emotions, and behaviors in relationships. However, "Bilal Al-Kubaisi's Attack" portrays these relationships extensively compared with prior videos. Figure 4.6 shows Al-Kubaisi praying with others as a man sings, "Every life dies and embarks on a journey." Figure 4.7 shows Al-Kubaisi embracing other militants. Both instances offer visual proof of the written text in AMC's founding statement that militants have become close and loving with one another in order to fight non-Muslims. For the first time since OMJ started releasing videos, we see a video in which all militants are dressed in the same uniform, as AMC appropriates practices normally associated with statehood.

FIGURE 4.6 A screenshot from "Bilal Al-Kubaisi's Attack." Al-Kubaisi is unmasked as other masked militants reinforce his resolve to commit a suicide mission by singing inspirational songs and praying with him.

Sequence 5

At 13:51, a slide introduces a segment titled "Carrying Out the Attack." A *nashīd* with the recurrent line "I will descend, I will descend" (*sau-fa-an-zil / sau-fa-an-zil*) conveys Al-Kubaisi's determination to act violently while the sounds of gunfire and explosions punctuate the soundtrack. The footage alternates between images of Al-Kubaisi in his truck and images of

FIGURE 4.7 A screenshot from "Bilal Al-Kubaisi's Attack." Militants take turns embracing and congratulating a smiling Al-Kubaisi before he embarks on his suicide mission.

explosions, offering visual proof of his attack's success. At 16:24, the video dwells on the ruins of his attack as the seventeenth verse of the Quran's eighth chapter, *Al-Anfāl*, is recited for authority:

> You did not slay them, but God slew them; and when thou threwest, it was not thyself that threw, but God threw, and that He might confer on the believers a fair benefit; surely God is All-hearing, All-knowing (Arberry 1996, 171).

Like OMJ, AMC relied on shared meanings of this verse to persuade audiences that the Quran justifies violent behaviors. At 18:27, a narrator reads out a text slide that lists the attack's casualties: two civilian vehicles, two military Humvees, as well as the entire building of Military Affairs and all forty people inside.

Sequence 6

At 20:38, the video ends by showing an adolescent and child clutching machine guns, as shown in figure 4.8.

After a brief *tahmīd* to God and praise to the prophet Muhammad as "the leader of the mujahideen," the adolescent draws contrasts between Muslims

FIGURE 4.8 A screenshot of an adolescent and child holding machine guns at the end of "Bilal Al-Kubaisi's Attack."

and non-Muslims: "Indeed, we are from this place. We say to the Crusaders and apostates, our God prepared the martyrs to migrate." He pledges allegiance to Abu Musab Al-Zarqawi, following which he and his companion fire their guns. The camera man says, "God is Great." According to one estimate, IS conscripted eighty-nine child soldiers between January 2015 and January 2016 (Bloom, Horgan, and Winter 2016). If radicalization encompasses the cognitive, emotional, and behavioral processes that predispose individuals to violence (Horgan 2008b, 2009), this video demonstrates that children have been internalizing AMC's violent group norms since at least 2006; this video is thus our first insight into the intergenerational diffusion of a militant cultural and psychological identity within Iraq.

"Bilal Al-Kubaisi's Attack" mediates disorder as a biographical documentary that reflects the diffusion of AMC's identity. The video relies on multiple mechanisms of persuasion: linguistic practices from the tradition of classical Arabic rhetoric, shared meanings from the Quran and Hadith to authorize violent actions, and recurrent contrasts between Muslims and non-Muslims. AMC features Al-Kubaisi as the prototypical group member who embodies faith, readiness to pursue violence, affection for in-group members, and hatred for out-groups. With deliberate sequencing, the video traces Al-Kubaisi's path on jihad as visual proof of his operation: Scouting his targets → planning the operation → reading out his last will and testament → carrying out the attack.

The sequences depict a shift in linguistic practices that reveal AMC's evolving self-conception from a militant organization into a state. At multiple points, AMC mediates disorder by positioning itself between individuals and society to call for the violent implementation of a caliphate and Sharia. "Al-Kubaisi's Attack" recalls OMJ's style of filmmaking, which emphasized the maintenance of violent in-group norms through positive interpersonal relationships: militants praying, singing, and embracing each other before missions. A brief concluding sequence depicts the spread of AMC's culture across generations with the inclusion of images of an adolescent and child holding machine guns.

"The Notice to Mankind of the Birth of the Islamic State"

In 2006, one month after the first Sunni "Awakening" Council, an AMC Sharia Committee member, Uthman bin Abd Al-Rahman Al-Tamimi, defended the declaration of ISI in a treatise to prevent Sunni tribes from collaborating with the U.S.-led coalition (Fishman 2007, 2009). Eventually, four thousand American soldiers, twenty-three tribal leaders from Anbar province, and more than one hundred thousand men from across Iraq participated in the Awakening, with tribal elites resenting AMC's control over lucrative smuggling networks that threatened their power (Katzman 2008; Long 2008; McCary 2009). In a section titled "What Will We Be Accused of and How Will We Respond?" Al-Tamimi (2006) addresses Sunni Muslims with the intent of constructing a common group identity, allowing us to observe the active diffusion of a militant culture throughout Iraq. It is an exemplary case study as the first known treatise of the group's attempt to justify its shift in identity to other Sunni mujahideen groups.

Al-Tamimi first cites the Quran and Hadith for authority:

> Texts from the book [the Quran] and Sunnah [the Hadith] indicate the necessities of coming together and forbidding sects and difference, as God—may He be exalted—said, "O, believers, fear God as He should be feared, and see you do not die, save in surrender. And hold you fast to God's bond, together, and do not scatter" (Al-Tamimi 2006, 55–56).

Al-Zarqawi cited this exact verse in his pledge to Osama bin Laden upon the formation of AQI, urging his audience to behave in strict conformity with God's orders. Like Al-Zarqawi, Al-Tamimi frames unity through a shared meaning of belief in God out of fear, contrasting an in-group of Muslims with an out-group of disbelievers. For additional authority, Al-Tamimi (2006) cites a Hadith:

> Ibn Jarir narrates through support from Abdullah ibn Masud—may God be pleased with him—that [the prophet] said, "Oh people, upon you is obedience and association. Indeed, it is tied by God who has ordered it, and what you hate in obedience and association is better than what you like in sects" (57).

Al-Tamimi uses the language of the Quran to promote shared meanings of Muslims forming a common in-group through association (*jamā'a*) and avoiding multiple sects (*firqa*). The word for "sect" (*firqa*) has a negative connotation and shares the same etymology as the verb "to scatter" (*tafarraqa*) in the Quranic verse cited previously. Through these meanings, Al-Tamimi mediates disorder by obliging his audience to obey *his* interpretation of God's orders.

A core assumption in social psychology is that individuals join in-groups to improve their self-esteem (Turner and Reynolds 2001). A common group identity is thought to result when individuals who formerly categorized each other as belonging to different out-groups recategorize each other as members of the same in-group and express positive emotions toward each other (Gaertner et al. 1993). "What you hate in obedience and association is better than what you like in sects" counters this classic tenet of social psychology. Instead, Al-Tamimi proposes that hatred for others, not positive self-esteem, is what will motivate the formation of a common Sunni identity.

As a variant of the mechanism of persuasion in which an author stipulates propositions for the audience, Al-Tamimi presents and then responds to objections from a hypothetical Sunni jihadist who shares his reverence for religious texts but does not think that AMC should have declared ISI. The text addressed real-time debates within the Islamist community, as Hamas and the Muslim Brotherhood denounced AMC for declaring ISI without first seeking consensus among reputed Sunni scholars around the world (Lynch 2010). Al-Tamimi (2006) addresses the need for territory before a state can be declared:

> It will be said: Your announced state lacks Sharia because it lacks the most important ingredient of a state and that is land. And with this, you oppose the tradition of your prophet who established his state after his consolidation of land and acquisition of power in Medina, and it was a clear and delimited territory. We do not see clear boundaries for you or its obvious appearance, as it is required among modern and sovereign nations (57).

In response, Al-Tamimi (2006) draws upon social proof to persuade his audience that Arab states in the Middle East also do not fulfill this requirement:

> We find that these states are threatened within the range of Israeli air weapons that look for every opportunity to disrupt their airspace and exert sovereignty over their airspace and lands. With our assertion that Israel is capable of striking any target that it wants inside these states at any time it wants—i.e., in military terms, the lands of the states neighboring Israel are confronted with a threat and weakening of their airspace—this does not make control over these lands before governing them ineffective or naïve (58).

Al-Tamimi also draws upon social proof of the Iraqi government's instability for persuasion: "The most skillful example of this is what is labeled the 'current Iraqi government.' It is a term of pitiful transformation, meager of meaning and strength. I do not say that it does not possess influence, but that it does not possess an existence in many regions of Iraq" (59). In essence, Al-Tamimi argues that AMC's in-group norms cannot be justified through contemporary political circumstances.

Instead, Al-Tamimi (2006) invokes the life of the prophet Muhammad to legitimize the founding of ISI:

> When the prophet—peace and prayers of God upon him—entered Medina and established it as the first Islamic state, there wasn't control over land through the understanding that many now living in modern states mean. With the beginning of the reign of the new state, missionaries (ashāb al-da'wa) perhaps did not constitute the majority in Medina, as there were hypocrites, Jews, and those who were waiting around until they saw business opportunities (60).

Al-Tamimi notes that allegiance to the state varied among the local population at the time:

> This did not prevent the announcement of an Islamic state over the land of Medina even though it formed a narrow stretch in relation to the wide area of land of the Arab peninsula; i.e., the prophet—peace and prayers of God upon him—announced a state in tight boundaries that was established among groups of people who differed in their level of support and loyalty to the fledgling state (60).

With this move, Al-Tamimi argues that the formation of a common group identity to support ISI can be gradual and does not have to happen instantly. He mediates disorder by positioning fear as central to the group's identity:

> This is what confirms that the prophet—peace and prayers of God upon him—and his noble companions were not fully secure in their first civil reign, but were carrying weapons and afraid, in that their control over the new society was deficient from the beginning (60).

Al-Tamimi's normalization of fear as an in-group norm challenges a fundamental tenet of psychiatry and psychology that the idealized self is rational, is in complete control, and does not experience negative emotions (Gaines 1992; Lloyd and Moreau 2011). For him, the Islamic State of Iraq is a psychological state as well as a political state.

Al-Tamimi (2006) next addresses objections that ISI could be a state without a bureaucracy:

> Among the ingredients of a state is the existence of institutions, government mechanisms, and the facilities of the state that are known today. Your state, which you have announced, does not present any of this and does not enjoy what we see regarding the manifestations of sovereignty that we have observed in modern states (66).

As before, Al-Tamimi cites the authority of the Quran and Hadith:

> The basis to which we return in our decisions and plans of action is the book [the Quran] and the *Sunna* [the Hadith]. The sayings that remarkable scholars mention are from predecessors and successors, and we do not find in these foundations a description of an Islamic State that requires the existence of mechanisms established along the lines of what the educated people see today in governments. There is no known evidence that requires the existence of mechanisms and facilities that modern states have, most of whose systems come from the Western infidel path and its political legacy (66).

By referencing "the Western infidel path," Al-Tamimi (2006) implicitly nods in the direction of social scientists like Max Weber who defined statehood through bureaucracy. Weber wrote, "All states may be classified according to whether they rest on the principle that the staff of men themselves own the administrative means, or whether the staff is 'separated' from these means of administration" (1991, 81). Instead, Al-Tamimi (2006) invokes Sharia as the sole cultural tradition that governs in-group psychological norms: "We say there is no evidence from the Sharia for a certain type of organization or institution that an emerging Islamic state requires" (66). For persuasion, the text contrasts states founded on "the Western infidel path" with the Islamic state, founded on Sharia, thus implying that Sharia is incompatible with secular principles. The repeated use of "we" underscores Al-Tamimi's ascription of a "we-dentity" to all Sunnis based on their adherence to his interpretations of the Quran and Hadith.

Finally, Al-Tamimi (2006) addresses objections surrounding ISI's lack of capital:

> It will be said: The modern state is not established except through funds that are set up with its foundation and establish its basis. Your declared state does not own sources of capital, strong financial resources, or stable and known economic supplies. Through this, you will carry a burden of poverty, despair, and suffering to the people (69).

For the cultural psychiatrist, this argument reflects a surprising realization that psychological disorders—"despair and suffering"—result from environmental challenges such as socioeconomic disadvantage, food insecurity, and unstable living circumstances (Lund et al. 2010; Iemmi et al. 2016). Al-Tamimi (2006) responds with an appeal for Sharia:

> The gap in needs between the state and the people will be filled, as it is a known and clear subject in the books of jurisprudence according to Islamic principles that are abandoned today. Returning to these principles for the present time and sphere of life will undoubtedly bring sustenance. Hope is pinned on the blessed Islamic state in stimulating these abandoned paths and institutions and reviving them after their knowledge has been forgotten under a mass of polytheistic institutions ruling the Muslim world (69).

Al-Tamimi emphasizes that ISI will interpret Sharia to create institutions that maintain in-group norms for thinking, feeling, and behaving. He cites the authority of Muhammad's life:

> The prophet—peace and prayers of God upon him—did not come to the people with economic welfare and a blossoming standard of living, but he—peace and prayers upon him—did what he could by way of distributing riches, spreading the bounties of alms, and establishing it [the state] with justice according to what was possible and destined. Rather, he—peace and prayers upon him—took wealth from the people for the sake of using it in jihad and the needs of the Islamic state (70).

If state institutions deliberately transform individuals into disciplined and industrious citizens (Mitchell 1991), Al-Tamimi's text articulates a conception of the self that fuses the individual's identity with that of the group.

"The Notice to Mankind of the Birth of the Islamic State" mediates disorder by disputing the very legality of the modern, secular nation-state as unfounded in Sharia, warranting violence against the official Iraqi government. Shared meanings of the need for Muslim unity justify animosity toward non-Muslim disbelievers to foster a common group identity. These shared meanings give way to shared emotions: fearing God and hating non-Muslims. Al-Tamimi deploys key mechanisms of persuasion to convince readers of behaving in conformity with his interpretations of the Sunni textual tradition: citing the authority of the Quran and Hadith, pointing to the instability of modern nation-states in the Arab Middle East as social proof that an Islamic state founded on Sharia would respond to God's commands, and invoking the life of Muhammad as a historical prototype whom all people must emulate. AMC mediates disorder by normalizing fear as an emotion to be expected when adopting violent jihad. Al-Tamimi regards Sharia as the sole cultural tradition that should govern group norms and the only foundation upon which to build institutions that reinforce the ISI's militant identity.

AMC's Mediated Disorder

The OCF framework reveals AMC's construction of a common group identity through shared meanings, practices, and symbols that subsumed the identities of six Sunni mujahideen organizations. Based on the texts analyzed in chapters 2 and 3, AMC clearly exhibits OMJ's cultural and psychological influences. All four AMC texts described in this chapter have justified jihad as a necessary practice, though in different ways: AMC's founding statement and "The Notice to Mankind of the Birth of the Islamic State" prioritized shared meanings of obedience to God's orders; "Fatima's Fiancé" portrayed violence as a reasonable response to violations of chastity and gender norms; and "Bilal Al-Kubaisi's Attack" deployed shared meanings of forsaking the pleasures of this material world in order to follow God's path. AMC has also used a wide array of symbols to promote a distinct worldview: Baghdad becomes the seat of a new caliphate in AMC's founding statement, wedding imagery compares would-be martyrs to bridegrooms who marry angels in "Fatima's Fiancé," and medieval vocabularies of conquest are applied to the current Iraq War in "Bilal Al-Kubaisi's Attack." Through these cultural resources, AMC mediated disorder by disrupting the audience's emotions to call for affection among Sunni Muslims, hatred toward all non-Muslims, vengeance and retribution to redress the humiliation of Muslim women, and steadfastness despite fear during violent jihad. Discourse analysis through the OCF framework allows us to empirically demonstrate these trends.

The choice of media platform also influences the mechanisms of psychological persuasion that AMC has employed to mediate disorder. Across all texts, drawing contrasts between a Muslim in-group and non-Muslim out-groups is a common mechanism of persuasion. The differential use of other mechanisms reflects the group's skillful manipulation of media. For example, written texts such as AMC's founding statement and "The Notice to Mankind of the Birth of the Islamic State" urged Sunnis to cultivate affection for each other, whereas its videos offered visual proof of attacks to persuade viewers of the positive relationships among in-group members. As a participatory documentary, "Fatima's Fiancé" depicted humor and camaraderie between Al-Shamali and his cameraman. The biographical documentary "Bilal Al-Kubaisi's Attack" showed militants singing, praying, and attacking together. Both videos represent a shift in the content of the group's messaging, with AMC focusing less on filming missions and more on showcasing militants as prototypical in-group members who embody norms to which others must conform. In both videos, AMC has tried to elicit likeability for its characters so that audiences feel transported into their worlds, establishing parasocial relationships and psychologically identifying with them. The group's use of linguistic persuasion remains evident in "Bilal Al-Kubaisi's Attack," with a concomitant shift in discourse that incorporates the language of statehood, presaging the group's declaration of ISI. The mechanism of persuasion in "The Notice to Mankind of the Birth of the Islamic State" whereby Al-Tamimi presents and refutes the arguments of a hypothetical opponent through lengthy written text would not be possible in videos or nashīds and is a style that is wholly suited to expository texts. AMC has thus used different mechanisms of persuasion depending on their choice of media platform.

"Bilal Al-Kubaisi's Attack" offers a glimpse into the cultural transmission of militancy throughout Iraq, with the video's last sequence portraying an adolescent and child announcing their commitment to jihad against enemy out-groups, pledging allegiance to Al-Zarqawi, and firing machine guns. Cultural transmission occurs through either direct, purposeful decision-making or indirect social imitation (Bisin and Verdier 2001); AMC's decision to depict an adolescent and child in a video demonstrates its attempts to actively spread the group's militant identity across generations, rather than only among adult men. Children learn to copy successful role models to enhance their social prestige (Henrich and Gil-White 2001), which may explain why both the adolescent and child pledged allegiance to Al-Zarqawi. The video shows an adolescent and child firing weapons as a form of play, a model for cultural transmission that reinforces positive experiences with peers during leisure that is more effective than didactic instruction from adults (Nielsen, Cucchiaro, and Mohamedally 2012). By internalizing physical and psychological dispositions that reflect known distinctions within society, children reproduce and maintain social differences in adulthood (Bourdieu 1977). Although this video showed both the adolescent and child speaking into the camera, we will see in chapter 7 that IS has since gone further, involving adolescents and children in suicide missions with the explicit support of their parents.

Moreover, "Bilal Al-Kubaisi's Attack" featured one militant as a prototypical in-group member whom Iraqi tribes should emulate. In its first issue of *Dabiq* after declaring its caliphate, IS included images of whole tribes pledging allegiance to Abu Bakr Al-Baghdadi as visual proof of the group's growing acceptance of mediating disorder and inciting violent against the Syrian state ("Halab Tribal Assemblies" 2014).

By focusing on tribes rather than individuals, IS mediates disorder more rapidly and pervasively against the state to spread its militant cultural and psychological identity. We will see in chapter 6 that images of groups of men pledging allegiance to IS reinforce the idea of an expanding in-group to which all individuals can belong.

Lastly, "The Notice to Mankind of the Birth of the Islamic State" promotes a view of the self that differs markedly from the idea of self-hood in contemporary psychiatry and psychology. In post-Enlightenment, secular, Euro-American societies, the self is perceived as emerging from shared meanings of individualism and shared practices of maximizing one's personal interests and desires, with a deficiency in either realm being construed as a form of mental illness. In contrasting people from individualistic versus sociocentric societies, the cultural psychiatrist Laurence Kirmayer (2007a) writes, "The preeminence of the self over other in both private psychological talk and public moral debate gives rise to an understanding of psychopathology as a failure of individuals to achieve full autonomy, to define their own goals and to achieve personal success" (10). If autonomy—the act of complying literally with one's "self (*auto*) law (*nomy*)"—defines the secular individualistic self, then AMC's common group identity propagates a distinct system of meanings and practices centered on what we could call "allonomy," complying with the law of the other (*allo*). This law of the other is the collection of divine precepts enshrined in religious scriptures that AMC contends it alone has the right to interpret. AMC's goal is clearly to promote *allonomous* selves so that individuals comply with the group's interpretations of Islamic law for thinking, feeling, and behaving. AMC does <u>not</u> want individuals to act autonomously so that they define their own goals and achieve personal success. I am not suggesting that individuals only act fully *autonomously*, without regard for others, or fully *allonomously*, without regard for themselves, but that these cultural ideals represent opposite ends of an asymptotic spectrum of selfhood as people struggle to negotiate their individual free will against group norms. Groups like AMC pull people toward *allonomy* in seeking to subjugate individual goals and measures of success to the group's.

Al-Tamimi repeatedly refers to the Quran and Hadith as the foundation of Sharia that governs AMC's in-group norms for thinking, feeling, and behaving. Before the European colonization of the Arab Middle East in the nineteenth century, Sharia oriented the totality of an observant Muslim's conduct in precolonial times:

> Islamic law governed the Muslim's way of life in literally every detail, from political government to the sale of real property, from hunting to the etiquette of dining, from sexual relations to worship and prayer. It determined how Muslims conducted themselves in society and in their families (Hallaq 2002, 1707).

The importance that pious individuals accorded to the Quran and Hadith exhibited a desire to live in strict conformity with religious texts, rather than according to individual reasoning, in order to resolve known social problems and avoid unwanted innovations in daily life that would deviate from the prophet Muhammad's practices (McAuliffe 2006).

In advocating for a return to this conception of an "allonomous" self, Al-Tamimi and AMC deactivate prohibitions against violent behaviors that lead to death by justifying all actions according to militant interpretations of Muhammad's life. This fundamentally transforms the relationship between individuals and the state, since AMC refuses to recognize any other form of law that it disdains as "human made." Unlike AQI's prioritization of jihad in the Arabian Peninsula, AMC's founding statement encourages all Sunni Muslims to migrate to Iraq *for* jihad, foreshadowing IS's claims in 2014 that

> it is a state where the Arab and non-Arab, the white man and black man, the easterner and westerner are all brothers. It is a *Khilafah* [caliphate] that gathered the Caucasian, Indian, Chinese, Shami [Syrian], Iraqi, Yemeni, Egyptian, Maghribi (North African), American, French, German, and Australian. Allah brought their hearts together, and thus, they became brothers by His grace ("Khilafah Declared" 2014, 7).

Belief in the group's interpretations of the Quran and Hadith becomes the sole determinant that defines in-group membership, as we shall see in chapters 5 through 7.

FIVE

The Islamic State of Iraq, 2006–2013

A Shift in Militant Identity

AL-ZARQAWI WAS killed on June 7, 2006, after the U.S. military bombed a safe house where he was meeting other militants. His death occurred sometime after the release of "Bilal Al-Kubaisi's Attack," in which an adolescent and child swore allegiance to him—they did not ask God formulaically to accept his martyrdom, so we know that he was alive then—and before the release of "The Notice to Mankind of the Birth of the Islamic State." To succeed him, AMC appointed Abu Ayyub Al-Masri (1968–2010), also known as Abu Hamza Al-Muhajir, as its head and Abu Omar Al-Baghdadi (1959–2010) to lead ISI.

This period in IS's evolution has elicited disparate accounts on ISI's group identity. Some have contrasted Al-Masri's leadership with Al-Zarqawi's:

> U.S. forces captured AQI's emir for southwestern Baghdad, who, in the course of his interrogation, spelled out what divided the two jihadist commanders. Al-Zarqawi, he said, saw himself in messianic terms, as the defender of all Sunnis against the Shia; al-Masri saw himself as a talent scout and exporter of terror, for whom Iraq was but one staging ground in the fight against "Western ideology worldwide." In this respect, al-Masri was closer to al-Zawahiri (Weiss and Hassan 2015, 63).

The cultural psychiatrist wants to know what defines "Western ideology worldwide," rather than assume what "Western" or its presumed opposite,

"Eastern," means. Al-Masri apparently enjoyed better relations with Al Qaeda than Al-Zarqawi had:

> The dual questions hanging over Zarqawi's successor were whether he would align AQI more closely with al-Qaeda's central leadership and whether he could strengthen AQI's relationship with Iraq's Sunni tribes. The new emir had deep ties with al-Qaeda and Zawahiri, but he was also an ideological hard-liner more disposed to executing attacks than delicate politics (Fishman 2016, 88).

For a cultural psychiatrist, being "an ideological hard-liner" requires empirical specificity whose meaning cannot be assumed. What ideologies did he have and what was so hard-line here?

Others have seen ISI as a "rebranding" effort that estranged Al Qaeda's central leadership from the outset: "Despite the rebranding, the group continued to be known and referred to as AQI. . . . Zawahiri subsequently conceded that he and bin Laden had not been consulted before ISI had been declared and that they had privately opposed it" (Gerges 2016, 93–95). To make matters worse, ISI's leadership did not advertise its allegiance to Al Qaeda, raising concerns in the Sunni jihadist community that it had gone rogue:

> The actual leader of the new Islamic State, Abu Ayyub al-Masri, assured his bosses that the "commander of the faithful," Abu Umar al-Baghdadi, had pledged an oath of allegiance to Bin Laden in front of the jihadist brothers in Iraq. They did not announce it publicly "due to some political considerations" (McCants 2015, 17).

The discontent was not limited to Al Qaeda, as other groups also resented ISI's brutality: "Rival insurgents appealed to Usama bin Ladin to rein in al-Qa'ida's Iraqi franchise, and they openly fought AQI fighters on the ground" (Siegel 2008, 5).

As a cultural psychiatrist, I'm not surprised at all that AMC's declaration of ISI would catalyze a shift in group identity; we know that context determines the categories that individuals use to define "us" versus "them" (Onorato and Turner 2004). We also saw in chapter 3 that Al-Zarqawi's pledge to bin Laden did not lead to OMJ's seamless assimilation within Al Qaeda upon the formation of AQI. On the contrary, OMJ's cultural and psychological identity dominated AMC. To me, the more fundamental questions are as follows: How did this group identity shift occur toward emphasizing governance? And what discernible group-level behavioral shifts in language use or systems of shared meanings, practices, and symbols do ISI's media reveal?

Two scenarios typically lead to identity shifts: (1) changes in circumstances that alter the shared meanings circulating in society through which people categorize in-groups and out-groups; and (2) changes in the types of identity that are activated simultaneously, leading people to prioritize one conception of the world over another (Burke 2006). In both cases, power influences the shift in identity by restricting the range of meanings available to categorize in-groups and out-groups (Todd 2005). AMC's declaration of ISI fulfills both conditions by changing local political circumstances such that the group repositioned itself from a militant organization (*jamā'a*) into a state (*dawla*) in compliance with Sharia. The previous chapters have shown that members throughout the group's evolution have activated various identities to mediate disorder. While all have appealed to Sunnis in a demographic sense, Al-Zarqawi reminded Sunnis of their historical competition with multiple out-groups; Al Qaeda's authors prioritized territorial affiliation—most notably with the Arabian Peninsula—to instigate violence against hypocritical rulers; and Al-Tamimi demanded an "allonomous" in-group identity such that all group members are to behave in full conformity with the group's interpretations of the Quran and Hadith. Which set of identities wins out in ISI, and how does this process influence the group's use of media to persuade audiences? How does this phase of IS's evolution inform its conception of itself and others?

In this chapter, I focus on ISI's construction of identity through a discourse analysis of three types of text: a speech from March 2007 in which Abu Omar Al-Baghdadi articulates the group's core values; a video in which ISI circulates new meanings, practices, and symbols that reflect its identity shift; and a cache of internal organizational documents known as the Harmony Documents, which were not intended to be read outside ISI but which the U.S. military collected from Iraqi battlefields. The Harmony Documents expose ISI's attempts to mediate disorder among militants seeking to join its in-group and rival Sunni out-groups that challenged its authority. By applying the OCF framework to these texts, we can trace the identity shift resulting from AMC's declaration of ISI and its efforts to maintain in-group norms for thinking, feeling, and behaving violently, among others.

"Say I Am on Clear Proof from My Lord"

In March 13, 2007, Al Qaeda's Al-Furqan Media released this speech, given by Abu Omar Al-Baghdadi. This speech is an exemplary case study of the group's new identity because of how Al-Baghdadi defines ISI's conceptions of in-group norms and targeted out-groups.[1] With its title, ISI attempts to persuade its audience by invoking the authority of the fifty-seventh verse from the Quran's sixth chapter, *Al-Anām*: "Say: 'I stand upon a clear sign from my Lord, and you have cried lies to it. Not with me is that you seek to hasten; the judgment is God's alone. He relates the truth, and He is the Best of deciders' " (Arberry 1996, 127). The speech begins with a *tahmīd* to God and praise for the prophet Muhammad:

> All praise is due to God whom we thank and from whom we ask for help and forgiveness. We seek refuge in God from the evil in us and our evil deeds. Whoever is guided by God cannot be led astray, and whoever is led astray cannot be guided. I bear witness that there is no God but God and that he has no partners. And I bear witness that Muhammad is his slave and prophet.

The text departs from the classical Arabic style of linguistic persuasion that Al-Zarqawi had employed. Instead of *saja'* or *izdiwāj*, Al-Baghdadi reserves his introduction for customary prayers of refuge from Satan's evil before reciting Quranic verses (Glassé 2008) and the Islamic profession of faith affirming God's oneness and Muhammad's status as God's prophet, known as the *shahāda*. Furthermore, Al-Baghdadi introduces an analogy of divine guidance to persuade the audience of his authority: Whoever is guided by God cannot be led astray → I bear witness that there is no God but God → I cannot be led astray. With this argument, he positions himself between the population and the state to mediate disorder.

Al-Baghdadi (2007) next combines two mechanisms of persuasion: He cites verses from the Quran for authority *and* verses that deliberately contrast an in-group of believers with an out-group of disbelievers. He first cites the thirty-eighth verse of the Quran's twenty-second chapter, *Al-Hajj*: "Assuredly God will defend those who believe; surely God loves not any ungrateful traitor" (Arberry 1996, 127). He then cites the 126th verse of the third chapter, *Āl-Imrān*: "Help comes only from God the All-mighty, the All-wise" (Arberry 1996, 61). Finally, he cites the sixty-first verse of the thirteenth chapter,

Al-Ra'ad: "Help from God and a nigh victory. Give thou good tidings to the believers!" (Arberry 1996, 581). With these citations, Al-Baghdadi mediates disorder in disrupting the audience's thoughts by categorizing his in-group solely through belief in God, which exists in zero-sum competition with all others. He insists that God's love comes only from "those who believe" in his path, highlighting shared in-group norms of obedience.

Al-Baghdadi (2007) continues to contrast his Sunni in-group against the Iraqi state:

> Oh bold and courageous mujahid in the jails of the polytheists! Lift your head up and laugh deep from your heart because you have brothers who will never accept injustices against you! They pledged to God to bring you back to their ranks (*sufūf*)!

This text treats audacity and fearlessness as core emotions expected of all in-group members. The word "ranks" draws upon a shared symbol of Muslims united in military combat against non-Muslims The word was also used by Al-Zarqawi in his pledge to bin Laden (discussed in chapter 2) and by AMC in its founding statement (discussed in chapter 4). Al-Baghdadi (2007) praises an operation by ISI militants to describe various types of in-group members, using the same vocabulary of "migrants" (*muhājirūn*) and "helpers" (*ansār*) that Al-Zarqawi introduced in 2003:

> They were in jail opening the doors for their brothers from the *muhājirūn* and *ansār*. More than 220 mujahideen were released by the grace of God. The enemy confessed only to 140 being freed, which is true because they only mentioned the *ansār* from Iraq even though the rest were *muhājirūn* to God in the Land of Two Rivers.

As another mechanism of persuasion, Al-Baghdadi (2007) mediates disorder by playing on fear to justify shared practices of jihad:

> How would jihad be possible in the Land of Two Rivers if there was no Assembly of the Mujahideen Council or Islamic State? How would things go if the Islamic State's soldiers laid down their weapons and discontinued jihad? The answer is known. Their [Sunnis'] honor would be violated. Their crops and cattle would be exterminated.

These appeals to fear persuade listeners to protect themselves against environmental threats, eliciting a high degree of message acceptance and substantial behavioral change, as the dangers named are specific (Shelton and Rogers 1981; Witte and Allen 2000). Al-Baghdadi exploits fear by pointing to the specific dangers of crop and cattle loss that would ruin the livelihoods of the Sunni Muslims whom he seeks to persuade.

Furthermore, Al-Baghdadi (2007) draws contrasts between ISI as the sole defender of Sunni civilians against Sunni rulers, especially the Saudis, whom he accuses of betrayal:

> The House of Salūl—the Saudis—are in a rush to build and strengthen the 'Saudi Hezbollah' under a different name with the blessing of the king's scholars ('ulamā al-sultān), especially those whose hostility against members of the Islamic movement was well known. Therefore, oil money flowed to them from Muhammad bin Nayef and from the merchants of religion.

In an insulting pun, Al-Baghdadi uses the phrase "Āl-Salūl" rather than "Āl-Saūd" to refer to the House of Saud, equating it with the Salūl family that guarded the pagan shrine of Mecca before the revelation of Islam (Jamestown Foundation 2005).

The implication is apparent: Saudi Arabia's rulers are disbelievers despite controlling Mecca and Medina, Islam's two holiest sites. Moreover, Al-Baghdadi mediates disorder by accusing Muslim scholars of selling their religious faith to defend the Saudi government's policies in exchange for wealth. In 1996, Osama bin Laden accused Saudi scholars of selling out religion to support King Fahd, who allowed the American military to establish a base in the country against Saddam Hussein's threats of encroachment (Lawrence 2005). Muhammad bin Nayef (b. 1959) headed the Saudi counterterrorism campaign as Deputy Minister of the Interior for Security Affairs and cracked down on Al Qaeda's in-country operations, all while publicizing his cooperation with Americans and Europeans ("Saudi Arabia's Ambitious Al-Qaida Fighter" 2005). Al-Baghdadi's use of this trope from bin Laden demonstrates Al Qaeda's influence on ISI in spreading a shared meaning of Sunni betrayal by Sunni Arab rulers.

Al-Baghdadi (2007) closes his speech by defining ISI's position on its ingroup, out-groups, and core values. He forgives Sunni for lapses in piety:

"We do not accuse any Muslim of disbelief from sins such as adultery, drinking wine, and stealing unless he claims that it is approved (halāl)." Cultural psychologists differentiate between group "tightness" and "looseness," which are "the strength of social norms, or how clear and pervasive norms are within societies, and the strength of sanctioning, or how much tolerance there is for deviance from norms within societies" (Gelfand, Nishii, and Raver 2007, 7). Al-Baghdadi's speech suggests a degree of cultural looseness in monitoring the behavior of Sunnis living in ISI territories as long as the Sunnis complied with two core values.

The first is Al-Baghdadi's (2007) demand that all people behave in conformity with ISI's interpretations of Sharia:

> It is compulsory to seek God's judgments in disputes by seeking recourse from religious courts and looking for them in cases of not knowing where they are because seeking judgment from polytheists based on secular and tribal laws invalidates one's Islam. God said, "Whoso judges not according to what God has sent down—they are the unbelievers" (Arberry 1996, 144).

Al-Baghdadi uses two mechanisms of persuasion here: imposing a stipulation with the phrase "it is compulsory" and citing the authority of the forty-fourth verse of the Quran's fifth chapter, Al-Māi'da. With these rhetorical maneuvers, he ascribes a "you-dentity" for Muslims by affixing religious identity upon acceptance of ISI's system of Sharia.

The second core value is Al-Baghdadi's (2007) imposition of jihad as a religious obligation:

> We consider jihad on the path of God as compulsory upon everyone ever since the fall of Al-Andalusia that relinquished Muslim lands. The greatest sin after not believing in God is prohibiting jihad on the path of God even though it is compulsory. Ibn Hazm said, "There is no greater sin after disbelief except prohibiting jihad against disbelievers."

As before, Al-Baghdadi uses the same mechanisms of persuasion—imposing a stipulation on the audience and referencing the authority of the Quran—though he cites the Iberian scholar Abu Muhammad Ali ibn Ahmad ibn Saʿid ibn Hazm (994–1064), who insisted on supporting the Umayyad Caliphate despite its waning power in medieval Europe (Wasserstein 2013). Through both mechanisms of persuasion, Al-Baghdadi mediates disorder by positioning the ISI over the government as the guarantor of law and order.

To further subvert the Iraqi government, Al-Baghdadi (2007) stipulates, "We consider freeing the prisoners and women of Muslims from the disbelievers compulsory, either by invasion or ransom. The prophet—peace be upon him—said, 'Free the prisoner.' And we consider helping their families and the families of martyrs compulsory." As before, Al-Baghdadi mediates disorder by using two mechanisms of persuasion: stipulating that prisoners and women must be freed— irrespective of their offenses—simply for being imprisoned among disbelievers, and citing the authority of the prophet Muhammad to justify violent behaviors against the state. The reference to helping women and families demonstrates ISI's efforts to diffuse its culture and psychology of militancy beyond its in-group of adult men who had been dominant in the group's media since 2003.

Finally, Al-Baghdadi (2007) draws contrasts with multiple out-groups. The first targeted group is the Shia: "The rejectionists are polytheists and a party of renegades." The second is secular Muslims: "We believe that secularism is clear disbelief despite the differences in flags and parties—such as nationalism, communism, and Ba'athism—in opposition to Islam. Anyone who practices it is not a Muslim." He targets supporters of the Iraqi government: "We consider anyone who supports the occupation and its supporters of any kind as disbelievers." Finally, he mentions members of other religions: "We consider the People of the Book as parties to war in the Islamic State today who are not honorable since they have broken their oaths in different ways. If they want to be safe and secure, they must renew their oath to the Islamic State." These out-groups are the same as those named by AMC in its founding statement, illustrating shared meanings of a Sunni in-group identity in opposition to all others.

Al-Baghdadi's speech mediates disorder by unifying different systems of meaning that justified jihad from the group's earlier iterations: Al-Zarqawi's articulation of a Sunni group identity that is polarized in contrast with multiple out-groups, Al Qaeda's shared meanings of Sunnis betrayed by their rulers, and Al-Tamimi's push for Sunnis to live life "allonomously" in conformity with AMC's interpretation of Sharia. This identity shift corresponds to the predominant mechanisms of persuasion that Al-Baghdadi uses throughout his speech: citing the authority of Quranic and Hadith texts, which form the basis of Sharia; imposing obligations upon his audience to behave according to these texts; heightening fear by naming the dangers that will befall Iraq's Sunnis if they abandon jihad; and contrasting multiple out-groups, including non-Sunnis and Sunni Arab rulers. Al-Baghdadi continues to use Al-Zarqawi's terms *sufūf*, *muhājirūn*, and *ansār* to equate Islam's early conquests with the current Iraq War, subverting the authority of Muslim scholars who interpret religious texts nonviolently. Al-Baghdadi intervenes between individuals and the state by forcing Iraq's Sunnis to seek redress from the group's covert Sharia courts, defying the Iraqi state's claims over law and order.

"Vanquisher of the Peshmarga"

This video was the most popular ISI video, with over thirty-four thousand views as of June 2017.[2] At fifty minutes and fifty-three seconds, this Arabic video[3] starts with a short *tahmīd* to God, "In the name of God, the beneficent, the merciful," and an image of the group's logo. The title refers to Kurdish peshmarga forces ("those who face death"), which began with thirteen thousand fighters defending the short-lived Republic of Mahabad from 1946 to 1947 in what is now Iranian Kurdistan (Abdulla 2011). After this republic collapsed, Mustafa Barzani (1903–1979) led the peshmarga to Iraq, with about thirty-five thousand working with Iraqi security forces and 190,000 allied to forces attached to Kurdish political parties (Beaumont 2014).

A graphic appears with the ISI flag planted on territory marked "Iraq," as shown in figure 5.1. The image mediates disorder by persuading the audience to visually accept the proposition that ISI, not the government, controls Iraq. No demarcation divides Iraq on the right from Syria on the left, conveying ISI's belief that international boundaries do not exist.

The video invokes the fifty-second verse of the Quran's ninth chapter, *Al-Tauba*:

Say: "Are you awaiting for aught to come to us but one of the two rewards most fair? We are awaiting in your case too, for God to visit you with chastisement from Him, or at our hands; so await; we are awaiting with you" (Arberry 1996, 213).

FIGURE 5.1 A screenshot from "Vanquisher of the Peshmarga." ISI promotes its flag as a shared symbol of group identity.

This verse refers to two possible outcomes for nonparticipants in the prophet Muhammad's military expeditions against the Romans: God's wrath or the wrath of the Muslims returning from war (Abdul-Rahman 2009). Like OMJ's "The Winds of Victory" and AMC's "Bilal Al-Kubaisi's Attack," ISI sequences this video to induce specific inferences. Unlike prior videos, ISI intersperses footage of the past with footage of the present, manifesting what one observer has identified as IS's creation of "multiple pasts to serve intellectual and sociopolitical interests perceived as being relevant for their present situations" (Bashir 2016, 136). By alternating between past and present, ISI reinforces that circumstances from Muhammad's time continue to be relevant now in an attempt to produce "allonomous" selves who adhere to ISI's interpretation of the Quran and Hadith.

Sequence 1

The video begins with footage of bombed buildings, visual proof of the Iraq War's destruction. Several mechanisms of persuasion are employed simultaneously to engage sight and sound. A narrator contrasts Muslims and non-Muslims: "This is the situation that has come to the pass for the

Muslim *ummah*: deviation from its religion, occupation of its land, robbery of its riches, imprisonment of its men, and desecration of its lands." The video shows Kurdish politicians who have supposedly deviated from religion by meeting with American officials, tanks in formation occupying Iraq, crops burning in a field to symbolize robbed riches, handcuffed and blindfolded men entering a prison, and Iraqi men kneeling before an American soldier to depict desecration. The narrator draws religious contrasts to mediate disorder by arousing anger and humiliation: "These are the results of the Crusader war against the Muslim ummah" (until 1:28). The narrator further contrasts Muslims from their rulers by chastising Sunni rulers for participating in "an alliance of Western disbelievers, with all of their countries and specters, and the hypocrites from our countries," as images appear of the United Nations General Assembly and Arab rulers meeting President George Bush.

Sequence 2

From 1:58 to 2:22, the narrator invokes the authority of a religious text that he reads aloud as its text scrolls on the top half of the screen, as shown in figure 5.2. The text comes from Abu Dawud Sulayman ibn Al-Ashath Al-Azdi Al-Sijistani (817–889 CE), who compiled a collection of Hadith on the sayings and doings of the prophet Muhammad (Brown 2009):

> The prophet said: The people will soon summon one another to attack you, just as people who are eating invite others to share their dish. Someone asked: Will that be because of our small numbers at that time? He replied: No, you will be numerous at that time: but you will be like the scum and rubbish that is carried down by a torrent. God will take the fear of you out of the breasts of your enemy and put *wahn* into your hearts. Someone asked: What is *wahn* [feebleness]? The prophet of God replied: Love of the world and the dislike of death [my translation].

The Hadith affirms these mechanisms of persuasion, which the narrator used moments before, contrasting believers with disbelievers and foreshadowing dangers for Muslims who avoid jihad. The last sentence mediates disorder by suggesting that sacrificing this existence for violent martyrdom

[117]

FIGURE 5.2 ISI attempts to mediate disorder by juxtaposing religious texts on the subjugation of Muslims with footage of atrocities committed during the Iraq War.

is the solution to psychological weakness or feebleness. In figure 5.2, the bottom half of the screen offers visual proof of atrocities committed against Muslims, equating Muhammad's past conquests with the Iraq War.

Sequence 3

At 2:24, the narrator recounts past injustices that non-Muslim colonial powers perpetrated against Sunnis as footage from World Wars I and II appears: "This Satanic alliance stimulated the fall of the Islamic caliphate and the division of Muslim lands into countries." The sequence introduces negative thoughts and emotions against non-Muslims, who are dehumanized as "Satanic." As the narrator speaks, an animation appears: visual proof to depict the formation of nation-states in the Arab world after the fall of the Ottoman Empire, as shown in figure 5.3.

The narrator vilifies non-Muslims for dividing Muslims:

They continued to occupy many of the Muslim states. They agreed among themselves to divide up nations and kingdoms, leading them, ordering them under their command, and setting them up according to their desires. That agreement is what is known as "Sykes–Picot" (until 3:16).

FIGURE 5.3 A screenshot from "Vanquisher of the Peshmarga" in which animation reinforces the contrast between a Sunni Muslim in-group and non-Muslim
out-groups. "1917" refers to the year the Ottoman Empire fell. In its place, the
flags of Turkey, France, and Great Britain show the division of Muslim lands into
nation-states.

The narrator contrasts democracy against Sharia: "They set up the biggest
idol of all among the greatest part of the population, called it 'democracy,' and
turned the Muslims away from their religion" (until 3:24). Al-Zawahiri appears,
a figure of authority meant to persuade viewers, as shown in figure 5.4.

FIGURE 5.4 ISI invokes Ayman Al-Zawahiri in "Vanquisher of the Peshmarga" as an
authoritative source of information. The books behind him are intended to offer
visual proof of his erudition.

Al-Zawahiri tries to convince the Kurds to join ISI:

> The Kurds are a mighty section of the Muslim ummah. Every Muslim is proud of
> their sacrifice and history. All Muslims sympathize with the injustices that they
> have suffered at the hands of the fanatical Ba'athist regime. I think that their
> brothers, the mujahideen in Iraq—whether they are Arab, Kurd, or Turkmen—
> understand many of their demands.

Al-Zawahiri tries to construct a common group identity by recategorizing
Arabs and Kurds through their shared belief in Islam, rather than through
their ethnicity. He mediates disorder by calling on his audience to revolt
against the Iraqi government: "What no Muslim—Kurd or not—can
possibly accept is that Iraqi Kurdistan be ruled by a secular government
that is loyal to the Crusaders and cooperating with the Jews" (until 4:45).
The narrator praises Kurdistan by invoking Salahuddin as an historical
prototype: "Indeed, Kurdistan is Salahuddin's. It is a part that cannot be
cut from the land of Islam."

Sequence 4

At 6:44, the video transitions to an image of a "vanquisher" of the peshmarga whose nom de guerre is Abu Omar Al-Muhajir. Sitting before the
camera, he reads out a *tahmīd* to God and praise for the prophet with *saja'*
as linguistic practices of persuasion:

> Praise be to God, the lord of the worlds (*rabb ul-ālamīn*). Peace and prayers upon
> the leader of the mujahideen (*qāid al-mujāhidīn*), our prophet Muhammad, and
> upon his family and companions altogether (*suhub-hi ajma'īn*).

He cites the fourteenth verse of the Quran's ninth chapter, *Al-Tauba*, for
authority: "Fight them, and God will chastise them at your hands and
degrade them, and He will help you against them, and bring healing to
the breasts of a people who believe" (Arberry 1996, 208). On this basis,
Al-Muhajir contrasts Muslims and non-Muslims: "The Crusaders, spiteful rejectionists [Shia], and the apostates have attacked the Sunnis. They

FIGURE 5.5 A screenshot from "Vanquisher of the Peshmarga" featuring footage of Al-Zarqawi's videos from the OMJ era at right and scrolling text of his speech at left.

have killed their kids and men." Al-Muhajir employs three mechanisms of persuasion to mediate disorder by inciting anger: linguistic practices from classical Arabic rhetoric, invocations of the Quran, and the drawing of contrasts with non-Muslims. Al-Muhajir calls on viewers to rise against the nation-state: "Fight on the path of God with your possessions and your souls!" (until 8:18).

Sequence 5

From 9:23 to 22:44, the narrator recounts the biographies of the pious Salahuddin and the treacherous Barzani, who cooperated with the Americans and Soviets, in punctilious detail, as the video shows images of both men. From 13:45 to 14:56, Osama bin Laden decries the Sykes–Picot Agreement—the accord signed by the British and French to demarcate spheres of influence in the Middle East after the end of the Ottoman Empire—as a Crusader–Jewish conspiracy. From 19:49 to 20:57, Al-Zarqawi cites texts from the Quran and Hadith on the need to "achieve unity" (*tahqīq al-tawhīd*), with footage of him from "The Heroes of Fallujah" playing, as shown in figure 5.5. By including Al-Zawahiri, bin Laden, and Al-Zarqawi in the same video, ISI offers visual proof that it has unified major Sunni mujahideen groups.

FIGURE 5.6 A screenshot from "Vanquisher of the Peshmarga" in which militants hoist and salute the ISI flag. The militants' faces have been blurred, a visual manifestation that no individual has a recognizable identity independent of the group.

Sequence 6

The video alternates between the past and present. From 22:45 to 23:21, the video shows Abu Omar Al-Muhajir discussing his suicide mission, and from 23:22 to 24:26, Al-Zawahiri warns Kurds against following the leaders of their secularist parties. At 25:45, the video shows ISI militants hoisting and saluting its banner of jihad, as shown in figure 5.6. The men contrast a Muslim in-group with a Jewish out-group through a chant: "*Khaybar, Khaybar*, Oh Jews! The Army of Muhammad is coming!" (*khaybar yā ya-hūd / jaish mu ha mad sau fa ya 'ūd*). In the year 628, Muhammad's armies defeated the Jews of Khaybar, taxing them half their annual date harvest in exchange for protection (Stillman 1979). The chant exemplifies ISI's use of shared meanings from the past to mediate disorder by calling for violence today.

Sequence 7

From 27:11 to 46:05, the video features an in-depth commentary of Al-Muhajir's attack on the peshmarga headquarters in Mosul. The narrator

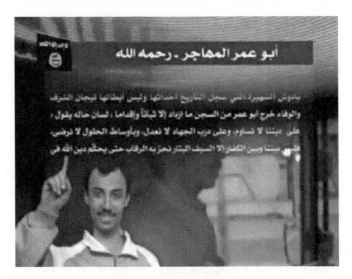

FIGURE 5.7 A screenshot from "Vanquisher of the Peshmarga." The text at the top of the screen translates to "Abu Omar Al-Muhajir, may God have mercy on him"; this is set next to the ISI flag. Al-Muhajir is shown holding up his right index finger to convey his belief in monotheism, a shared practice that originated with OMJ. The background images show footage of his attack.

idealizes Al-Muhajir as a prototypical in-group member who fulfilled expectations of violent behavior: "Abu Omar Al-Muhajir was from the peninsula of Muhammad, peace and prayers of God upon him. His heart was tender. He knew the value of jihad and its gift." ISI emphasizes Al-Muhajir's sacrifice of worldly pleasures to join the group: "He left, migrating to his Lord, thinking of Iraq as the land of heroism and sacrifice." Al-Muhajir becomes a parasocial character whose narrative transports the audience, with whom they can establish a relationship and psychologically identify. ISI uses a split-screen effect to praise him: scrolling text at the top of the screen and video of him at the bottom, as shown in figure 5.7. Depicting Al-Muhajir alongside Al-Zawahiri, bin Laden, and Al-Zarqawi visually reinforces his in-group conformity.

As Bilal Al-Kubaisi did in "Bilal Al-Kubaisi's Attack," Al-Muhajir recites his last will and testament, scouts his target, and executes his attack. There is no footage of him embracing other militants or smiling with others.

As with AQI's video "All Religion Will Be God's," the only time more than one man appears on screen is during footage of the attack.

Sequence 8

At 46:06, the video depicts militants training, visual proof of their rigorous preparation for jihad. At 46:36, Al-Baghdadi declares,

> This is my call to all regions of Kurdistan: Join the Islamic State of Iraq in the Land of the Two Rivers, especially since squadrons from Kurdistan have returned to their families in the mountains. The blessed operations have begun against disbelief with God's permission. Its time has been appointed—despite numerous, various obstacles—with our far-reaching operations in Erbil and Makhmour, just as our operations in Sulaimaniyya and its mountain comprised many dangerous sides. The lions of the mountain were able to rip apart the ties between the two secular parties that are hostile to Islam and its people with the Americans supporting them.

The "two secular parties" referred to are the Kurdish Democratic Party and the Patriotic Union of Kurdistan.

"Vanquisher of the Peshmarga" mediates disorder by alternating footage of the past and present to reinforce ISI's shift in identity, now producing individuals who behave "allonomously" according to the group's literalist interpretations of the Quran and Hadith. Given this identity shift, ISI relied on persuading individuals through textual references that valorize jihad, recurrent contrasts between Muslims and non-Muslims, and footage of innocent casualties injured or killed by non-Muslims in the colonial and postcolonial periods. Screens juxtapose religious texts with footage from the Iraq War to strengthen ISI's claim that the solution to today's problems lies in conforming to in-group norms of emulating the prophet Muhammad's life. By calling attention to past humiliations—the division of Muslim lands, the introduction of secular over religious law to govern societies, and the installation of Arab rulers hostile to Islam—during the post–World War II international order, ISI positions itself between individuals and the state to call for the implementation of a Sharia-based caliphate through violence.

The Harmony Documents

In contrast to "Say I Am on Clear Proof from My Lord" and "Vanquisher of the Peshmarga," the Harmony Documents were not intended for public consumption. These texts were collected from Iraq's many battlefields and are stored in a publicly accessible U.S. Department of Defense database (Combating Terrorism Center at West Point 2015b). As a corpus of bureaucratic texts, the Harmony Documents uncover ISI's significant challenges in shifting its identity and trying to maintain in-group norms for violent thoughts, emotions, and behaviors within relationships and institutions. One method to explore whether people identify with social norms is to examine the connection between group discourses and individual behaviors (Lambert and McKevitt 2002). The Harmony Documents illustrate how individuals internalized ISI's discourse.[4]

For example, ISI had a whole labor-management chain. ISI expected its middle managers to conform to group norms more than the potential fighters whom managers directly oversaw. One document announces that "all properties, big and small, must be computed, and a report is submitted, whereas we keep a copy with us" (NMEC-2007-657926). To persuade others to conform to in-group norms, the text invokes shared meanings of the fear of God's retribution: "Every brother is responsible for these properties before God. He will be accountable, and his case will be referred to the local leader (amīr), regardless of how small it may be" (NMEC-2007-657926). The same text emphasizes the need for records of all people who enter and exit the group: "We will collect information on any individual who joins the Islamic State of Iraq," with the next sentence declaring, "We will collect information on any individual who leaves the Islamic State of Iraq" (NMEC-2007-657926).

In situations characterized by the chronic threat of violence, groups exert a high degree of cultural tightness by demanding conformity to in-group norms and punishing deviance (Gelfand 2012). Successful individuals learn to internalize social norms to garner prestige among other in-group members and obtain rewards, unlike those who do not identify strongly with the group's identity or conform to its norms (Gelfand, Erez, and Aycan 2007). These texts show that ISI fostered great cultural tightness among middle managers expected to conform to in-group norms, but not among recruits who would become potential fighters. The responsibilities for managerial documentation led to unintended consequences; an unnamed author of a highly self-critical document titled "Analysis of the State of the ISI" (NMEC-2007-612449) writes, "It is discovered that a brother requests the administrator on a daily basis for luxuries, including sandpaper, Pepsi, clothes, and excess 'necessities' which the brother would not think of buying if they were from his own pocket" (23).

This distinction between managers and recruits recurs in a one-page welcome memo that ISI's Salahuddin Security Office issued to foreign fighters. The text begins by invoking a Hadith for authority to persuade recruits to conform to in-group norms: "The Hadith 'There are conditions between Muslims' is not hidden from you, and Muslims must agree to each condition. The Sharia did not emerge through violations of this, so religion and obligation are compulsory on both sides" (NMEC-2007-636916). This text attempts to implement Al-Tamimi's "we-dentity" of "allonomous" selves who comply with ISI's interpretations of Sharia. ISI allowed militants to decide whether to pledge allegiance to Al-Baghdadi:

> After you have explored the place and spent a sufficient amount of time in it to form a general impression of it, the circumstances, and our prospects, we ask those who do not get acclimated to the conditions to approach us within a period of no greater than twenty-four hours after reading this message so that we can safeguard departure from here to a safe place, surrendering him to the brother responsible for him (NMEC-2007-636916).

In determining whether to join a group, individuals evaluate the trade-offs between behaving autonomously and conforming to in-group norms (Turner et al. 1994). Here, ISI introduced a grace period for recruits to decide whether they wished to join the group and uphold in-group norms to behave violently.

After pledging allegiance, foreign fighters completed a standard form. These single-page documents recorded basic information that ISI deemed essential. Some forms illustrate the nature of relationships between in-group members, as in this section of a form for a Saudi fighter named Hatim Ahmed Hamdan Al-Shamrani (NMEC-2007-657829):

How did you reach Syria: *by plane*

Stages of arrival to Iraqi Territory: *to Syria to the borders to Iraq*

Who are the people you met in Syria: *Louie*

What are his characteristics: *thin, delicate, white haired*

The way that the coordinator treated you in Syria: *Not good. Louie took the money from them and they were not pleased. He gave them $200.*

How much money was on you: *$1,000/1,000 riyal with his friend*

How much did they take from you in Syria:

Why: *They said these were orders.*

Al-Shamrani expresses plain dissatisfaction that Louie, his Syrian coordinator, confiscated most of his money under the pretext that "these were orders." Others echoed Al-Shamrani's frustration; the author of "Analysis of the State of the ISI" (NMEC-2007-612449) criticizes coordinators for deviating from in-group norms: "We learned that many of those who worked to coordinate entry into Iraq from abroad are one of two types [of people]: they are migrants (*muhājirūn*) who have never lived with the experience of jihad, or observers of the situation in Iraq and its crises from afar" (4). The author accuses the coordinators of cowardice:

Many of this type—among the local supporters (*ansār*) who work as coordinators for entering the land of jihad—do not possess any religious inhibitions, fear meeting God who is their Keeper on the Day of Judgment, and stay behind with those who are left [living] without permission from the emirate (4).

Such coordinators deviated from in-group norms without fearing punishment, exhibiting an unintentional degree of cultural looseness within ISI.

ISI could not rely on its recruits to know the specific religious meanings and practices that Al-Tamimi and Al-Baghdadi emphasized from the Quran and Hadith. Two Harmony Documents (MNFT-2007-005315, MNFT-2007-005318) asked foreign fighters about the number of scriptures that they had committed to memory. The following box summarizes this information from one document (MNFT-2007-005315):

Religious Proficiencies Among ISI's Recruits

Name	Year of Birth	Quran Verses Memorized	Hadith Memorized
Abu Uthman Diyar	1981	Several	Several
Abu Hadhifa	1985	None	None
Abu Adil	1975	None	None
Abu Abd Al-Rahman	1980	Several	Several
Abu Umar	1980	Several	Several
Abu Abdullah Nashat	1984	Several	Several
Abu Dujana	1986	[blank]	[blank]
Abu Al-Hasan	1987	Several	Several
Abu Muhammad	1982	[blank]	[blank]
Abu Awad	1984	None	None
Abu Farhad	1975	[blank]	[blank]
Abu Adnan	1965	[blank]	[blank]
Abu Tayyar	1986	[blank]	[blank]
Abu Husain	1988	[blank]	[blank]
Abu Muhammad	1982	[blank]	[blank]
Ali	1977	Several	Several
Abu Anis	1985	Several	Several
Abu Jafar	1985	Several	Several
Abu Abdullah	1985	4	3
Abu Yusuf	1979	Several	Several
Abu Salim	1988	Several	Several

The ages of these recruits ranged from nineteen to forty-two, with most in their early twenties. Only one recruit had memorized more than three texts from the Quran or Hadith. Ten recruits listed "several" as responses, and ten listed either "none" or left the answer blank. No recruit prioritized memorizing scriptures as central to their religious identities, which is noteworthy since all these fighters spoke Arabic natively. This discrepancy between the group's aspirations to shift its identity and real-world realities frustrated the author of "Analysis of the State of the ISI" (NMEC-2007-612449) such that he acknowledged the consequences of ISI's mediated disorder: "They are influenced by the media and propaganda and by CDs [compact discs] with high expectations" (10). He censured foreign fighters for choosing to memorize ISI's media over religious texts: "Some do not know anything but *Al-Fatiha* [the Quran's first verse] and other prayers of protection even though they memorize jihadist movies and songs very well" (15).

ISI recognized that many recruits experienced what I called equivocation in chapter 3. Some individuals voiced their similarity or identicalness with others to acculturate to the group's identity while privately thinking, feeling, and behaving with ambivalence. A template form for recruits to become suicide bombers, "The Brother Martyr's Pledge" (NMEC-2007-657925), exhibits this tension. ISI asks individuals to commit to death: "My entry in Iraq and my demand to carry out a martyrdom operation have sprung from my deep personal desire. I have no intention of changing into a fighter (*muqātil*) after entry. I swear this to God." By invoking the authority of God for persuasion and asking individuals to sign their names, the text mediates disorder by inciting individuals to commit violence against the nation-state and preventing them from becoming fighters not assigned to suicide missions. The second condition reveals how ISI maintains violent thoughts, emotions, and behaviors within relationships: by demanding that recruits "listen to and obey the *amīrs*, in good times and in bad." However, the third condition introduces the possibility of equivocation: "In case I back away from carrying it out, the organization does not owe me anything except evacuating me from Iraq in the way it sees fit." Unlike videos featuring angry militants who have embodied group norms of audacity and sacrifice, this condition recognizes that would-be suicide bombers may change their minds.

In fact, the group's emphasis on full obedience to hierarchy angered the author of "Analysis of the State of the ISI," who argued for greater cultural looseness. In recommending a new structure for ISI, he championed the oversight of local leaders (*amīrs*):

> Exchange or replace the *amīrs* who issued bad decisions that had personal or ideological effects on the group. For example, any important decisions made by an *amīr* without reference to the State or the Missionary and Coordination Committee must be held accountable. Introduce the idea that obeying the state doesn't necessarily mean staying in it forever and that obedience doesn't oblige the obedient person to obey less credible people or someone who was previously under his command (35).

The possibility that individuals would not have to stay in ISI forever contradicts Al-Tamimi's stance that an Islamic State should be declared even though individuals within its territory may pledge differing degrees of loyalty; Al-Tamimi's text suggests that all individuals would support an Islamic State, not leave it. To persuade his internal audience of ISI members, the author of "Analysis of the State of the ISI" cites Muhammad's example for authority:

> They must be reminded of the prophet's actions when he replaced one of the *amīrs* in charge of the city with a young man who had not yet reached his eighteenth birthday during one of the most dangerous battles and military decisions that the Muslims experienced (35).

This text illustrates the gap in scriptural literacy between ISI's leadership and its recruits and how the group struggled to find a solution.

In "Say I Am on Clear Proof from My Lord," Al-Baghdadi (2007) demanded that Muslims comply with God's judgments by seeking out ISI's religious courts for arbitration. ISI faced resistance from other Sunni mujahideen who challenged this imposition. A letter from one ISI militant complains that another group, the Islamic Army, avoided ISI's Sharia courts (NMEC-2007-637011). A third group, known as the Mujahideen Army, tried to assassinate an ISI judge (NMEC-2007-636973). The most detailed glimpse into ISI's challenges with its identity shift toward governance comes in a letter from rival Ansar Al-Islam's Bureau of Sharia and Jurisprudence (NMEC-2007-637001), which blamed ISI for exacerbating tensions with Sunnis who did not pledge allegiance to ISI or accept Al-Baghdadi's authority:

> We have repeatedly called your attention before to the behaviors of some of your individuals through whom evil thinking and treatment had reached our brothers. Such that they issued misleading and fabricated statements to the extent of voiding the legality of jihadist activity for brothers opposing you on the proof that they had not pledged allegiance to your leader or joined the newly announced organization. Some of the individuals had even received approval to shed blood against those opposing this [announcement] (1).

Ansar Al-Islam's writer mocks ISI for obliging Sunnis to follow its interpretation of Sharia by tracing the group's evolution:

> The proof for murder at this time: Why did you not join the Assembly of the Mujahideen Council? Before the Assembly, the only legal organization in Iraq was the

Al Qaeda Organization. And before that Organization, it was compulsory to pledge allegiance to the migrants in the Organization of Monotheism and Jihad! (1)

The writer denounces ISI's appeals to Sharia:

We inform you once again of developments on this issue in the Diyala region where the slogans "Allegiance and Caliphate" have been raised and edicts have been issued, explaining that whosoever does not pledge allegiance to the leader of the State will be killed and that it [allegiance] is mandatory (1).

Not to be outdone, this writer invokes the authority of the thirty-third verse of the Quran's seventeenth chapter, *Al-Isra*, for persuasion to shame ISI: "Do you shed the blood of innocent souls through Islam even though God— mighty and majestic is He—says, 'And slay not the soul God has forbidden, except by right'?" (Arberry 1996, 277) (1).

Instead, Ansar Al-Islam's writer cites another scholar for authority:

Shawkani said, "After the spread of Islam, it was known that each place—or places—became provinces of a leader or ruler, and it [the spread] happened in many places like this. An order or prohibition was not binding for people in one place that came from the province of another" (NMEC-2007-637001, 2).

Muhammad ibn Ali ibn Muhammad ibn Abdullah al-Shawkani (1759–1839) believed that the Quran and Hadith were the sole texts that Muslims should use to define their religious lives (Haykel 2003). With this citation, Ansar Al-Islam's author challenges ISI's authority over other Sunni mujahideen groups. He continues:

Although we have not considered ourselves from the beginning to be among those who call for multiplicity (*ta'duddīya*) in jihadist activity, and no other orga- nization has appeared to support this, the fact of multiplicity must be dealt with upon a Sharia foundation and stipulations as the scholars have mentioned. We have not seen any scholars issuing an edict that allows for internal fighting or using Sharia terminology that is not applicable to the current situation (3).

Ansar Al-Islam argues that shared meanings of the unity (*tawhīd*) of the mujahideen ranks or the application of Sharia to present circumstances are invalid, threatening ISI's project of creating "allonomous" selves. The author warns ISI against sowing dissension: "We genuinely advise you not to be responsible for dividing the ranks, scattering the mujahideen, and cooling the passion or isolating the mujahideen from the Muslim masses with these behaviors" (3).

The Harmony Documents provide a penetrating look into ISI's problems shifting its identity from that of a militant organization to that of a state governing populations and territories. ISI could not take the in-group acceptance of shared meanings from the Quran and Hadith for granted, either from foreign fighters who had not memorized religious texts or from Sunni mujahideen out-groups who challenged ISI's interpretations of Sharia. Even within its in-group, individuals resisted ISI's attempts to create "allonomous" selves. Without the ability to enforce accountability among local leaders and jihad among recruits who equivocated over suicide attacks, ISI was unable to successfully maintain in-group norms for violent thoughts, emotions, and behaviors. Cultural looseness pervaded the group, and recruits came and went at will, with ISI facilitating their evacuation. The Harmony Documents reveal substantial discrepancies between ISI's media discourse and the actual behaviors of its members.

ISI's Mediated Disorder

The OCF framework reveals the discrete strands of jihadist thought that motivated ISI's shift toward an identity based on governance: Al-Zarqawi's construction of a polarized Sunni identity in opposition to all other out-groups, Al Qaeda's allegations that Sunni Arab rulers have betrayed their populations, and Al-Tamimi's cultivation of "allonomous" subjects who conform to ISI's interpretations of the Quran and Hadith. In "Say I Am on Clear Proof from My Lord," Al-Baghdadi uses these themes to mediate disorder by spreading violent thoughts that God helps only believers who follow His obligatory path of jihad and by postulating that God's love arises only through self-sacrificial obedience. "Vanquisher of the Peshmarga" adds to these themes by demanding that Muslims overthrow an international state system that had developed between secular Muslim politicians and European colonizers who turned Muslims away from Sharia.

As part of its identity shift, ISI sought to construct a common group identity with the Kurds by recategorizing them as members of the in-group based on religion. Despite this attempted recategorization, the title "Vanquisher of the Peshmarga" reflects ambivalence regarding whether the Kurds are considered allies or adversaries. This ambivalence persists today, as is evident in a notification that IS issued for Kurds to leave its former Syrian capital, Raqqa:

> In view of the Crusader war on the Islamic State and the alliance of the Kurdish parties with them in this war, we inform you that it has been established for us that in your midst are those who have cooperated with the Crusader alliance. Thus, and so that there is no confrontation between us and you on account of some of the foolish ones among you, we ask you to leave Wilayat al-Raqqa within 72 hours towards Wilayat Homs (Tadmur) and all who remain after this time will be arrested and exposed to Shari'a inquiry and trial" ("Notification for Kurds to Leave Raqqa City" n.d.).

This memo is notable for drawing distinctions between "foolish" and non-foolish Kurds by offering the Kurds safe passage, coming as the U.S. military publicized its partnership with Kurdish peshmarga and Iraqi security forces (Garamone 2016). It treats the Kurds ambivalently, unlike Christians, Jews, and the Shia, who are all treated as hostile out-groups. Rather than risk confrontation, the memo requests all Kurds to leave IS's Syrian capital. This memo, and a video described in chapter 6, demonstrate IS's failed attempts to diffuse its militant cultural and psychological identity among Iraq's Sunni Kurds.

The choice of media platform determined the mechanisms of persuasion ISI used to mediate disorder. As with the other texts examined in this book, each text contrasts a Muslim in-group with non-Muslim out-groups and cites the Quran and Hadith for authority. Through these actions, ISI elevates the prophet Muhammad as a historical prototype whose military strategies are solutions to contemporary problems, consistent with the desire to produce "allonomous" in-group members who behave in conformity with the group's interpretation of Sharia. In addition to these mechanisms, "Vanquisher of the Peshmarga" also offers visual proof: Animation and graphics support the narrator's points; footage alternates between past and present so that the audience draws inferences that Muhammad's military battles must be emulated during the present Iraq War; split-screen effects present texts from the Quran and Hadith alongside contemporary footage; and Al-Muhajir acts as a parasocial character who embodies prototypical ingroup norms. Visual proof is absent in speeches and bureaucratic documents as a mechanism of persuasion. However, bureaucratic documents ask recruits to sign their names, requiring the demonstration of active commitment to the group's tasks—unlike passively listening to speeches or watching videos.

The Harmony Documents reveal that in-group and out-group members disputed ISI's attempts to monopolize authority among Sunni Muslims. Some analysts have applied economic models of selfhood to the Harmony Documents (Combating Terrorism Center at West Point 2006), contending that terrorist groups face two fundamental trade-offs. The first is between operational security and financial efficiency. Groups that spend money on middle managers to ensure that operations are successful because fighters may not carry out attacks lose out on financial efficiency. Spending such money to add personnel then increases security risks.

The second trade-off is between operational security and tactical control. In this trade-off, spending money on more managers decreases the likelihood that fighters can act spontaneously if attacks do not go as planned (Combating Terrorism Center at West Point 2006). It has been hypothesized that "agency problems," how individuals act according to their own will in groups, emerge because the "cognitive dynamics of underground organizations will lead operational units to see the world differently than their leaders" (Combating Terrorism Center at West Point 2006, 19). This analysis assumes that "operational units" of followers could exhibit agency by behaving in ways other than their leaders would hope.

I believe these authors are overstating the degree of cognitive similarity among members in cultural groups. Drawing on extensive fieldwork conducted by herself and others, the anthropologist Katherine Ewing (1990) disputes the possibility that all people within a culture ever see the world similarly, whether they are leaders or followers:

This assumption of a single culturally constituted concept of self rests on a further assumption that, until very recently, has been the prevailing paradigm in cultural anthropology: that "cultures" themselves are coherent systems. Anthropologists have understood cultures to be organized sets of symbols, resting on distinctive underlying principles and constituting a global reality for those raised in a particular cultural tradition (257).

Consistent with social representations theory (discussed in chapter 2), Ewing suggests that the presence of shared meanings, practices, and symbols within a cultural tradition does not mean that they are uniformly accepted as "coherent systems"; they are negotiated through contests of meaning making. Despite ISI's attempt to produce "allonomous" selves, its welcoming memo, suicide attack pledge for recruits, and "Analysis of the State of the ISI" all convey in-group equivocation and cultural looseness.

In the 1970s and 1980s, psychologists spoke of cultures as possessing traits of cultural tightness and looseness, consistent with a conception of culture as homogeneous and unchanging (Triandis 1989), which is not how we understand it now. To retain the metaphor of tightness and looseness while updating the idea of culture as constantly created and debated, we can characterize how cultural groups tolerate or punish deviance from social norms as *cultural tightening* and *loosening*, recognizing that cultures are dynamic and negotiated, not monolithic entities through which people cognize the world uniformly.

Juxtaposing the first and last text in this chapter proves that ISI struggled to punish deviance from in-group norms through a process of cultural tightening. Al-Baghdadi sought to mediate disorder by demanding that Muslims seek out the group's Sharia courts at the risk of apostasy. However, the Islamic Army, the Mujahideen Army, and Ansar Al-Islam rejected ISI's claims to power. A common group identity that emerges organically, rather than being imposed, facilitates conflict resolution, since individuals want to feel that their primary in-groups are better than those of others (Eggins, Haslam, and Reynolds 2002; Crisp, Stone, and Hall 2006). By imposing a common group identity based on conformity to its interpretations of Sharia, ISI ironically reinforced the in-group–out-group distinction among Sunni mujahideen groups. This struggle reflects what Comaroff and Comaroff (2006) have called lawfare, defined as "the resort to legal instruments, to the violence inherent in the law, to commit acts of political coercion," (30) such that criminal organizations "appoint shadow judicial personnel, duplicate legal rituals and processes, and convene courts to try offenders against the persons, property, and social order over which they exert sovereignty" (34). Like ISI, Ansar Al-Islam also waged lawfare by appointing shadow personnel through a Bureau of Sharia and Jurisprudence. Discourse analysis through close readings of these texts shows that ISI tried to define knowledge of Sharia and maneuver for power over other mujahideen groups.

These debates over ISI's ability to interpret Sharia explain why IS promoted Sharia institutes in its first print publication in 2014. Consider this statement:

> Given that the process of changing a society begins in the *masjid* [mosque], the leadership of Wilayat Ar-Raqqah [Raqqa province] sought to establish educational seminars to train and prepare *du'aat* [missionaries], *imams* [mosque leaders] and *khateebs* [public speakers] in order to undo the damage of the regime, which corrupted the minds of the people one generation after another ("Propagating the Correct Manhaj" 2014).

Such seminars have disseminated IS's militant cultural and psychological identity. Shortly thereafter, IS publicized details of its Sharia court system so that individuals would not have to go searching for them:

> We have a *Shar'ī* [expert in Sharia] who works specifically with the Islamic Police, is affiliated with the Wilaya's [province's] general Shari'ah body, and has a direct relationship with a judge from the Islamic court. Our work specifically deals with breaking up disputes ("Interview with Abul-'Abbas Ash-Shami, Head of the Islamic Police, Wilayat Ar-Raqqah" 2014).

Learning from ISI's mistakes, IS founded Sharia courts to maintain the group's violent psychological norms through institutions.

Finally, IS has publicized pledges of allegiance from rival groups, including Ansar Al-Islam, as in the fourth issue of *Dabiq*:

> One of the most recent pieces of good news was that the group "Ansār al-Islam in Iraq," including both its leaders and its soldiers, has pledged allegiance to the Islamic State. The *bay'ah* took place on the twenty-ninth of *Shawwāl* [August 25, 2014], and was accompanied by the announcement that their banner would be dissolved, and that all their troops, weapons, and capabilities would be placed at the disposal of the Islamic State ("Ansar Al-Islam Pledges Allegiance to the Islamic State" 2014).

Such announcements resemble AMC's founding statement, publicizing a common group identity. We shall see in chapter 6 that ISIS learns from ISI's mistakes by cultivating "allonomous" subjects across generations through cultural tightening and the control of social institutions once it gains territory in Syria.

SIX

The Islamic State of Iraq and Syria

Militant Cultural Diffusion

ISI LEARNED to adapt as it spread from Iraq into Syria. U.S. troops began withdrawing from Iraq in 2009, until ISI killed hundreds of civilians in carefully planned attacks in from April through October. In response, coalition forces assassinated more than 80 percent of ISI's leadership in 2010, including its top two officials, Abu Omar Al-Baghdadi and Abu Ayyub Al-Masri (Hashim 2014). From 2008 to 2011, the group went underground. IS's future "caliph" and Al-Baghdadi's deputy, Abu Bakr Al-Baghdadi (no relation), regrouped with other jihadists (Chulov 2014).

In March 2011, thousands of people across Syria protested the state-sanctioned torture of fifteen boys who had destroyed a police kiosk and posted graffiti against the regime ("In Syria, Crackdown After Protests" 2011). The regime had miscalculated, believing that a brutal crackdown on civilians would end the demonstrations (Fahim and Saad 2013). By July 2011, thousands of Sunnis were participating in weekly marches ("Syria: 'Hundreds of thousands' join anti-Assad protests" 2011), and thousands of Shia and Christians were holding demonstrations in support of the government, fearing the rise of Sunni Islamists (Bakri 2011). Abu Bakr Al-Baghdadi dispatched operatives into Syria in August 2011, including Abu Muhammad Al-Jawlani, who later pledged allegiance to Al Qaeda after forming the rival group Jabhat Al-Nusra (Weiss and Hassan 2015).

A theme from this phase of ISI's transition into the Islamic State of Iraq and Syria (ISIS) is the expansion of its forces. ISI continued to smuggle hundreds of militants into Syria after the United States pulled out its combat forces from Iraq throughout 2012 (Carlino 2012; Jones 2013). Hundreds of Jordanian militants also immigrated to fight the Syrian regime (Al-Shishani 2013). By 2011, Australians, Europeans, and North Americans comprised 10 percent of a sixteen thousand–strong foreign militant pool in Syria (Doornbos and Moussa 2013; Pantucci 2013; Schmitt 2013). The numbers swelled rapidly: The Soufan Group (2015) estimates that up to thirty-one thousand people from eighty-one countries had joined ISIS. About sixteen thousand of those came from North Africa and the Middle East, ten thousand came from Western Europe and the former Soviet republics, one thousand eight hundred came from Southeast Asia and the Balkans, and the rest arrived from North America and elsewhere.

However, few have shown how ISIS created a single cultural and psychological identity to unite individuals from all these different backgrounds. Some have hypothesized that they were bound by a commitment to militant Islam:

> Jihadists, especially foreigners who travel to fight in distant lands, call themselves "strangers." They are strange, they claim, because they adhere to the true Islam that most Muslims neglect. They are strange because they have abandoned their countries for foreign lands to fight the final battles against the infidels (McCants 2015, 100–101).

Others see multiple motivations:

> For many, perhaps most, jihadists, religious motivations are necessary but not sufficient to explain the leap to violent action. Some mix of political sentiment, religious belief, and personal circumstance is required. Parsimonious explanations, which focus only on single external factors, whether religious or political, cannot explain why one sibling becomes a jihadist and another a doctor (Stern and Berger 2015, 83).

Both explanations use the individual as the unit of analysis.

In contrast, Fawaz Gerges (2016) speculates on the role of group identity in ISIS's recruitment:

> Of all variables empowering ISIS and like-minded Salafi-jihadi groups in Iraq and Syria, the anti-Shia, anti-Iranian factor tops the list. ISIS has successfully

developed a narrative rooted in a pan-Sunni identity that is intrinsically opposed to what it portrays as an aggressive and expansionist Shia ideology that has infiltrated as in engulfing the Islamic world. ISIS's anti-Shia, anti-Iranian program is the most powerful card it has played in Iraq and Syria, and it has so far proved to be a potent recruitment tool (219).

We've seen the group's identity emerge and shift. As a cultural psychiatrist, I want to know how ISIS manufactured a common militant identity to accommodate thousands of natives and foreigners who spoke different languages and belonged to different ethnicities. How did the group transmit this identity to others? After a group establishes a coherent identity, three processes enable its diffusion. First, *demographic swamping*: Groups produce new members faster than others to uphold certain meanings, practices, and symbols (what we call "cultural traits"). Second, *intergroup competition*: Groups compete for resources through warfare, with certain traits proliferating over others based on what benefits they confer. Third and last, *prestige-based selection*: Individuals copy the traits of others who receive higher social payoffs (Henrich 2004). Media disseminates cultural traits by highlighting valued in-group norms and persuading others to align their thoughts, emotions, and behaviors with those of the in-group (Biglan and Embry 2013; Mullins, Whitehouse, and Atkinson 2013).

In this chapter, I look at the diffusion of ISIS's cultural and psychological identity through discourse analysis by applying the OCF framework to two types of text: Abu Bakr Al-Baghdadi's speech on ISIS's competition with Al Qaeda and a number of short videos from the series "Windows Into the Land of Epic Battles." The videos discussed in earlier chapters have featured footage of adult men committing suicide attacks in Iraq. In contrast, these videos—which I present by targeted age group—depict life during the Syrian Civil War. ISIS represents itself as *the* model Islamic community for all sectors of society: children, adult men, older men, and foreign fighters. By analyzing ISIS's customized messaging for these populations, we can explore its diffusion of a common militant identity.[1]

"Remaining in Iraq and Syria"

In June 2013, Abu Bakr Al-Baghdadi released this speech[2] to declare ISIS's stance on other militant groups involved in the Syrian Civil War and as a response to a speech from Al Qaeda's Ayman Al-Zawahiri[3] demanding that Al-Baghdadi restrict himself to Iraq and Al-Jawlani restrict himself to Syria under the leadership of Al Qaeda. The speech is an exemplary case study, as Al-Baghdadi uses it to differentiate ISIS from other Sunni mujahideen groups, clarifying ISIS's transmission of a militant identity through intergroup competition. His speech begins with the same text used in Al-Zarqawi's 2004 speech "A Message to the Ummah and the Mujahideen in Fallujah" (discussed in chapter 3) and includes a militarized *tahmīd* to God, praise for his prophet, *saja'*, and parallel grammatical phrases (*izdiwāj*):

> Praise be to God, the fortifier of Islam with his assistance (*bi-nasri-hi*), the vanquisher of polytheism with his subjugation (*bi-qahri-hi*), the expediter of his affairs with his order (*bi-amri-hi*), the tempter of the infidels with his hatred (*bi-makri-hi*), who appointed the days of fortune with his justice (*bi-'adli-hi*), who produced a good result for the pious with this grace (*bi-fadhli-hi*). And peace and prayers upon the one whom God raised as the lighthouse of Islam with his sword (*bi-saifi-hi*).

In this entire passage, only one phrase had not appeared in Al-Zarqawi's speech from 2004: "who produced a good result for the pious with this grace." With this rhetorical tribute at the beginning of his speech, Al-Baghdadi positions himself as Al-Zarqawi's successor within the mujahideen.

For persuasion, Al-Baghdadi (2013) draws contrasts between an in-group of believers and an out-group of disbelievers, referencing shared emotions of steadfastness in belief:

> We have become accustomed over the past ten years of bloodshed not to overcome hardship, without God—may He be exalted—imposing a similar or harder one. This is the established way of God—may He be exalted—upon his mujahideen servants. We have become stronger in facing these hardships. Therefore, they break without breaking us.

He invokes the authority of the group's former leaders to demand unswerving adherence to ISIS's path of jihad: "Our elderly (*mashāyikh*) who came before us, left us on the road in which they had decisive word on such matters and kept an eye on our interests despite what others would consider ruin, which they would not pay attention to." For persuasion, Al-Baghdadi cites the sixty-ninth verse of the Quran's twenty-ninth chapter, *Al-'Ankabūt*: "But those who struggle in Our cause, surely We shall guide them in Our ways; and God is with the good-doers" (Arberry 1996, 104).

On the basis of this verse and out of respect for the example set by the group's deceased leaders, Al-Baghdadi (2013) commits himself to violent jihad:

> The Islamic State of Iraq and Syria will remain as long as we have a pulse that courses or an eye that blinks. It remains (*bāqīya*). It remains. We will not bargain it away or back down until God—may He be exalted—raises it or we die within it. It is a state that *Shaykh* Abu Musab Al-Zarqawi wanted and is mixed with the blood of the *Shaykhs* Abu Omar Al-Baghdadi and Abu Hamza Al-Muhajir.

In his introduction, Abu Bakr Al-Baghdadi hearkened to Al-Zarqawi by imitating his style of linguistic persuasion; here, he explicitly elevates Al-Zarqawi, Abu Omar Al-Baghdadi, and Al-Muhajir (a.k.a. Al-Masri) as historical prototypes worthy of emulation. He mediates disorder by calling for the destruction of the international state system through violence, based on the exact reasoning used in ISI's "Vanquisher of the Peshmarga" (discussed in chapter 5):

> We have gone beyond the borders that were drawn by the evil hands through the lands of Islam to restrict our movements and force us to stay within them. We work to remove them with the permission of God, may He be exalted. This blessed march will not stop until we put the final nail in the coffin of the Sykes-Picot conspiracy.

Al-Baghdadi (2013) then draws a contrast between himself and Al-Zawahiri to position ISIS as the legitimate successor to Al-Zarqawi's legacy:

> As for the message attributed to *Shaykh* Ayman Al-Zawahiri—may God preserve him—we have several legal (*shar'ī*) and methodological (*manhajī*) issues with it. The servant [Al-Baghdadi is referring to himself] was given a choice between following the command of his Lord and the command that opposes his Lord. After consulting with the Assembly Council of the Islamic State in Iraq and Syria from among the migrants and helpers (*muhājirūn w'al-ansār*) and raising the issue

with the Sharia Committee, I decided to behave according to the command of my Lord.

Since chapter 2, we've seen that Al-Zarqawi used the terms *muhājirūn* and *ansār* to draw an analogy between Muhammad's early battles and the Iraq War. In doing the same, Al-Baghdadi tries to persuade his audience that he is behaving in full conformity with shared meanings of the need to behave according to the Quran and Hadith, a way of behaving established by Al-Zarqawi but which Al-Baghdadi believes Al-Zawahiri himself violated by limiting himself to the Sykes–Picot Agreement. He cites the 103rd verse of the Quran's third chapter, *Āl-Imrān*: "Hold you fast to God's bond together, and do not scatter" (Arberry 1996, 87). Al-Zarqawi cited this exact verse in his pledge to bin Laden nine years before Al-Baghdadi's speech; Al-Baghdadi's reference is used to demonstrate the power imbalance between a weaker Al Qaeda and a stronger ISIS.

Al-Baghdadi (2013) concludes by calling for violence against Shia outgroups:

> Rise, Oh lions of the Islamic State of Iraq and Syria! Cure the frustration of the believers and attack the spiteful Rejectionists, the criminal Nusayris, the Party of Satan [a reference to Hezbollah, which refers to itself as "the party of God"], and those who come from Qom, Najaf, and Tehran.

With this sentence, Al-Baghdadi connects various Shia out-groups: the Assad regime, Hezbollah, and the Iranian backers of both Assad and Hezbollah. During the 1980s, the Syrian government backed the Iranian Revolution, its proxy militia, Hezbollah, in Lebanon, and Iran during the Iran–Iraq War, leading Iran to reciprocate during the Syrian Civil War by supporting the government, training fifty thousand militants, and releasing $600 million to $700 million per month in aid (Sajadpour 2013). Iraqi Shia militias sent thousands of volunteers who were vetted by Iranian and Syrian officials to fight for the Syrian government (Smyth 2013). Al-Baghdadi mediates disorder by exhorting Sunni youth to behave violently against the Shia and overthrow the nation-state:

> Give to your ummah the news of victory, and do not be weak! Pray and submit to He who supports the heavens and earth! As for you, Oh youth of Islam, answer

the call for blessed Syria, the land of migration (*hijra*), jihad, and fortification (*ribāt*)! Come to your state to raise its foundation!

The use of command verbs—"give, "pray," "submit," "answer the call," "come"—treats migration to ISIS territories as an act of religious devotion that emphasizes shared emotions of obedience to God's commands.

Like Al-Zarqawi, Al-Baghdadi uses elements of classical Arabic rhetoric to convince his audience through linguistic practices of persuasion: the *tahmīd* to God, praise for His prophet, *saja'*, and repeated parallel sentences. Like Al-Zarqawi, he also uses the terms *muhājirūn* and *ansār* to draw an equivalence of contexts between past and present circumstances in emphasizing a militant identity for ISIS recruits. He employs three mechanisms of psychological persuasion: invoking the authority of the group's deceased leaders as historical prototypes for in-group members to follow, citing the Quran for authority, and drawing contrasts with enemy infidels like the Shia and Al Qaeda. Like Al-Zarqawi, Al-Baghdadi uses his speech to call for shared emotions of collective determination and shared meanings of conformity to the Quran and Hadith, not the nation-state system established by European colonizers. In the process, he argues that Al-Zawahiri has wavered in his commitment to Sharia by agreeing to abide by the human-made laws of the Sykes–Picot Agreement rather than God's law. His last sentences stir the audience to violent action and invite mass migration to ISIS territories to fight the Syrian government.

Videos Featuring Children

ISIS videos featuring children illustrate cultural diffusion through the processes of demographic swamping, intergroup competition over scarce resources, and prestige-based selection. All the children are shown modeling the in-group behaviors of adults, thus portraying the spread of a militant identity across generations. Girls appear in only two videos, each of children memorizing the Quran in public missionary forums (one is analyzed below); this complies with ISIS's orders that adult women not appear in public without being completely covered from head to toe or accompanied by adult male relatives (Islamic State in Iraq and al-Sham 2014).

FIGURE 6.1 A screenshot from the sixth video of the "Windows into the Land of Epic Battles" series showing a child stocking a truck with food to deliver to civilians.

Children Stocking Supply Trucks

At two minutes, thirty-eight seconds, this video[4] features multiple shots of trucks delivering food. The lack of dialogue heightens the visual proof of ISIS's ability to deliver aid to civilians during times of civil war. Children and adolescents help men stock trucks with supplies, as shown in figure 6.1.

Younger boys wear civilian clothes, but older boys wear military fatigues that match the men's. Children acculturate to in-groups by imitating socially desirable behaviors (Henrich 2004; Legare and Nielsen 2015); the video illustrates this concept by depicting the intergenerational transmission of in-group norms from adults to adolescents. Only three sentences are audible in the video: A man says "God bless you" to children stocking a truck at 1:19; a man off frame responds, "I don't know," at 1:39 when a child asks what is being delivered; and a man off frame states, "The Islamic State of Iraq and Syria is distributing supplies to Muslims in the countryside of Aleppo" at 2:13. This video offers visual proof that ISIS's militants constitute an in-group whose members cooperate to protect other Muslims based on shared emotions of loyalty. By showing trucks departing from warehouses to deliver food to civilians, the video communicates ISIS's resource advantage over other militant groups and the Syrian government during the Civil War.

A Girl Reciting the Quran

At three minutes, thirty-one seconds, this video[5] features a missionary encouraging a young girl to recite the Quran at a public missionary forum hosted by an ISIS media center. From 00:17 to 00:35, they exchange names and greetings, and the man laughs after the girl makes a slight error in pronunciation, which causes her to cry, as shown in figure 6.2. The girl is draped in ISIS's flag, a visual metaphor of her individual identity being enveloped by the group. In featuring only two protagonists who engage in a casual, coherent sequence of events, the video features the two as para-social characters to whose world viewers can feel transported, establishing relationships and identifying with them.

FIGURE 6.2 A screenshot from the seventh video of the "Windows into the Land of Epic Battles" series in which a girl draped in the ISIS flag recites verses from the Quran in front of an audience with help from a missionary. More ISIS flags fly at the upper left and right corners of a tent set up by a media center.

From 00:36 to 0:55, the girl recites the final chapter of the Quran, *Al-Ikhlās*, which has four verses: "Say thou: He Is Allah, the One! Allah, the Independent, He begetteth not, nor Was He begotten. And there hath never been co-equal with Him anyone" (Arberry 1996, 353). The Sunni tradition equates three recitations of this chapter with the benefit of reciting the entire Quran (Rahmaan 2016). In contrast to ISI, which took scriptural memorization for granted among new recruits, the video depicts ISIS's creation of "allonomous" selves who comply with its interpretations of the Quran and Hadith by targeting young children for instruction.

The missionary asks the girl, "Can you recite another verse?"

She smiles and says, "Yes." From 0:55 to 1:33, she cries through the second recitation after forgetting the words. Rather than reprimand her, the man whispers the words into her ear, which she then repeats. This is more visual proof of the missionary's likeability. After the girl ends the recitation, he exhorts the audience to yell "God is great." At 1:56, he asks the girl, "Why are you crying?"

She shrugs her shoulders and says nothing.

He smiles and hugs her. "Would you like a prize?" he asks.

She nods her head. She walks to the media center, receives several objects, and returns to the audience. The presence of the media center conveys that the group's identity is maintained in institutions to which the public has access. Completion- and performance-based rewards positively reinforce socially desirable behaviors among children and adolescents (Deci, Koestner, and Ryan 1999); ISIS's missionaries thus ensure conformity to in-group norms by distributing completion-based rewards to all children who participate in its activities. In showing this girl winning prizes on the basis of effort and not perfection, the group engages in prestige-based cultural diffusion, with children learning to copy peers whom they perceive as receiving higher social payoffs.

An ISIS School in Syria

At four minutes, thirteen seconds, this video[6] begins with children talking and laughing as they enter the gates of a school. The caption "An Islamic school in the Jarablus area of Aleppo province" appears. A teacher stands among children in a classroom, as shown in figure 6.3. The school is clearly gendered; no girls appear as students and no women as teachers.

FIGURE 6.3 A screenshot from the twenty-eighth video of the "Windows into the Land of Epic Battles" series depicting ISIS's successful opening of a school for boys.

The video offers visual proof of ISIS's control over resources during the Civil War, demonstrating cultural diffusion through the control of social institutions. From 00:37 to 00:47, the teacher instructs the boys in a grammar lesson. At 00:48, the teacher speaks into the camera, listing the curriculum: "The subjects that we teach them are the glorious Quran, the *Tuhfat Al-Atfāl Fī 'Ilm Al-Tajwīd* [*The Gift to Children on the Knowledge of Reciting the Quran*], Arabic grammar, and English grammar." From 1:12 to 1:36, children recite verses of the Quran in unison, and, from 1:37 to 2:07, a boy recites a verse perfectly by himself.

At 2:40, another man describes the syllabus for older boys: "They study some instructional texts, including the text of Abu Shuja' from the *Shafi'* school of jurisprudence and the *Sullam Al-Wusūl Ila 'Ilm Al-Usūl* [*The Steps of Arrival for Knowledge of Jurisprudence*] of Hafidh Ibn Ahmad al-Hakami." "Abu Shuja'" refers to Shihabuddin Ahmad ibn Al-Husain ibn Ahmad (c. twelfth century), an Iraqi judge whose concise text *Al-Mukhtasar* (*The Abridgement*) has been memorized for centuries as an introduction to Sharia (Messick 1993). This video portrays the creation of "allonomous" selves who conform

[148]

to ISIS's interpretations of the Quran and Hadith through the group's educational system.

At 3:33, the video mediates disorder by exhorting people to migrate to Syria and support ISIS. A child speaks into the camera: "Peace, mercy, and the blessings of God be upon you. I direct my message to all of our brothers in the east and the west. We are in need of you and your knowledge, so come to us."

Presenting the "Cubs" to the Public

At twelve minutes, four seconds, this video[7] consists of five sequences to congratulate adolescent boys who have graduated from ISIS's schools. As we've seen since chapter 2, the group refers to men as "lions"; the term "cub" (ashbāl) disseminates this shared symbol across generations.

SEQUENCE 1 The video begins with a missionary on stage asking questions of an audience composed mostly of children: "Do we worship Muhammad or God?"

"God!" the children shout.

"Where is God?"

"In heaven," they reply.

The missionary smiles. "Yes, of course. Heaven."

By asking questions the audience can answer correctly, the missionary establishes initial propositions for his argument that are unlikely to elicit objections. At 1:41, he cites the authority of a Hadith: "If you go back through Arabic literature, we have noble Hadith such as the collections of Bukhari and Muslim. We have Hadith on the conquest of Rome." He uses the word "Rome" as a Christian symbol since the Vatican Church is headquartered there. He mediates disorder by convincing his audience that behaving in conformity with ISIS's interpretations of the Quran and Hadith will result in the defeat of Christians: "Rome will be conquered again once we succeed in obeying the book of God and the prophet of God, peace and prayers upon him."

SEQUENCE 2 At 2:05, the missionary introduces the "cubs": "Today, we will present the fruits of what the cubs of the Islamic State of Iraq and Syria

FIGURE 6.4 A screenshot from the fortieth video of the "Windows into the Land of Epic Battles" series in which four "cubs" in fatigues sit in an ISIS public missionary forum.

have acquired, especially since they are the source of our honor." Adolescent boys in military fatigues sit in the front row, as shown in figure 6.4. The boys take turns reciting the Quran by themselves and in unison, demonstrating visual and aural proof of their training.

SEQUENCE 3 At 3:29, the video shows the "cubs" receiving prizes from older men, as shown in figure 6.5. By showing the boys coming onto the stage one by one, ISIS treats them as prototypical members who embody in-group norms that other children should emulate.

Like the video of the girl reciting the Quran, this video diffuses cultural traits through prestige-based imitation, featuring "cubs" as in-group members who receive higher societal payoffs than untrained children. The soundtrack here is a *nashīd*, which mediates disorder by ascribing a militant "you-dentity" to the children: "You are from the people of Badr; you are faithful to Khaybar" (*min ah-li ba-da-rin / in-ta am-in khay-bar-in*). We've seen in past chapters that the group holds both these battles in high esteem, and this *nashīd* also recalls the prophet Muhammad's historical victories to reinforce behavioral conformity to ISIS's interpretation of the Quran and Hadith.

FIGURE 6.5 A screenshot from the fortieth video of the "Windows into the Land of Epic Battles" series showing a "cub" accepting a reward from an older ISIS member.

SEQUENCE 4 At 4:27, another missionary addresses the audience to promote shared meanings of Muslim unity:

> Many people are now saying that there are Muslim groups. There is only one group, and there is only one caliph, as God wills—may He be exalted. There is only one pledge of allegiance. It is important that there be only one banner, the banner of "There is no God but God, and Muhammad is his prophet."

With these sentences, the missionary positions ISIS as the sole group that represents Muslims. At 5:36, he invokes religious authority for persuasion: "The most beloved thing is God and his prophet, more beloved than oneself, one's people, one's parents." Here, the missionary is trying to convince the children to abandon their families to follow the path of violent jihad. He mediates disorder by urging the children to shun non-Muslims: "Avoid the disbelievers, Oh you who believe! There are some Muslims who associate with America, with Israel, with the disbelieving rulers, with criminals." He cites the twenty-fourth verse of the Quran's ninth chapter, *Al-Tauba*:

> If your fathers, your sons, your brothers, your wives, your clan, your possessions that you have gained, commerce you fear may slacken, dwellings you love—if

these are dearer to you than God and his Messenger, and to struggle in his way, then wait till God brings his command; God guides not the people of the ungodly (Arberry 1996, 209).

The ISIS missionary contrasts God's commands and Muhammad's example with all earthly attachments, including to one's family.

SEQUENCE 5 At 8:11, the video shows young men pledging allegiance to Abu Bakr Al-Baghdadi. The placement of this sequence following the commemoration of the "cubs" induces inferences that the men are imitating the adolescents who have just received public rewards, resulting in prestige-based cultural diffusion. The video offers visual proof that violent thoughts, emotions, and behaviors to act against the official Syrian government will be maintained within the group's relationships across generations.

Videos Featuring Adult Men

Unlike videos showing children absorbing in-group norms through educational institutions, videos showing adult men depict the diffusion of the group's cultural and psychological identity in different settings of social life. Adult men are portrayed in the company of other men, never with women or their families. This suggests a high degree of cultural tightness that encourages conformity with in-group norms maintained through relationships with other men.

A Group Pledge of Allegiance to ISIS

At two minutes, twenty-one seconds, this video[8] begins with a shot of a turbaned man standing amid a group of men of many ages, as shown in figure 6.6. He recites a brief *tahmīd* and praises the prophet to frame his speech: "In the name of God, the beneficent, the merciful. Peace and prayers upon the prophet Muhammad." The turbaned man cultivates likeability with the audience: He smiles and jokes with others until everyone has taken their places. "This is a group pledge of allegiance to the Islamic State of Iraq and Syria. This is one of the hundreds of pledges among the tribes,"

FIGURE 6.6 A screenshot from the first video of the "Windows into the Land of Epic Battles" series. A Twitter account is shown in the lower left corner of the screen. The caption reads, "A group pledge of allegiance to the Islamic State of Iraq and Syria." The group's banner hangs on the wall behind the men.

he states (until 00:44), which suggests that tribal pledges are shared practices through which ISIS diffuses its culture via demographic swamping. He invokes religious authority to justify the pledge: "This pledge is to the Islamic State and its correct and steadfast methodology, which Islam will ennoble if God wills. The banner of monotheism will be raised."

The man mediates disorder by asking the others present to pledge allegiance to ISIS, not to the nation-state (starting at 1:30). He speaks slowly, no more than five syllables at a time, so that the men can repeat after him: "I pledge allegiance to the Commander of the Faithful, Abu Bakr Al-Baghdadi Al-Hussayni Al-Qurayshi, based on listening to and obeying [him], in pleasant and unpleasant situations, at any time and any place, and to be steadfast in this." The video uses two mechanisms of persuasion simultaneously. First, it imposes the proposition that Al-Baghdadi leads all the world's Muslims. Second, it offers visual proof that violent thoughts, emotions, and behaviors are maintained within social relationships such as tribal structures. This video points to a strategy of cultural diffusion by targeting tribes, not just individuals, which perhaps explains how ISIS could act publicly in Syria rather than covertly in Iraq.

FIGURE 6.7 A screenshot from the third video of the "Windows into the Land of Epic Battles" series in which the imam of a mosque addresses adult men in the Syrian city of Aleppo.

A Sermon on Jihad at a Mosque

At five minutes, fifteen seconds, the video[9] features the imam of a mosque addressing a congregation of men, as shown in figure 6.7. The imam begins by invoking religious authority through repeated recitations of the *takbīr*—"God is great"—for the first thirty seconds of his sermon.

He situates his speech against several propositions of God's omnipotence: "We know with certainty that God is the greatest, mighty and majestic is He. God the greatest is what united the Muslims through the religion of God, mighty and majestic is He" (00:40–00:54). The imam's frequent expressions of "God the greatest" and "mighty and majestic is He" are linguistic practices used in sermons to inculcate devotion (Saddhono, Wardani, and Ulya 2015). Under Sharia, adult men must attend Friday prayers at a local mosque, and imams have used sermons throughout history to call for religious unity based on shared meanings of the prophet Muhammad's unification of pre-Islamic Arab tribes (Borthwick 1967). The imam cites the 102nd and 103rd verses of the Quran's third chapter, *Āl-Imrān*: "O believers, fear God as He should be feared, and see you do not die, save in surrender. And hold you fast to God's bond together, and do not scatter" (Arberry 1996, 86–87). Al-Baghdadi cited the same verse in his speech "Remaining in Iraq and Syria" to praise Al-Zarqawi's efforts to unify the mujahideen; here, the imam promotes shared meanings of in-group unity through religion and shared emotions of obedience through fear of God.

At 1:13, the imam mediates disorder by provoking his congregation to forsake the pleasures of this world, including their families: "Oh beloved brothers! Indeed, we know that there is no joy through the transitory wares of this world. Never. There is no joy through a wife, children, or possessions. Joy is through the mercy of God, through the acceptance of God." ISIS positions itself between men and their families to provoke disenchantment with domestic life, just as it calls on children to relinquish their families for jihad.

At 2:32, the imam imposes an obligation upon the congregation to conform to ISIS's interpretation of religion: "Joy, by the grace of God—mighty and majestic is He—comes from adapting ourselves to this religion." He cites the authority of the third verse of the Quran's fifth chapter, *Al-Māida*: "Today, I have perfected your religion for you, and I have completed My blessing upon you, and I have approved Islam for your religion" (Arberry 1996, 128). He equates the past and present:

> Oh brothers, when we know that in this [the Quran] there is a great explanation, the explanation of victories, the explanation of the Battle of Badr and Mecca—this is a great explanation. God, mighty and majestic is He, has bestowed victory upon us brothers in the Islamic State of Iraq and Syria despite our paucity of numbers.

Since OMJ's founding, the Battle of Badr has served as a symbol for the incitement of violence, and the imam here draws a contrast with the Syrian government: "If a comparison were drawn with the Nusayri Alawite regime, then they [ISIS] were few in number. But we have the assistance of God, mighty and majestic is He. We are stronger and greater with his cooperation and assurance." The imam ascribes a "we-dentity" to his congregation as God's chosen people and a "you-dentity" to the Assad family, which belongs to the Alawite sect of Islam but has promoted itself as secular to garner mass political appeal (Goldsmith 2012).

The imam concludes by drawing contrasts between an in-group of Sunni Muslims and the Syrian government, contending that a recent ISIS attack was successful because the attackers had conformed to God's will by sacrificing their lives:

> They [ISIS] killed more than fifty Alawites. They left safely and with spoils (*sālimīn wa ghānimīn*). By God, the greatest of victories! When we take a look at how this happened, we see a person, a Muslim brother, who became a bullet. He was killed, and when he was killed, he was happy, prostrating to God, mighty and majestic is He. He was targeted, so he prostrated, his soul departing, bearing witness, abstemious, and fighting for God.

This part of the imam's sermon demonstrates ISIS's public diffusion of violent thoughts, emotions, and behaviors against the Syrian state. The imam's address at a public mosque confirms that ISIS possesses enough resources to spread its militant culture and psychology through the control of institutions despite competition with other parties during the Civil War.

Providing Social Services to Civilians

At four minutes, fifty-four seconds, this video[10] begins with a caption that explains the purpose of dozens of cardboard boxes stacked against a wall: "Distributing relief supplies to the needy in the countryside of Aleppo province." Unlike the previous two videos, which consisted of single shots, this video has three sequences.

SEQUENCE 1 From 00:29 to 00:57, the video features long shots of rice and flour pouches, as shown in figure 6.8. Men off camera speak inaudibly for the last thirteen seconds of the segment. The relative silence of the footage and the close focus of each shot emphasize ISIS's access to scarce resources during the Syrian Civil War.

SEQUENCE 2 From 00:58 to 1:16, masked men load supplies onto trucks. A cardboard sign outlines the provisions allotted to each family: five kilograms of rice, four kilograms of sugar, and four kilograms of olives. At 1:17, militants in different uniforms travel by truck to deliver the supplies, as shown in figure 6.9. As in the previous segment, silence accentuates the visual proof of ISIS's generosity to civilians. Keeping the men masked

FIGURE 6.8 A screenshot from the twenty-ninth video of the "Windows into the Land of Epic Battles" series showing stored food supplies that ISIS members will distribute to villagers.

FIGURE 6.9 A screenshot from the twenty-ninth video of the "Windows into the Land of Epic Battles" series in which ISIS militants travel by truck to distribute food supplies to villagers.

underscores their total identity fusion with the group. Both sequences convey that ISIS possesses vital resources, such as warehouses, vehicles, personnel, and supply chains, to assist civilians during the Civil War.

SEQUENCE 3 The video shows thirteen instances of masked militants delivering supplies to households. People from a wide cross-section of society accept the deliveries: young children, people with disabilities, elderly women, and able-bodied men, as shown in figure 6.10. Only three sounds are audible: the roar of the truck's engine, militants knocking on doors, and civilians thanking the masked men for the deliveries. The two militants act as parasocial characters transporting viewers from house to house. The video tries to inculcate likeability by showing the men struggling to lift heavy bags and accepting compliments through silent, humble nods—even though these are men who carry machine guns.

The video mediates disorder by positioning ISIS as the guarantor of the population's well-being rather than the official government, illustrating

FIGURE 6.10 A screenshot from the twenty-ninth video of the "Windows into the Land of Epic Battles" series showing a man thanking a masked ISIS militant for delivering food supplies.

that its methodology of jihad also includes ensuring food security for civilians. In 2012, Jabhat Al-Nusra began to win Syrians over by providing public services such as sanitation pickup and food distribution and by providing people with factory work (Sherlock 2013). Viewed against Jabhat Al-Nusra's earlier initiatives, this video provides visual proof that ISIS's militants constitute an in-group whose members like each other, cooperate to safeguard civilians during the Civil War, and act generously toward others.

The Execution of a Muslim Traitor

At three minutes, fifty-nine seconds, this video[11] features two sequences demonstrating ISIS's implementation of law and order based on its interpretations of Sharia.

SEQUENCE 1 An ISIS judge chastises a prisoner whose hands are tied for colluding with the Syrian government. A caption explains the setting: "Carrying out the Sharia order against a suspected collaborator of the Nusayri regime after his repentance." This caption uses two mechanisms of persuasion: stipulating that ISIS's actions comply with Sharia and drawing contrasts with the Syrian government on the basis of religion. The judge invokes religious authority to persuade the prisoner of his wrongdoing: "This is between you and God, mighty and majestic is He. God, mighty and majestic is He, will have mercy on you" (until 00:52). He encourages the prisoner to repent: "Seek forgiveness. Seek forgiveness for what you have done" (00:58–1:01). The video mediates disorder by showing ISIS intervening between individuals and the state to contend that supporting the official government is tantamount to apostasy.

SEQUENCE 2 Militants accompany the prisoner to a forest, as shown in figure 6.11. By depicting the men together, ISIS communicates that adult men maintain in-group norms for violent thoughts, emotions, and behaviors within their relationships. We saw in chapter 5 that ISI's relative cultural looseness led to different types of deviance from in-group norms; in contrast, this video depicts ISIS's cultural tightening in its punishment of deviant behavior.

FIGURE 6.11 A screenshot from the thirty-seventh video of the "Windows into the Land of Epic Battles" series showing a group of men maintaining in-group norms to act violently against government informants.

In two sentences, the prisoner admits to passing on information to the Syrian government that led to the bombing of ISIS's military positions. An executioner forces him to kneel, stating, "I condemn you with the sentence of death for the overwhelming apostasy that has occurred. We ask God for peace and forgiveness." The executioner identifies himself as "the Official for General Sharia in the Islamic State of Iraq and Syria in Idlib Province." Another militant executes the prisoner as the men cry, "God is great!"

This video mediates disorder by normalizing violent thoughts, emotions, and behaviors against the Syrian government. Social theorists have classically defined the state as a political entity with the authority to exercise control over the lives and deaths of inhabitants within a given territory (Foucault 1978; Weber 1991). This video offers visual proof that ISIS, not the Syrian government, exercises lawfare to monopolize control over life and death. By filming the execution, ISIS conveys the high cost of punishment for those refusing to conform to its in-group norms (Henrich and Boyd 2001) and disseminates the group's shared meanings of loyalty through cultural tightening.

Videos Featuring Foreign Fighters and Elderly Men

The foregoing sections have shown how ISIS customizes its messaging by age group. Children become "allonomous" selves in public missionary forums and schools. Adult men learn about references to jihad in the Quran and Hadith during Friday sermons from missionaries who lead collective pledges of allegiance to Abu Bakr Al-Baghdadi and from Sharia officials who enforce conformity to in-group norms. In contrast, foreign fighters demonstrate the group's shared practice of abandoning family to pursue jihad. By honoring foreign fighters, ISIS promotes prestige-based cultural transmission.

A Message from Iraqi Kurdish Fighters

At five minutes, forty-seven seconds, this video[12] opens with masked Kurdish militants in a forest addressing the camera, as shown in figure 6.12. Prior iterations of the group have expressed ambivalence

FIGURE 6.12 A screenshot from the twenty-sixth video of the "Windows into the Land of Epic Battles" series, which features Kurdish militants.

toward the Kurds: Al-Zarqawi condemned them for cooperating with foreign powers, whereas Al-Zawahiri tried to establish a common in-group identity with them through religion during the ISI era. A caption informs viewers that the video is "a message from the Kurdish mujahideen in the Islamic State." The portrayal of the fighters standing together conveys that violent thoughts, emotions, and behaviors are maintained in collective relationships.

A militant speaks into the camera in Kurdish, with captions providing the Arabic translation. He first invokes authority by asking for God's assistance: "We ask God—may He be praised and exalted—for assistance, improvement in the ummah's condition, guidance, and rectitude based on this true religion." He cites the 111th verse of the Quran's ninth chapter, *Al-Tauba*, for persuasion: "Yet if they repent, and perform the prayer, and pay the alms, then they are your brothers in religion; and We distinguish the signs for a people who know" (Arberry 1996, 208). He addresses Kurds who do not belong to ISIS as a polarized out-group of disbelievers: "This is a brief message to all apostates of the Democratic Party of Kurdistan, the Kurdistan Workers' Party, and all secularists in Kurdistan, especially those who are enthralled by the War on Terror."

Next, he mediates disorder by trying to strike fear in this out-group of Kurds: "With the permission of God, the weapons that we have placed on our shoulders will be how we return to Kurdistan." Recalling the trope of being outnumbered from the Battle of Badr, he promises that ISIS will be victorious: "Despite the strength of their weapons and their greater numbers—praise be to God—we will defeat them with our 'God is great' as they flee." Finally, he calls on all Muslims to conform "allonomously" to ISIS's interpretations of the Quran and Hadith:

> When we have become sincere to God—may He be exalted—we will be more powerful than them day after day. God—may He be praised—will select men from among us who are capable of avenging the blood of our martyrs who have been killed on the path of God.

His speech closes with the men around him repeatedly yelling, "God is great!" This video shows that ISIS films foreign fighters to diffuse the cultural trait of abandoning family to undertake violent jihad.

A Message from an Elderly Fighter

At eight minutes, fifty-eight seconds, this video[13] consists of two sequences that venerate two elderly militants as prototypical in-group members. As the content is similar in each sequence, I analyze only the first militant's depiction.

SEQUENCE I The video begins with the shelling of buildings, visual proof of the men's participation in battle. A text slide reads, "A meeting with the oldest fighters" with a date of "Eid ul-Adha 1434 *h*" (October 15, 2013). The only sounds are of men shouting "God is great" and firing their weapons, aural proof of the men at war. Other text slides establish initial propositions that Muslims in Syria live peacefully because of the sacrifices of men such as the ones featured in this video:

> They are among those who spend their days and nights in the trenches and tunnels so that the Muslims live with peace in the streets of Aleppo and its outskirts. Indeed, they are the stationed ones (*murābitūn*) whom the people are ignorant of and whose determination the Lord of men has set. They are men of the Islamic State of Iraq and Syria.

The last sentence elevates the two men as prototypical figures who embody in-group norms of anonymous sacrifices. Al-Baghdadi used the term *ribāt* ("fortification") in his speech "Remaining in Iraq and Syria," and this video offers visual proof of older fighters deployed in fortifications.

SEQUENCE 2 At 1:10, an elderly man speaks into the camera holding a machine gun, as shown in figure 6.13. A caption identifies him as "the brother Abu Hamza Al-Albani, may God protect him," his surname indicating that he is from Albania. Approximately five hundred Albanians had migrated to fight in Iraq and Syria as of March 2015, with one study concluding that those most susceptible to radicalization were those aged between twenty-one and twenty-five years (Shtuni 2015). This video suggests that there may have been more elderly fighters than previously identified. Another study has identified twenty-seven images of older adults eulogized in IS media between August 2016 and March 2017 (Horgan et al. 2017); this video proves

FIGURE 6.13 A screenshot from the twentieth video of the "Windows into the Land of Epic Battles" series, which features interviews with elderly militants.

that adults over sixty years of age fought with ISIS before its declaration of the caliphate in 2014.

Employing multiple mechanisms of persuasion, Al-Albani addresses the audience in Albanian, with captions providing the Arabic translation. He invokes religious authority to justify the Civil War: "I address you from Syria, which God has blessed as we have come to jihad on the path of God in obedience to God's wish." He tries to cultivate likeability to persuade his audience of conforming to shared meanings of jihad based on his own example: "I have turned seventy years old. I call you, Oh Muslims, whom God has tried to turn into believers of the Quran." He mediates disorder by demanding that his audience undertake violent actions, stipulating that avoiding jihad is tantamount to apostasy: "Act steadfastly on your order, and raise yourselves for jihad on the path of God, which is obligatory upon you through Islam! Make yourselves believers!" After establishing a "you-dentity" for his audience of fellow Muslims, he draws contrasts with non-Muslims: "Oh disbelievers, you are now the most vile! God will make us victorious upon you! By God's permission, we will defeat you and be victorious over you!" In treating elderly militants with reverence, ISIS attempts to diffuse militant cultural traits by cultivating prestige-based imitation.

ISIS's Mediated Disorder

By applying the OCF framework through a discourse analysis of ISIS's various texts, we can trace the social processes through which the group has diffused its militant identity. Chapter 4 introduced Al-Tamimi's goal of creating "allonomous" selves who comply fully with the group's violent interpretations of the Quran and Hadith. The Harmony Documents (discussed in chapter 5) exposed ISI's disappointment that foreign fighters could not memorize sections of the Quran and Hadith even at the most elementary level. The texts in this chapter indicate how the group has learned from its past to better diffuse its identity. In "Remaining in Iraq and Syria," Abu Bakr Al-Baghdadi repeatedly invokes "the command of God" to call for steadfastness in jihad, the destruction of state boundaries established under the Sykes–Picot Agreement, and full obedience to Sharia law, extolling youth to migrate to ISIS-controlled territories. Videos featuring children have progressed beyond "Bilal Al-Kubaisi's Attack" (discussed in chapter 4), which showed two boys pledging allegiance to Al-Zarqawi. ISIS demonstrates its emphasis on forming "allonomous" selves by rewarding young boys and girls for reciting the Quran in public competitions. Similarly, videos of adult men in mosques depict imams invoking select verses of the Quran that demand the abandonment of worldly pleasures and family to behave in full conformity with ISIS's interpretation of religious texts. Justifications for shared practices of jihad have gone from revenge against the U.S.-led coalition for inflicting civilian casualties in OMJ's "The Winds of Victory" to complying with ISIS's interpretation of select passages from the Quran and Hadith. The data here differ from Gerges's conclusion that "ISIS's anti-Shia, anti-Iranian program is the most powerful card it has played in Iraq and Syria" (2016, 17); while it is true that ISIS has disparaged the Shia as an enemy out-group, ISIS's most powerful card has been to persuade others that only it can correctly interpret the Quran and Hadith.

In fact, these texts prove that ISIS has mediated disorder by intervening between individuals and the state to disrupt traditional sources of social authority: for men, this is the tribe; for children, their parents; for all people, their families. Prior studies of IS media have noted that the group has customized its messaging based on whether mainstream Sunni interpretations of Sharia support or differ from the group's interpretations (Pelletier et al. 2016). In this chapter, I have shown that the group has also customized

[165]

its messaging by age group. Socially polarizing movements with high cultural tightness promote internal cohesion by intimidating and indoctrinating members that all human needs can be met within the group (Curtis and Curtis 1993; Feldmann and Johnson 1995).

A commonality across all these videos is that ISIS members reiterate that only the group, not people's families, determines norms for acceptable thoughts, emotions, and behaviors. This has allowed ISIS to integrate native and foreign fighters on the basis of religion, which may not have been possible if the group had framed jihad more narrowly in nationalist terms as revenge against Iraqi or Syrian civilian deaths. An internal document from 2014 leaked to the press confirms this strategy: "Unifying the life of the mujahid and his language and culture is the guarantor for unifying the rank of the mujahideen and realising their total belonging in the Islamic State that includes muhajireen from every corner of the earth" ("The ISIS Papers: A Masterplan for Consolidating Power" 2015). These videos also corroborate findings from interviews with foreign fighters in Syria: Whereas jihad used to be a time-limited activity in earlier conflict zones such as Afghanistan and Bosnia, IS has transformed jihad into a lifestyle (Nilsson 2015). I believe that such transformation occurs through the intentional production of "allonomous" selves. For the first time, the group's media depicts total control over institutions that normalize violent thoughts, emotions, and behaviors. Accordingly, cultural transmission has occurred in two key ways: control over critical resources from hostile groups such as the Iraqi or Syrian government and demographic swamping by expanding the group's reach to nonmembers such as civilians in the territories that it controls.

In chapter 5, we saw that Abu Omar Al-Baghdadi urged Iraq's Muslims to "seek God's judgments in disputes by seeking recourse from religious courts and looking for them in cases of not knowing where they are." The texts here demonstrate that the turmoil in Syria has allowed ISIS to exert sovereignty and social order through lawfare. It has opened new schools for the children of English-speaking foreign fighters (Islamic State 2014a) and mandated remedial Sharia sessions for teachers before they can enter classrooms (Islamic State 2014b). By implementing compulsory education for children from grades 1 through 9 (Islamic State 2014c), the group ensures children receive instruction in its interpretations of the Quran and Hadith, while banning subjects from the social sciences and humanities such as history and psychology (Islamic State 2013). All mosques must be registered in territories under its rule (Islamic State 2016), and the group forces men to attend dawn and evening prayers by recording attendance (Islamic State n.d.-a). In Syria, ISIS mosques have awarded prizes to those who correctly recite and memorize parts of the Quran (Islamic State 2014d). In addition to educational and religious institutions, ISIS controls medical and bureaucratic institutions, in which employees are forced to pledge allegiance to Abu Bakr Al-Baghdadi or face death (Zelin 2016). ISIS mediates disorder by using media to persuade individuals to behave violently against the state while depicting control over social institutions. The philosopher Michel Foucault (1995) defines discipline as "a type of power, a modality for its exercise, comprising a whole set of instruments, techniques, procedures, levels of application, [and] targets" such as "specialized institutions," including schools and hospitals (215). Discourse analysis of ISIS's media uncovers its power over institutions to define everyday knowledge of religion.

As we've seen in previous chapters, the choice of media platform determines the mechanisms of persuasion for mediating disorder. As before, drawing contrasts with despised out-groups and invoking authority through citations of religious texts is common across speeches and videos. Nonetheless, there are notable differences. Abu Bakr Al-Baghdadi began "Remaining in Iraq and Syria" by paying tribute to Al-Zarqawi's style of linguistic persuasion through a militarized *tahmīd* to God, praise for his prophet, *saja'*, and parallel grammatical phrases (*izdiwāj*). In hewing tightly to Al-Zarqawi's oratorical performances, he positions himself as the successor to Al-Zarqawi, Abu Omar Al-Baghdadi, and Al-Masri, all of whom he elevates as in-group prototypes. In contrast, the multimodal nature of film allows for other mechanisms of persuasion. Visual proof convinces viewers of the group's resources: children and men stock trucks for food deliveries, whole tribes pledge allegiance to Abu Bakr Al-Baghdadi, ISIS controls mosques with dozens of men visibly in attendance, and operatives murder nonconformists in a demonstration of cultural tightening. Videos also cultivate the likeability of certain ISIS protagonists and missionaries, yet another mechanism of persuasion. The videos attempt to induce likeability by presenting images of successful children and elderly militants as prototypical in-group members who act as parasocial characters with whom viewers can identify, disseminating a militant identity through prestige-based cultural selection.

Through the analysis of still images, researchers have identified that IS recruits children through a six-step process: (1) passive exposure to group culture through media and public events; (2) direct exposure to IS members; (3) individualized attention from recruiters; (4) physical and psychological subjugation such that individuals fuse their individual identities with that of the group; (5) receiving task-based, specialized training; and (6) role assignment and deployment (Horgan et al. 2017). The videos analyzed in this chapter expand our understanding of this acculturation process by representing the range of activities that support these six steps. For example, peripheral participation includes acts of social service such as delivering food to civilians. Direct exposure to IS personnel may occur through education in IS schools, such that enrolled children attract the attention of senior leaders. Finally, role assignment and deployment can lead to the presentation of "cubs" in public missionary forums to catalyze prestige-based cultural transmission. The recruitment of young boys for suicide operations shows that ISIS does not believe in human rights for children (National Coordinator for Security and Counterterrorism and the General Intelligence and Security Service 2017), rights that ISIS would deem "human made" rather than God given.

Social media applications prove that IS has mediated disorder by exposing children at ever-younger ages to its media in order to mold their thoughts, emotions, and behaviors violently. Children can learn letters and numbers through the group's various *nashīd*s. A video released on September 3, 2017, illustrates the application's use.[14] In chapter 7, we'll see how IS normalizes the transmission of violent thoughts, emotions, and behaviors within families to champion jihad across the lifespan.

SEVEN

The Islamic State

The Transmission of Militancy in Families

IS'S CAPTURE of the Iraqi city Mosul in June 2014—where Al-Baghdadi declared himself the caliph of a new "Islamic State" that would not respect international state boundaries—provoked the United States to send 3,600 military personnel to advise Iraqi forces, gather intelligence, and secure American interests (Katzman et al. 2015). Many Americans were introduced to IS through extensive news coverage of its bloodthirsty spree across northern Iraq in the summer of 2014 when it beheaded opponents, freed Muslim prisoners as ISI's Abu Bakr Al-Baghdadi had promised, and staged a $425 million heist from Mosul's central bank (McCoy 2014).

On August 7, 2014, President Obama authorized air strikes to halt IS's advance and rescue tens of thousands of Yezidi refugees from genocide, with Kurdish peshmarga supplying ground support (White House Office of the Press Secretary 2014a). The United States worked with Iraq's new president and prime minister through August 2014 so that Sunni Arabs would feel politically enfranchised and not join IS (White House Office of the Press Secretary 2014b). In September 2014, the United States expanded air strikes into Syria as part of a forty-member coalition (White House Office of the Press Secretary 2014c).

Throughout 2015 and 2016, the coalition captured major areas with high concentrations of Sunnis. In Iraq, these territories included Ramadi (U.S. Department of Defense 2015a) and Salahuddin province (U.S. Department of Defense 2015b), where Al-Zarqawi had recruited hundreds of militants.

In October 2016, the coalition collaborated with the Turkish government and Syrian opposition fighters to capture Dabiq (U.S. Department of Defense 2016), a city of great importance to IS based on a Hadith predicting its location as the final battleground between Muslims and non-Muslims ("Introduction" 2014). The United States coordinated with Iraqi security forces to liberate Mosul in July 2017 (U.S. Department of Defense 2017), and, by month's end, IS had lost 73 percent of its territory in Iraq and 65 percent of its territory in Syria compared with its peak in August 2014 (Global Coalition 2017a). Despite these setbacks, in August 2017, IS negotiated a truce with the Syrian Army, the Lebanese Army, and Hezbollah to evacuate its militants from the Lebanon–Syria border to IS-controlled areas in Syria, proving its force capabilities (Nordland 2017).

Research on IS's media output has increased since President Obama condemned the 2014 beheadings of American civilians James Foley and Steven Sotloff. Most studies have focused on themes in IS's periodical *Dabiq* such as the construction of a group identity, the fusion of religious and political authority to legitimize IS's caliphate, and IS's announcements of military conquests against rivals (Gambhir 2014; Vergani and Bliuc 2015; Ingram 2016). Other studies have shown that IS advertises a consistent worldview in *Dabiq*'s articles despite its shifting fortunes (Wignell et al. 2017). These findings confirm what we've seen in the group's media since Al-Zarqawi announced the formation of OMJ in 2003: In all phases, the group has promoted shared meanings, practices, and symbols to forge a distinct in-group identity, invoke the authority of religion to persuade audiences to behave violently, and draw contrasts with out-groups through a polarized in-group conception of the world.

Research has also demonstrated that IS customizes its messaging by gender. In theory, Sunni Islamists who interpret the Quran and Hadith literally are to oppose the involvement of women in violent jihad except under extraordinary circumstances (Lahoud 2014). In practice, Islamist groups have differed over whether to allow women to commit suicide attacks (Cook 2005). Anita Perešin (2015) describes IS's narratives as normalizing life for would-be migrants:

> Narratives about individual experience of life in the "Caliphate" have proven to be a very effective tool for luring Western women to join the group. By presenting

their daily activities, such as cooking, making Nutella pancakes, doing house-work, playing with children or posting pictures of romantic sunsets in Syria, online promoters are offering a picture of life under ISIS'[1] rule that is positive and attractive to would-be followers (26).

Julia Musial (2016) has examined narratives in *Dabiq* aimed at women:

Clear complementary roles are expressed leaving no doubt that a women's place is home and her role is limited to be a mother and wife. However, the platform to act independently in terms of religion may compensate [for] the conservative setting. The narrative of jihadist feminism offers women a function as guardians of the ideology (77–78).

Simon Cottee and Mia Bloom (2017) state that IS resists using women as combatants at all costs:

It [IS] also takes great pride in eulogizing its martyrs in videos and online banners, regardless of whether they're very young or craggy and old. But nowhere on its social media, encrypted platforms or internal discussions has ISIS acknowledged the use of female suicide bombers—no images of burqa-clad warriors, no infographics in which they take credit for inflicting damage on the enemy.

We saw in chapter 6 that the group has created media to transmit a common cultural and psychological identity of militancy across genera-tions. Videos featured young children, adolescent boys, and adult men, but not adult women, which is likely due to IS's prohibitions against women appearing in public without male relatives. As a cultural psychiatrist, what I want to know is this: How do these people from different age groups come together to form families? And how does the family represent a locus for the transmission of militancy? Within cultural psychiatry, we've realized that unmet role expectations and uncertain life conditions in the family cause psychological stress across cultures, especially for women and chil-dren, who occupy the lowest ranks of hierarchy in patriarchal societies (Douki et al. 2007; Kastrup and Niaz 2009). The medical anthropologists Arthur Kleinman, Veena Das, and Margaret Lock (1997) caution that mental disorders cannot describe the effects of social, political, and economic upheaval:

> The grouping of human problems also defeats categorization of such issues as principally psychological or medical and, therefore, *individual*. Instead, it points to the often close links of personal problems with societal problems. It reveals too the interpersonal grounds of suffering: in other words, that suffering is a social experience (ix, original emphasis).

An alternative is to identify the social determinants of health:

> The theory of social suffering collapses the historical distinction between what is a health problem and what is a social problem, by framing conditions that are both and that require both health and social policies, such as in urban slums and shantytowns where poverty, broken families, and a high risk of violence are also the settings where depression, suicide, post-traumatic stress disorder, and drug misuse cluster (Kleinman 2010, 1519).

As I mentioned in chapter 1, without direct clinical examinations we cannot opine on whether suicide attackers suffer from any pathology. In this chapter, I want to focus on how broken families become staging grounds for suicide attacks. Without ever condoning the actions of these attackers or depriving their victims of justice, how can we view suicide attacks as extreme forms of social suffering in IS's media? How does this media reflect IS's disintegration of the family unit to normalize violent thoughts, emotions, and behaviors?

In this chapter, I apply the OCF framework through a discourse analysis of three texts—an article in *Dabiq* encouraging women to urge their husbands to pursue jihad, a video of a man preparing his son for a suicide attack, and a video of elderly men who follow their "martyred" sons in jihad—to demonstrate IS's transmission of a militant identity in families.[2] The videos discussed in chapter 6 featured children and foreign fighters as ideal group prototypes whom all adult men should emulate in jihad. Here, the spread of a militant identity within families to universalize violent behaviors redirects our attention to suffering as a social experience rather than only an individual problem, raising questions about the nature of the family inside the so-called caliphate.

"A Jihād Without Fighting"

"A Jihād Without Fighting," written by an unknown author under the pen name Umm Sumayyah Al-Muhājirah, appears in the eleventh issue of Dabiq. This is the only text in Dabiq that details a woman's familial responsibilities (Musial 2016) and is therefore a notable case study of IS's transmission of a militant identity within families. The name of the author, which translates to "the Mother of Sumayyah, the Migrant," itself conveys a militant identity for women. Sumayyah bint Khayyat (550–615 CE) was the seventh convert to Islam and the Muslim community's first martyr, dying after being tortured for refusing to renounce her faith (Halverson, Goodall Jr., and Corman 2011). The word Al-Muhājirah is the female form of al-muhājir, which we've seen throughout this book as a shared symbol conveying in-group loyalty by migrating to assist other Muslims.

Al-Muhājirah (2015) begins the article by establishing an initial proposition that women have vied with men to participate in jihad: "Indeed, when Allah obligated jihād for His cause upon his male slaves and placed a tremendous reward in it not found in other duties, some women became jealous and envious" (41). She then cites the Quran and Hadith:

> The Mother of the Believers, Umm Salamah—may God accept her—asked the Prophet, peace and prayers upon him, according to the hadīth of Mujāhid, "O Messenger of Allah, the men go out to battle and we do not go out to battle. . . ." So Allah—may He be praised and exalted—revealed: {And do not wish for that by which Allah has made some of you exceed others} [An-Nisā': 32] (Al-Muhājirah 2015, 41).

Here, Al-Muhājirah emphasizes shared meanings that men must pursue jihad's rewards and that gender differences are ordained by God, leading to different responsibilities for men and women. This text grounds speculation that IS has envisaged noncombat roles for its women migrants (Perešin and Cervone 2015).

As another mechanism of persuasion, the author imposes the proposition that women play critical roles in jihad:

> The absence of an obligation of jihād and war upon the Muslim woman—except in defense against someone attacking her—does not overturn her role in building

the Ummah, producing men, and sending them out to the fierceness of battle. Therefore, I write this article for my Muslim sister, the wife of a *mujāhid* [combatant] and the mother of lion cubs (Al-Muhājirah 2015, 41).

This style of argument reflects early social science scholarship that considered female identities only in relation to men, in which women possessed distinct, complementary, but subordinate responsibilities (Shields 1975). Al-Muhājirah constructs a "you-dentity" for her "Muslim sisters" who function without a primary independent identity, existing only relationally as wives and mothers of male relatives who will inevitably leave for battle. Her argument justifies shared practices of reproduction to produce militants for IS's caliphate. For persuasion, Al-Muhājirah (2015) cites another Hadith that considers female identities in relation to men: " 'O Messenger of Allah, what wealth should we seek to possess?' He said, 'Let one of you possess a thankful heart, a tongue that remembers Allah, and a wife that helps him in the matter of the Hereafter' " (41). Women exist in IS's families only to support men in religious endeavors.

Al-Muhājirah (2015) anticipates objections from women about their male relatives leaving for war:

Why do we find some of the *mujāhidīn*'s wives complaining about their lives? If she hears of an imminent battle that he will be in, she gets angry. If she sees him putting on war armor, she gets upset. If he goes out for *ribāt* [deployment], she gets in a bad mood. If he returns late, she complains. O my sister, who deluded you and told you that the life of *jihād* is one of comfort and ease? Do you not love *jihād* and its people? (41).

The text exhibits cultural tightening in that Al-Muhājirah condemns any deviance from in-group expectations for women: The wives she references are upset but do not stop their husbands from putting on war armor, going to battle, or returning home late. She invokes religion to encourage shared emotions of steadfastness and devotion:

You are in *jihād* when you await the return of your husband patiently, anticipating Allah's reward, and making *du'ā'* [prayer] for him and those with him to attain victory and consolidation. You are in *jihād* when you uphold your loyalty to him in his absence. You are in *jihād* when you teach his children the difference between the truth and falsehood, between right and wrong. Indeed, you, my precious sister, are today the wife of a *mujāhid* [fighter], and tomorrow you might be the wife of a *shahīd* [martyr] (Al-Muhājirah 2015, 41).

In societies around the world, governments have enlisted women to serve as biological reproducers of the citizenry and cultural reproducers of state ideologies to ensure the docility of children (Anthias and Yuval-Davis 1989). Al-Muhājirah insists that women participate in jihad through shared practices of waiting loyally for their husbands, praying for battlefield successes, and transmitting shared meanings of jihad to their children. The phrase "his children"—rather than "your" or "our" children—denies women claims to their offspring. The phrase "you might be the wife of a *shahīd*" normalizes martyrdom as an in-group expectation, deactivates familial prohibitions against violence, and frames widowhood as a socially privileged status.

Next, Al-Muhājirah (2015) contrasts a woman seeking divorce with a woman who has stayed married to illustrate steadfastness:

After days it reached me that she herself could not tolerate hardship, that she wanted divorce, and that her family were not involved in this issue at all. Some people might say this is her right if she fears for herself. So I tell them, yes this is her right, but between this right and patience are levels and meanings which none comprehends except for souls made of pure gold (43).

Mainstream Sunni and Shia interpretations of Sharia regard marriage as a contract that can be annulled by either party, and multiple passages from the Quran and Hadith grant women autonomy without the need for permission from male relatives (Engineer 1992; Awde 2013). Al-Muhājirah's claim that there are "levels and meanings which none comprehends except for souls made of pure gold" offers proof that IS mediates disorder by compelling its subjects to behave "allonomously" in conformity with *its* interpretations of Sharia, subverting traditional religious scholarship. Al-Muhājirah contrasts this woman with another who is worthy of emulation as an ideal in-group prototype:

I know a prisoner's wife who is a school of patience, faithfulness, and steadfastness. Lofty as a high mountain, she raised his children and made of them lions and lionesses. She lives on his memory and waits to meet him. Ten years have passed while he is in prison. Yes, ten complete years, and she has neither changed nor wavered (2015, 43).

Here, the author lists core values demanded of women: patience, faithfulness, and steadfastness. She returns to the propositions of her introduction by concluding, "How good she is, and her reward is with Allah" (43). Al-Muhājirah mediates disorder by calling on women to raise "lions and lionesses" for violent jihad and send their husbands into battle so that women can reap God's rewards.

Al-Muhājirah (2015) concludes by discussing in-group expectations of ideal mothers. As before, she proposes that women should act as biological and cultural reproducers for the caliphate: "What will make you know what the mother of lion cubs is? She is the teacher of generations and the producer of men" (44). She cites the authority of a Hadith here: "I inform you of the statement of the Prophet—peace and prayers upon him—'Every one of you is a shepherd, and everyone is responsible for his herd. . . . And the woman is a shepherd in her house and is responsible for her herd' " (44). Expectations of domestic routines are culturally determined, with patriarchal societies placing domestic responsibilities disproportionately upon women (Andermann and Fung 2015); here, Al-Muhājirah emphasizes that women must fulfill domestic responsibilities according to IS's in-group norms. She specifies how to transmit shared meanings of jihad against disbelievers to children:

> Give your children a righteous upbringing upon clear *tawhīd* [monotheism], a correct *'aqīdah* [belief], *kufr bit-tāghūt* [disbelief through polytheism] and worship of Allah alone, teaching them the heart-softeners, the remembrance of Allah, the Prophet's biography, and the *fiqh* [jurisprudence] of *jihād* (45).

Al-Muhājirah (2015) exhorts women to seek out IS institutions that propagate violent thoughts, emotions, and behaviors: "Before you are the *Sharī'ah* institutions, training camps, and even the kindergartens. All of them in our state—may Allah support it—are upon the methodology of prophethood" (45).

"A Jihād Without Fighting" mediates disorder by constructing a militant identity for women. Al-Muhājirah establishes initial propositions that promote shared meanings of the obligation of jihad for men, which inevitably

[176]

leads to God's rewards. She invokes the authority of the Quran and Hadith to reinforce shared meanings of gender, treating female identities only in relation to husbands, who must be encouraged to act violently through steadfastness and loyalty, and in relation to children, who must receive instruction on the distinction between Muslims and non-Muslims. By anticipating the audience's objections to a life of difficulty, Al-Muhājirah calls on women to act "allonomously" according to IS's interpretations of the Quran and Hadith, rather than invoke their rights to divorce, demonstrating IS's unconventional understandings of religious texts. She normalizes the eventual martyrdom of all male relatives as an in-group norm, acclaims the social status of widowhood, and encourages women to maintain violent thoughts, emotions, and behaviors within familial relationships. Al-Muhājirah urges women to seek support from IS social institutions that propagate the group's militant identity, such as training camps, Sharia institutes, and even kindergartens, which offer transportation services to ensure that children receive instruction in the group's beliefs (Islamic State 2015). IS's caliphate has weaponized the family, treating all men as ammunition in a war against disbelievers, which all women must support dutifully.

"My Son Has Preceded Me: A Martyr's Story"

The ISIS videos discussed in chapter 6 depicted the intergenerational transmission of a militant identity by including footage of children participating in group activities like loading delivery trucks with food, learning the group's interpretations of the Quran and Hadith in schools, and graduating as "cubs" in public forums. The video discussed here, "My Son Has Preceded Me: A Martyr's Story," illustrates the final stage of deployment for a suicide mission after an adolescent has received militant training. At twenty-three minutes, six seconds, the video[3] begins with a brief *tahmīd*—"In the name of God, the beneficent, the merciful"—followed by a narrator reading text on screen:

> In the land of the caliphate where a new generation has arisen, they live among the flames of bombings and the sounds of guns and aircraft. They live, and what is most beloved is the roar of tanks and the flame of explosions. So they live with the meaning of honor and are trained in the readiness to make sacrifices (until 00:29).

This text adopts several mechanisms of persuasion. First, the narrator invokes social proof of the Syrian Civil War by summoning imagery of bombings, guns, aircraft, tanks, and explosions. Second, he imposes propositions that children must uphold shared meanings of honor and shared practices of self-sacrifice. The narrator mediates disorder by illustrating the role of parents in inspiring violent thoughts, emotions, and behaviors:

> In the land of the caliphate where a father emboldens his children, he says to him, "Oh, child, advance! Go there before me! Oh, child, indeed I love you, but I love the religion of God more than you! Advance, oh, child, as we will meet where there is true life! Oh child, I separate from you so that we meet there" (until 1:06).

The narrator draws two contrasts to persuade viewers of violent thoughts, emotions, and behaviors. First, he pits a parent's love for religion against love for a child. Second, he contrasts a violent life in this world with a "true life" that implicitly describes heaven. IS mediates disorder by intervening between children and parents to promote a militant identity *within* the family.

Sequence 1

At 1:39, a narrator describes the setting: "We are in the year 1437 [2016], and the epic battles (*malāhim*) in the land of Syria intensify day by day. After more than five years, jihad in the land of Syria continues without stopping, which started after the uprising against the Nusayri, disbelieving, and tyrannical ruler" (until 2:02). The narrator contrasts IS's pious in-group of subjugated Muslims with an infidel Shia out-group in power. The narrator portrays the relentless regime through yet more contrasts: Phrases such as "The Nusayris attacked the people of Syria with everything they own" and "They killed thousands of Muslims in this blessed land" reinforce thoughts that the regime consists of Shia who are not Muslims (until 2:24).

At 2:25, the narrator valorizes the mujahideen as the video shows men donning uniforms: "The sincere migrants (*muhājirūn*) from all corners of the earth came to assist the people of Syria. They sacrificed themselves and their possessions." Militants rally under IS's banner and march in formation, conveying that shared meanings of sacrifice and shared practices of jihad are maintained within tight in-group relationships. Footage of seven suicide attacks across Iraq and Syria provide visual proof of the shared practice of self-sacrifice.

Sequence 2

At 3:30, the narrator describes traveling to Aleppo to meet would-be suicide attackers (*istishhādiyūn*). At 4:08, he introduces Abu Ammara as the first protagonist, as shown in figure 7.1: "We met this young boy who had not yet turned fifteen years old." Abu Ammara takes the narrator and cameraman to his city.

The narrator describes their journey: "We continued on our way to the city of Al-Bab when we encountered violent bombing from the Nusayri regime. But this city is no different from any other, as life continues amidst the bombing." Bombs fall from the sky as people run for cover, visual proof of the regime's attacks. After the bombing, a bulldozer clears debris from the street, a man sweeps the sidewalk, masons carve new bricks, and construction workers rebuild storefronts, imagery meant to be visual proof

FIGURE 7.1 A screenshot from "My Son Has Preceded Me: A Martyr's Story" featuring a fourteen-year-old boy exhorting other children to emulate him by committing suicide attacks.

of IS's claims to protect Muslims. By interspersing Abu Ammara's biography with footage of attacks from the Syrian government, IS disorders the thoughts and emotions of the audience by inducing inferences that retaliatory attacks are justified.

Sequence 3

At 5:37, the narrator describes meeting Abu Ammara's family: "We finally reached Qabassin and asked Abu Ammara to meet him while he goes for the last time." The narrator portrays him as the prototypical in-group member: "Abu Ammara used to dream about taking part in the epic battles of Dabiq and being a martyr in them because the martyrs in the epic battles are the best of martyrs" (until 6:04). Both walk up a hill in the Syrian city of Dabiq. The video attempts to induce inferences that Abu Ammara and other IS militants are acting out prophesy from the Hadith during the Syrian Civil War. At 6:42, Abu Ammara explains his decision to commit an attack: "It was my father who encouraged me, who advised me, to accept a martyrdom mission."

The narrator asks, "How are you feeling about your mission?"

Abu Ammara responds, "My feelings are the best."

The narrator asks, "What do you think is the path of the suicide mission?"

Abu Ammara answers with a smile, "It is the path to heaven, if God wills."

Finally, the narrator asks, "Do you have a message for your father?"

Abu Ammara mediates disorder by urging his father to behave violently: "I advise my father: Be patient and have forbearance! Fight!" He concludes, "We will meet in heaven, if God wills."

By featuring Abu Ammara discussing his decisions, IS transports viewers into his world, allowing viewers to establish a parasocial relationship with him and align their thoughts and emotions with his. The screenshot in figure 7.2 shows Abu Ammara petting a rabbit, a moment of disarming tenderness, meant to persuade viewers of his likeability.

Sequence 4

The narrator asks to meet Abu Ammara's father, whom he praises as a prototypical in-group member for teaching core in-group values to his

FIGURE 7.2 A screenshot from "My Son Has Preceded Me: A Martyr's Story" that attempts to induce likeability with the protagonist, Abu Ammara. Showing Ammara petting a rabbit, the video contrasts Ammara's message of violent jihad against the United States, Syria, and other out-groups with his caring spirit for vulnerable beings.

children such as "the meaning of bravery and sacrifice, how the Muslims are all part of a single body, establishment of the caliphate, implementing Sharia, and expelling occupiers from the land of Islam, an obligation upon all Muslims across the world" (until 12:42). The narrator emphasizes that Abu Ammara's father was an IS militant who had been injured multiple times and that he repeatedly refused to be interviewed until the narrator persisted, an attempt to persuade viewers of the father's humility and likeability. Figure 7.3 shows Abu Ammara and his father being interviewed by the video's narrator.

Abu Ammara explains, "Any person is fearful of their father but fears the hellfire even more. By God, this martyrdom mission is a key to heaven, with God's permission" (until 13:47).

The narrator asks his father whether he has a message for others in IS's territories. The father responds, reiterating shared in-group meanings: "The first thing is that they should believe in God themselves. The path of jihad is obligatory for every human who is a Muslim. Entrust God with your children" (until 14:29). As another means of persuasion, Abu Ammara's

FIGURE 7.3 A screenshot from "My Son Has Preceded Me: A Martyr's Story," which features a prototypical father–son relationship, with both individuals committing to jihad.

father anticipates objections that IS unique in mandating jihad upon Muslims: "It is not the Islamic State that has made it obligatory. It is the peak of the summit for Islam" (14:42). The narrator asks Abu Ammara's father if he would feel sad after his son's mission, to which the father responds, "I only feel sad that he [will have] preceded me. That's all" (15:34).

Sequence 5

The video shows father and son playing with each other at home, as captured in figure 7.4. By depicting Abu Ammara and his siblings laughing, the video offers visual proof that violent thoughts, emotions, and behaviors are maintained in familial relationships through love, not coercion. The narrator extols Abu Ammara for teaching the Quran to "brothers who will also set off on his path."

The narrator accompanies Abu Ammara on his mission, praising his decision "to tear apart his body on the path of defeating America and the West" (until 17:21), another contrast between a Muslim in-group and a non-Muslim

FIGURE 7.4 A screenshot from "My Son Has Preceded Me: A Martyr's Story" show-ing the protagonist arm-wrestling his father. The children in the background are Abu Ammara's brothers; they wear IS headbands, indicating their acculturation within the group.

out-group. The narrator honors Abu Ammara's father for guaranteeing the success of the mission: "Abu Ammara's father was reassured about the flaw-lessness of the car. He wanted to be confident that his son would carry out the action to reach the heaven of the Beneficent, with God's permission. The father carried his son." Figure 7.5 shows Abu Ammara's father helping him into the car as he says, "God was in need of the sacrifice of heroes" (until 18:09). Abu Ammara promises his father that they will meet in heaven. Abu Ammara drives toward his target, and then an explosion appears at a dis-tance, providing visual proof of his mission.

"My Son Has Preceded Me: A Martyr's Story" mediates disorder as a biographical documentary that reflects the transmission of IS's militant cultural and psychological identity within families. The video relies on several mechanisms of persuasion: invoking social proof of the Syrian Civil War, establishing propositions that Muslim men must uphold shared meanings of honor and sacrifice through violent jihad, drawing contrasts with the American and Syrian governments as enemy out-groups, and presenting extensive visual proof of the Syrian government's attacks and

FIGURE 7.5 A screenshot from "My Son Has Preceded Me: A Martyr's Story" showing Abu Ammara's father helping his son into the car he will use for a suicide attack.

IS's reconstruction efforts. IS does *not* rely on extensive quotations of the Quran or Hadith to justify its actions; as in "Fatima's Fiancé" (discussed in chapter 4), IS tries to cultivate likeability for its protagonists as a mechanism of persuasion. Viewers feel transported into the protagonists' world, establishing parasocial relationships and psychologically identifying with them. IS portrays Abu Ammara and his father as prototypical in-group members who pledge a love for God over their love for each other, a desire for the afterlife over this life, and a dedication to jihad as the "key" to entering heaven.

IS mediates disorder by positioning itself between individuals and society to demand the implementation of a caliphate and Sharia that will abrogate the nation-state system. Societies differ in their cultural expectations of when children initiate self-directed behaviors (Rousseau, Measham, and Bathiche-Suidan 2008). This video emphasizes the maintenance of violent in-group norms within the family as Abu Ammara teaches his brothers about IS's interpretations of the Quran and Hadith in a self-directed manner to produce "allonomous" selves.. "Bilal Al-Kubaisi's Attack" (discussed in chapter 4) concludes with a sequence of two boys firing weapons and pledging allegiance to Al-Zarqawi; this video depicts the consequences of such actions when boys like this grow up.

"The Caravan of Lights 2"

At fifty-six minutes, seven seconds, this video[4] features footage of multiple suicide attackers emulating relatives who have died in suicide missions. The video begins with a brief *tahmīd*—"In the name of God, the beneficent, the merciful"—with two text slide declaring the location as Mosul in "Nineweh Province." I analyze only the first half of the video since the second half duplicates the video's themes.

Sequence 1

At 00:16, excerpts from Abu Bakr Al-Baghdadi's "Remaining in Iraq and Syria" speech provides the soundtrack for footage of Mosul's buildings being bombed, as masked and armed militants take cover. The first speech excerpt emphasizes shared meanings of steadfastness and constancy: "The Islamic State of Iraq and Syria will remain as long as we have a pulse that courses or an eye that blinks. It remains. We will not bargain it away or back down until God—may He be exalted—raises it or we die within it." The sequence draws contrasts with multiple Shia out-groups for persuasion: "Rise, Oh lions of the Islamic State of Iraq and Syria! Cure the frustration of the believers and attack the spiteful Rejectionists, the criminal Nusayris, the Party of Satan, and those who come from Qom, Najaf, and Tehran" (until 00:52). The video mediates disorder by calling on all Sunnis to commit violence: "Tear them apart! Inform us of meeting them as they are cowards! Join your days with your nights, becoming bullets during the days and rockets during the last third of the night!" Al-Baghdadi ascribes a militant "you-dentity" to his in-group with this command to wage war during all waking hours, equating his population to ammunition. The phrase "last third of the night" refers to shared practices for expressing piety; several Hadith note the benefits of praying just before daybreak, after one has slept: Prayer in the last third of the night is considered optional, unlike the five prayers of daytime (Heck 2007). Al-Baghdadi calls on militants to treat violent jihad as a form of prayer, similar to Al-Zarqawi's exhortation that "your slaughter is your prayer" in "The Heroes of Fallujah" (discussed in chapter 2).

From 1:15 to 6:04, the video features dozens of attacks as visual proof of IS's successes, including aerial shots from drones, an example of which is

FIGURE 7.6 A screenshot from "The Caravan of Lights 2" showing aerial footage from drones to provide visual proof of IS's military sophistication. The caption at the top translates to "the first target," and the caption below translates to "the second target."

shown in figure 7.6. Documents retrieved from battlefields in Mosul show that IS has had an institutionalized drone program in place since 2013, with the Iraqi provinces of Nineveh and Salahuddin experiencing the most drone activity (Rassler, al-'Ubaydi, and Mironova 2017). This video depicts IS's drone capabilities to supplement street-level footage of attacks, a perspective unique to the media platform of film. As this footage appears, a *nashīd* provides a soundtrack that reinforces the video's title:

> The convoy of light has called us. Take the initiative, our hand-mill [of war] has turned. The bond of religion is calling, Oh, our brother, Oh, our brother. Accept the burden and arise together; it [the bond of religion] only has us today. We are descendants of noble ones, who subdued disbelief for a time (Al-Tamimi 2016).

"The Winds of Victory" (discussed in chapter 2) introduced the symbolism of a caravan of lights in comparing suicide attackers to martyrs on an illumined path to heaven. This *nashīd* mediates disorder by inciting violent behaviors with verbal commands—"take the initiative," "accept the burden," "arise together"—conveyed through two mechanisms of persuasion: stipulating that listeners respond to a "burden" established through the "bond of religion" and warning against a future danger of disbelief. In claiming that listeners are "descendants of noble ones," the *nashīd* insists that violent thoughts, emotions, and behaviors have been maintained within families for generations, foreshadowing themes that will emerge in this video.

Sequence 2

At 6:04, the video features a man named Abu Iman Al-Urduni, whom the narrator describes as a prototypical in-group member: "He memorized the book of God [the Quran] while he was in the autumn of his fourteenth year. He towered above his peers in his religious and worldly studies" (until 6:55). Al-Urduni exemplifies shared meanings of sacrifice and perseverance over other IS militants: "He excelled beyond his peers, he was the most beloved of his soldiers, and he was appointed the overseer of Damascus. He was rich in blessings and deployed to Salahuddin where he was known for his determination, for his high perseverance and his strong steadfastness" (until 7:37). Despite his injuries, his dedication to jihad has not wavered. The video also portrays the normalization of violent thoughts, emotions, and behaviors within his family: "He saw the men who preceded him and each other toward the landing areas of immortality, among whom were his brother and his son" (until 8:03). He plans an attack with other militants, who lift him into a car because he cannot walk independently, as shown in figure 7.7. By beginning the video with Al-Baghdadi's words that the Islamic State "will not back down" and then showing Al-Urduni functioning despite significant injuries, the video infers that Al-Urduni embodies IS's value of steadfastness despite affliction.

At 8:23, Al-Urduni justifies shared practices of suicide attacks through two mechanisms of persuasion: claiming that suicide missions are necessary for asymmetric warfare and contrasting an in-group of Muslims against an out-group defined as "the enemies of God": "Indeed, the martyrdom mission is the strongest and deadliest weapon against the enemies of God, mighty and majestic is He, especially as we do not possess what they possess by way of weapons. Instead, we possess faith in God, which is the best and the greatest of rewards." As we have seen, this proposition hearkens to the Battle of Badr, in which Muslims defeated a better-equipped army of disbelievers

FIGURE 7.7 A screenshot from "The Caravan of Lights 2" showing men lifting a disabled IS militant into a car. A handle of the militant's wheelchair is visible at the bottom of the screen.

purely through faith. Al-Urduni imposes another proposition to persuade men of sacrificing their families for jihad: "Whosoever enters this state and tastes the actions of jihad and combat, by God, he puts aside and risks all of his children so that the can spend years in this jihad and combat. I swear to God, he will not give up this action." He smiles and touches his tongue to emphasize the physical sensation of taste, indicating his enjoyment of violence. By using an impersonal construction of the subject—"whosoever" rather than "I" or "we"—Al-Urduni attempts to universalize his joy in combat as a shared emotion, one possible for all men in IS's territories.

At 10:28, Al-Urduni recites his last will and testament to his children, as shown in figure 7.8. He defends the attacks of their brother and uncle through "their religious education and the command that was mandatory for them" (until 10:44). He says, "I will also leave today," as the boys cough, take deep breaths, and wipe away tears, demonstrating how IS mediates disorder by intervening within families to call for violence.

The youngest boy collapses into his father's lap, crying. Al-Urduni smiles sympathetically, running his hand through the boy's hair: "Come on! You're going to be one of the mujahideen if God wills! Is it not? You're going to be a martyr, right? Why are you crying?" He hugs and kisses the boy, as shown in figure 7.9. This segment adopts two mechanisms of

FIGURE 7.8 A screenshot from "The Caravan of Lights 2" showing a militant sitting with his children, preparing them for his suicide mission. The militant's teenage son is wearing a uniform, a sign of his acculturation into the group. Scenes like this depict the transmission of a militant cultural and psychological identity within IS's families.

FIGURE 7.9 A screenshot from "The Caravan of Lights 2" showing a young boy crying after his father tells him that he will be leaving to commit a suicide attack.

persuasion. First, IS mediates disorder by providing visual proof of fathers urging sons to emulate them through violent jihad. The video normalizes violence against oneself and others through prestige-based cultural transmission: Al-Urduni congratulates his sons as future "martyrs." Second, the video cultivates the likeability of Al-Urduni and his children by depicting Al-Urduni's compassion for his children and his children's vulnerability. Al-Urduni consoles his family without deviating from his mission, suggesting that others can imitate his behaviors despite the toll on their families. The sequence ends by showing him climbing into a car and a drone filming his attack.

Sequence 3

From 16:00 to 25:16, the video features footage of dozens of attacks. Ground and aerial views offer visual proof of the militants' successes. The soundtrack is two *nashīds*, one of which reinforces the symbolism of light: "You are the light of guidance, you are for the truth of the banner. They controlled the leadership of wastelands. Spread the light of Muhammad!" (*in-tu-mu nū-ral-hi-dā-ya / in-tu-mu lil-haq-qal rā-ya // ha-ki-mu qai dal qi-wā-ya / in-sha-ru nū-ra mu-ham-mad*). The phrase "light of guidance" refers to shared meanings of Muhammad's illustrious status as God's last prophet, who guided all people to His path (Schimmel 1985). The *nashīd* ascribes a militant "you-dentity" to listeners by demanding that they emulate Muhammad's militarism, contrasting an in-group of believers with an out-group of rulers for psychological persuasion. Explosions offer visual proof of the militants proceeding to God in a caravan of lights.

Sequence 4

At 25:16, the video features testimonies from four militants whose sons have committed suicide attacks. For persuasion, the narrator contrasts the customary father–son relationship with IS's interpretation of this bond: "It is not surprising when fathers are good examples for their sons. But it is surprising when fathers choose the paths of their sons. In the epic battles of Nineveh, the fathers quickened their pace toward their sons who preceded

FIGURE 7.10 A screenshot from "The Caravan of Lights 2" showing a father weeping as he recounts the suicide missions of his sons.

them as martyrs." The reference to sons as "martyrs" promotes the prestige-based cultural transmission of suicide attacks, and the phrase "epic battles" persuades viewers that the men are acting out prophesies in present times.

At 25:41, the first militant, Abu Saif Al-Iraqi, speaks: "My children chose the same path, the same way. My second son was the brightest of the swords; he pledged allegiance before me." He praises his son's courage: "He went off, praise be to God. And after him, my smallest son, Muhammad . . ." He trails off, beginning to weep, as shown in figure 7.10. This segment attempts to persuade viewers of Al-Iraqi's likeability by conveying the pain of a father losing his son

Al-Iraqi regains his composure and explains his son's influence on him: "His uncle and I went to the place for pledging allegiance and received him. He came to me within a day and said, 'Oh father, I have learned how to operate so-and-so weapon. I am going to carry it and learn to use it.'" He honors his sons' sacrifices: "He and his brother preceded me to God, may He be praised and exalted, and I ask God to accept them and this action." Bureaucratic documents smuggled from IS territories indicate that men who pledge allegiance to the group must attend "Shari'i and training sessions" (Islamic State n.d.-b), thus illustrating how IS molds "allonomous" selves to comply with its interpretations of the Quran and Hadith.

At 27:43, the second militant, Abu Omar Al-Mosulawi, speaks into the camera. Unlike Al-Iraqi, Al-Mosulawi describes a deep loyalty to IS before signing up for a suicide mission: "I had served this religion for years as a preacher, imam, and a missionary at times, but I found myself that this was not sufficient for serving this religion. Instead, this religion is in need of more and more." Al-Mosulawi's voice hesitates upon recalling his son's sacrifice: "Some of the youth made me brave during the sermons and demonstrations for pledging allegiance and killing the apostates, polytheists, and Crusaders. One of them was my son, Abu Azhar. . . . I ask that God accept him among the martyrs." He does not weep like Al-Iraqi, but he pauses in distress after saying his son's name.

At 28:24, the third militant, Abu Muwaz Al-Safri, describes his older son's circuitous route to a martyrdom operation: "He was always in touch with us and spoke to us. He told me, 'I don't want to stay in Turkey. I want to return to Mosul city.' " His father agreed with his decision: "He went to the Office of the Military, and it did not take long for him to sign up for a martyrdom operation. He embraced the obligation of a martyrdom mission inside the city of Baghdad. He carried out the operation by the grace of God, mighty and majestic is He." Al-Safri describes his older son's effect on his younger son: "Similarly, my younger son, Sayf Al-Iraqi, pledged allegiance, as he used to work in the Office of Services. He wanted to be transferred to the Office of the Military." Al-Safri praises his younger son for carrying out an operation inside Baghdad.

At 29:53, a fourth militant, also named Abu Omar Al-Mosulawi, describes his sons' participation in jihad:

> Praise be to God. My sons participated in the battles of the [Arabian] Peninsula, and my oldest son, Omar, participated in the conquest of Mosul. The first of my sons who was killed was Amir. Then Tamir followed him, and Imran followed both of them, may God accept them. I will catch up to them with God's permission.

Al-Mosulawi describes his joy on hearing of Imran's death: "I heard news about him, and I was gladdened. I decided to join them—if God wills—and put myself down for a martyrdom mission." Suddenly he cries while addressing his wife: "My last will and testament to Omar's wife: You will hear about me just like you have heard about the examples of Amir and Imran. Perseverance is perseverance. Our meeting will be in the highest company, with God's

FIGURE 7.11 A screenshot from "The Caravan of Lights 2" showing an aerial view of the area where Abu Saif Al-Iraqi will undertake his suicide attack. The IS flag waves in the upper right corner. Al-Iraqi's photo and name appear in the lower right corner. The small circle to the left of the photo is a blinking light identifying the location of his car as he proceeds to the location of his attack.

permission. Look after the children." His message affirms Al-Muhājirah's (2015) advice in "A Jihād Without Fighting" for women to remain steadfast in widowhood.

At 31:32, the video features drone views of the attacks by all four fathers. Figure 7.11 illustrates the aerial perspective that follows the attackers who drive cars to their targets. A portrait of each attacker appears on screen during his attack. The footage provides visual proof of fathers following their sons on the path of martyrdom; the repeated explosions reinforce the symbolism of a caravan of lights.

"The Caravan of Lights 2" mediates disorder by filming the impact of suicide attacks on families. Men emulate relatives, thus transmitting IS's militant cultural and psychological identity. The video uses multiple mechanisms of persuasion: drawing contrasts with the Shia, imposing obligations on men to wage violent jihad in obedience to God's commands, warning that disbelievers threaten Muslims, and offering visual proof of IS's missions. As in the last video, the men do *not* cite the Quran or Hadith to justify their actions. Instead, this video tries to cultivate the likeability of its protagonists such that viewers feel transported into their world, establishing parasocial relationships and identifying psychologically with them. IS depicts the fathers as prototypical in-group members who embody piety through self-sacrifice, a symbolic convoy of lights defeating a better-equipped army of disbelievers. The video illustrates the maintenance of violent in-group norms within families: All men commemorate their sons by adopting shared practices of violent jihad, "allonomously" conforming to IS's interpretations of the Quran and Hadith.

Societies devise cultural solutions to the loss of independence and self-reliance that accompany aging (Hurwicz 1995; Schulz and Heckhausen 1999); this video reveals IS's solution: Involve elderly men in militancy.

IS's Mediated Disorder

Applying the OCF framework through a discourse analysis of IS's texts on families uncovers the group's diffusion of a militant cultural and psychological identity through kin relationships. In chapter 6, I showed how ISIS mediated disorder by customizing messages for children, adult men, elderly men, and foreign fighters. In its current phase, the group continues to experiment with new forms of media production by targeting familial relationships. The texts presented in this chapter extol jihad in different ways: "A Jihād Without Fighting" insists that women must produce and dispatch men for battle; "My Son Has Preceded Me: A Martyr's Story" shows fathers who prioritize their love for God over their love for their children; and "The Caravan of Lights 2" illustrates the perhaps surprising path of fathers choosing the path of jihad later in life, after being inspired by their martyred sons. When analyzed together, these texts disclose IS's gender and parenting norms for families.

Again we see that the media platform determines the mechanisms of persuasion used to incite violent thoughts, emotions, and behaviors. In all three texts discussed in this chapter, authors impose obligations on the audience by ascribing a "you-dentity" that foregrounds religion. However, there are relevant differences. "A Jihād Without Fighting" conforms to IS's norms of not depicting images of adult women. As a written text, it employs mechanisms of persuasion that engage readers cognitively through lengthy quotations from the Quran and Hadith and preempt arguments from opponents. The two videos exploit the multimodality of sight and sound for maximal persuasion through visual proof of IS's attacks, reconstruction efforts, and representations of the father–son relationship. Both videos transport the viewer to the worlds of their protagonists to establish parasocial relationships with them. All three texts acknowledge the social nature of suffering as relatives commit suicide attacks: Al-Muhājirah tries to shift the attention of readers from thoughts of divorcing husbands to celebrating widowhood; "My Son Has Preceded Me: A Martyr's Story" tries to impose the obligation of jihad upon all Muslim men, even at the cost of relationships; and "The Caravan of Lights 2" shows children and fathers sobbing at the loss of loved ones.

This militarization of kin relationships challenges long-standing cultural and psychological theories that the family unit is entrusted with disciplining individuals so that they might become productive members of society. Michel Foucault (2008) connects families to state power through the discourse of mental health, what he terms the "Psy-function": "The family requested confinement and the individual was placed under psychiatric discipline and supposed to be refamilialized. Then, gradually, the Psy-function was extended to all the disciplinary systems: school, army, workshop, and so forth" (86). Foucault (2008) explains that the state deems families responsible for a relative's abnormal behaviors, whether suicide or homicide:

> When an individual could not follow school discipline or the discipline of the workshop, the army, and, if it comes to it, of prison, then the Psy-function stepped in. And it came in with a discourse attributing the individual's inability to be disciplined to the deficiency and failure of the family (86).

Foucault (2008) characterizes twentieth-century mental health services as a "familiarization of the therapeutic milieu for the clinics on one side, and, on the other, disciplinarization of the family, which at that point becomes the agency of the abnormalization of individuals" (114). Modern psychiatry demonstrates a familiarization of the clinic, with researchers creating family interventions to prevent suicide in the very groups that IS has targeted, such as adolescents (Hawton et al. 2015), war veterans (Hoge et al. 2016), and elderly adults (Lapierre 2011).

IS media overturns these cultural and psychological assumptions. Its so-called caliphate relies even now on the family to inculcate discipline, but the outcome is radically different. The texts covered in chapters 6 and 7 reveal a goal of *defamiliarization*, not *refamiliarization*, as IS intervenes to create distance between individuals and their relatives. School instructors, imams, foreign fighters, and now parents and siblings encourage defamiliarization through detachment from all biological relationships: Mothers and fathers dispatch their adolescent children for attacks, and adolescents exhort siblings and fathers to follow their lead. The texts in this chapter come from IS's portrayals of life in Iraq and Syria, though journalists have reported that online recruiters also try to separate potential recruits from their families by hiding all correspondence from relatives (Callimachi 2015b). Defamiliarization and the substitution of biological relationships with in-group relationships to maintain violent thoughts, emotions, and behaviors expose one pathway for IS's transmission of a militant cultural and psychological identity.

In fact, IS has recognized the threat that refamiliarization poses. In several articles, it condemns its opponents—even the relatives of suicide attackers—as "apostates" (Chowdhury 2016; "Wala and Bara, O Women" 2017). One article targeted to women subtly encourages defamiliarization:

> We do not incite you, O bondwoman of Allah, to abandon your family and relatives except in the case of those whose apostasy has become clear to you through a statement or deed of theirs which takes one out of the religion. This type of individual is to be abandoned and disavowed before Allah with absolutely no alternative, such as one who supports the enemy, even with a single word, or makes *du'a* [prays] for the Islamic State to suffer ruin and loss in its war against its enemies, or wishes for the rule of the Shari'ah to come to an end ("Wala and Bara, O Women" 2017, 24).

This text aims to persuade readers that even the slightest criticism of the group "takes one out of the religion," illustrating a process of cultural tightening as IS demands that recruits shun anyone who deviates from its in-group norms for religion, even family.

To be sure, counter-media that promote refamiliarization will not end the forced conscription of men over fourteen years of age in places like IS's capital of Raqqa (Islamic State 2014e), but such media may prevent fathers and sons from volunteering for suicide attacks. This strategy could offer one potential health and societal solution to the problem of social suffering in IS territories gripped by political violence and broken families.

EIGHT

Toward a Science, Policy, and Practice of Militant Counter-Messaging

AS I WRITE this conclusion, the Islamic State (IS) has released the thirteenth issue of *Rumiyah* to coincide with the sixteenth anniversary of the September 11 attacks. Although IS is losing territories in a global war against a coalition of sixty-nine states and four international bodies (Global Coalition 2017b), its media output continues. I have drawn from cultural psychiatry's multidisciplinary nature (Kirmayer 2007b) to integrate key insights from anthropology, psychiatry, and psychology—that media is central to our everyday lives, to our ability to reconfigure individual and group identities, to the alteration of our basic psychologies, and to the subversion of traditional sources of authority such as religious scholars or the nation-state—in developing my theory of *mediated disorder*.

The study of mediated disorder disentangles group culture and individual psychology by investigating how militant groups use media to disrupt the thoughts and emotions of audiences while acting as intermediate between individuals and society to incite violence against others. The qualitative research tradition in cultural psychiatry offers a pragmatic strategy of using exemplary case studies and maximum variation sampling to solve the problem of multimedia overload. Rather than take culture or psychology for granted, I have conducted a discourse analysis of each text by adapting standardized variables from the Outline for Cultural Formulation (OCF) framework: shared meanings, practices, and symbols that constitute group culture, psychological mechanisms of persuasion, and the social context of interpersonal relationships and institutions. These approaches can advance our understanding of the culture and psychology of militancy by providing a framework to examine media communication and allowing us to avoid the tendency to "default to individual, trait-based explanations, if not explicitly negative dispositional qualities" (Horgan 2017, 628). The persuasive effects of communication, not individual traits, explains why I briefly fell under the sway of Abu Talha Al-Yamani.

I organized this book's chapters chronologically to trace thematic convergences and divergences in the Islamic State's culture and psychology over time. Media from the phases of the Organization of Monotheism and Jihad (OMJ), Al Qaeda in Iraq (AQI), the Assembly of the Mujahideen Council (AMC), and the Islamic State of Iraq (ISI) exhibit greater intragroup divergences than in the phases of the Islamic State of Iraq and Syria (ISIS) and the Islamic State (IS). I attribute the increased cohesion over time to the phenomenon of *cultural tightening.*

In chapter 2, I interpreted Al-Zarqawi's construction of an entirely new cultural and psychological identity for OMJ in speeches, videos, and *nashīds* through the theory of *social representations.*

In chapter 3, I contrasted texts from OMJ and Al Qaeda before and after their merger to discover behavioral shifts in language use and systems of shared meanings, practices, and symbols during the groups' *acculturation* process of forming AQI.

In chapter 4, I selected written documents and videos to empirically delineate AMC's *common group identity.*

In chapter 5, I compared the extent to which ISI's *identity shift* manifested differentially in a speech, a video, and bureaucratic documents.

In chapter 6, I presented the diffusion of ISIS's militant identity through *cultural group selection* in multiple videos portraying life amidst the Syrian Civil War.

Without excusing suicide bombers or their actions, I showed in chapter 7 how IS's transmission of a militant identity has broken families through *social suffering.*

Interpreting IS's evolution in this manner has several advantages. First, these theories continue to animate research in cultural mental health and can generate an evidence base for cross-cultural comparisons across militant and nonmilitant groups. This may be useful to scholars and practitioners of political science, international relations, counterterrorism, and security studies by providing working terms and concepts of culture that many of us already use. Reciprocally, militant media forces those of us in the social and behavioral sciences to contend with cultural life and psychological operations at the extremes of life and death. Our theories are useful insofar as they help us interpret the world with greater accuracy, and militant media furnishes us with novel data to think with for iterative theory building, which I've pursued in each chapter.

Discourse analysis allows us to avoid assumptions about IS's uniformity since 2003. Let's return to the definition of culture as "the shared meanings, practices, and symbols that constitute the human world" (Rabinow and Sullivan 1987, 7). "Shared" does not mean unitary, and discourse analysis clarifies "the divergences, the distances, the oppositions, the differences" within groups through a granular examination of each individual text (Foucault 1991, 55). By starting from the individual text as the unit of analysis rather than the our perception of how the group is organized according to some trait (such as "terrorist" or "Islamist" groups), we avoid the reduction of identity to abstract categories like race, ethnicity, or religion that may not necessarily be relevant for the people involved (Guarnaccia and Rodriguez 1996).

For example, OMJ introduced shared meanings for recruits to adopt a conception of the world based on a defensive jihad against the U.S.-led coalition, the annihilation of historical foes like the Kurds and Shia, the implementation of a Sharia-based caliphate, and the emulation of the prophet Muhammad's militarism. The AQI phase exposed fault lines in shared meanings between OMJ and Al Qaeda, some of whose members *equivocated* over how to treat the Kurds and Shia and whether to prioritize jihad in Iraq or the Arabian Peninsula. AMC drew upon shared meanings of honor and chastity for women while presenting jihad as an option for substituting a worldly existence with a heavenly one. With ISI, jihad transformed from a defensive strategy into an obligation upon all Muslims to act "allonomously" in line with the group's interpretations of the Quran and Hadith, which elicited conflicts with other Sunni mujahideen groups like Ansar Al-Islam. After a period of dormancy, ISIS emerged during the Syrian Civil War to transmit its identity across generations by wresting resources over rivals. In its current phase, IS disciplines families to maintain a steady supply of male suicide bombers. Dismissing the group as "terrorist" or "Islamist" would have risked overlooking pertinent differences in identity that have important consequences beyond the academy. As a practical example of how to construct counter-narratives, a strategy to dissuade recruits from violent jihad on the basis of love for their families may not be as successful today, with IS encouraging *defamiliarization*, as it may have been during the OMJ and AQI phases, when shared meanings of violent jihad to defend families were prominent.

Despite differences in meanings, there are similarities across the phases of IS's evolution. Through discourse analysis, we have seen how cultural and religious vocabularies—such as *anfāl, muhājirūn, ansār, fitna, ahzāb, murtadd,* and *munafiqīn*—acquire new meanings to divide in-groups from out-groups. We have also seen how symbolic tropes such as the Battle of Badr, the medieval hero Salahuddin, the martyr's wedding to angels, and the caravan of lights equate current wars in the Middle East with past battles. Across all chapters, a theme of emulating the prophet Muhammad's bravery and steadfastness against better equipped, non-Muslims forces recurs. This finding corroborates a core assumption of discourse analysis: that the world inside texts reflects the world outside. Interviews conducted during the battle for Mosul with captured IS fighters, Kurdish peshmarga, Kurds in the Iraqi Army, and Arab Sunnis in militias found that the "relative spiritual formidability of groups, compared to relative physical formidability, is more related to willingness to sacrifice" (Gómez et al. 2017, 674). Specifically, captured IS fighters "disregarded consideration of ingroup and outgroup physical formidability" in favor of " 'strength of belief in what we are fighting for' and 'what is in our heart,' " especially among would-be suicide bombers (Gómez et al. 2017, 674). Despite these important findings, we do not yet know how they relate to media consumption. For instance, we do not know whether militants were persuaded to fight before or after consuming IS media.

Furthermore, I have demonstrated the group's differential use of psychological mechanisms of persuasion across time and media platform. Most texts relied on invoking the authority of religion either through scriptural references or historical prototypes, drawing contrasts between Muslims and non-Muslims and imposing obligations of action upon the audience. In each phase of IS's development, *nashīd*s have aestheticized militancy through short rhyming messages that ascribe "you-dentities" and "we-dentities" to listeners.

Variations have also occurred as the group has evolved. Abu Musab Al-Zarqawi's speeches deployed ornate techniques of linguistic persuasion drawn from classical Arabic rhetoric during the OMJ and AMC phases, calling attention to the creation of culture through *sociolinguistic representations*. AQI's written texts dispensed with this style altogether. In each phase, however, videos have consistently used visual proof to induce inferences that mediate disorder by depicting innocent casualties and militants training together for jihad; some videos also show militants embracing before their attacks. By the AMC phase, persuasive strategies included the presentation of suicide attackers as likeable figures so that viewers feel transported into their worlds, establishing parasocial relationships and identifying with them. The characters within all these videos embody tight social norms that the group projects as worthy of emulation: From the OMJ through the ISI phases, we only see adult men, but younger children and the elderly appear during and after the ISIS phase. From this point, the videos also convince viewers of the group's penetration into the everyday lives of the people under its rule: Children and men deliver food to civilians, tribes pledge allegiance to Abu Bakr Al-Baghdadi, boys attend IS-run schools, men gather in mosques to hear the messages of imams, and in-group members rebuild cities bombed by the Syrian government. What intrigues me most about the videos is that the ISIS and IS phases replace extensive quotations from the Quran and Hadith with an emphasis on empathetic characters: Religious scriptures did not pull me into Abu Talha's world, but his carefree spirit and companionship with others did. *Jundullah*'s catchy hymn and lyrics kept me pondering the video long after watching it. IS has masterfully exploited the psychology of persuasion by media platform, and so should we.

This raises a fundamental question: What should our response be? I support a strategy that develops a data-driven science, policy, and practice of counter-messaging, but I restrict my recommendations to my area of expertise: the field of cultural mental health.

Science

The OCF framework builds on an ongoing collaboration between cultural psychiatrists and interpretive medical anthropologists. This partnership began in the 1970s to ethnographically inquire into experiences of health and illness, normal and abnormal psychology, without assuming that secular Euro-American concepts of mental health are valid (Kleinman 1987). As

I've shown elsewhere (Aggarwal 2015), mental health professionals involved in the War on Terror have too often assumed that suicide bombers are rife with pathology without appreciating the cultural justifications that underpin violent thoughts, emotions, and behaviors. The advantage of the OCF framework is its established status within cultural mental health. Researchers, practitioners, and administrators have written extensively on its prior (Mezzich and Caracci 2008) and current versions (Lewis-Fernández et al. 2014). It is the most common cultural assessment tool taught to psychiatric trainees in North America (Hansen et al. 2013; Mills et al. 2017). Psychiatrists have long wondered how to meaningfully contribute to counterterrorism efforts (Bhugra 2017), and the OCF furnishes us with an evidence-based tool to analyze the relationship between group culture and psychological persuasion in militant media, for IS and other groups. Cultural psychiatrists can partner with colleagues in counterterrorism studies to conduct focus groups—a methodology common to both fields (Ahmad et al. 2012; Ekblad and Bäärnhielm 2002)—to elicit reactions on which psychological mechanisms are most persuasive in a given unit of media. Such science can hone effective counter-messages to violent extremism by media platform.

Policy

Psychiatrists have increasingly called for a public mental health approach to developing counter-messages to violent extremism in order to prevent terror attacks (Bhui et al. 2012; Weine et al. 2017). While I appreciate that the intent of this initiative is to serve society, I have reservations about its implementation. The National Academies of Sciences, Engineering, and Medicine (2017) in the United States support this model despite acknowledging that there is no consensus on a standardized definition for counter-messages to violent extremism, the causes of violent extremism, the ability to predict who will act on violent impulses, or outcomes to measure. Other criticisms come from public health models that are now in place. Since 2011, the United Kingdom's National Health Service has mandated that mental health professionals screen all patients for signs of militant activity and report suspicious individuals to the police, such that the entire domestic population is under surveillance (Heath-Kelly 2016). The burden of society's protection has fallen on clinicians who have become mandated reporters, not on law enforcement and national security agencies, which reinforces concerns that mental health professionals are elevating state interests over those of individuals while stigmatizing minorities (Foucault 1995).

My experiences writing this book convince me that public health screening—not for law enforcement but to treat individuals—could help in two areas: mediatized trauma and addiction. Evidence is emerging of a link between exposure to violent media, such as footage of terrorist attacks, and the development of symptoms suggestive of traumatic stress disorders (Comer et al. 2016; Pfefferbaum et al. 2016; Monfort and Afzali 2017). Social media's addictive properties have been described as a habitual desire for mood alteration (Ryan et al. 2014); IS may be trying to manipulate biological arousal and pleasure pathways by releasing time-limited content that people can access only if they stay online (Bloom et al. 2017). Mental health clinicians could screen patients to assess whether they consume militant media, and, if so, whether they have symptoms of distress that are concerning for trauma and addiction. By way of illustration, let's relate these findings on the psychological effects of social media to two screening tools used widely across medicine.

First, we could modify the Primary Care Post-Traumatic Stress Disorder Screen for DSM-5 (PC-PTSD-5) (Prins et al. 2016). This is a screening questionnaire to help determine whether individuals are experiencing PTSD. We could adjust the first question slightly to introduce the key issue: "Sometimes people are exposed to violent media from militant groups, which can be unusually or especially frightening, horrible, or traumatic. Have you ever experienced this kind of event?" If a person answers no, there is no need to proceed further.

However, if a respondent answers yes, we could elicit more history with the next question of the PC-PTSD-5 (Prins et al. 2016):

In the past month, have you:

(1) had nightmares about the event(s) or thought about the event(s) when you did not want to?
(2) tried hard not to think about the event(s) or went out of your way to avoid situations that reminded you of the event(s)?
(3) been constantly on guard, watchful, or easily startled?
(4) felt numb or detached from people, activities, or your surroundings?
(5) felt guilty or unable to stop blaming yourself or others for the event(s) or any problems the event(s) may have caused?

Anyone who answers yes to three of these five questions could be referred for more extensive PTSD evaluation.

Similarly, we could modify the CAGE questionnaire (Ewing 1984) to assess for media addiction. This is another questionnaire commonly used to assess individuals for substance addiction, and it is worth considering whether it can be applied to militant media. Here are possible adaptations:

(1) Have you ever felt you needed to cut down on watching violent media from militant groups?
(2) Have people annoyed you by criticizing you for watching violent media from militant groups?
(3) Have you ever felt guilty about watching violent media from militant groups?
(4) Have you ever felt you needed to watch violent media from militant groups first thing in the morning?

Any respondent who answers yes to two of the four questions could be referred to assess addiction to violent media.

These are not necessarily the only or even the best ways of assessing the mental health sequelae of watching violent media. I wish only to suggest that studies increasingly demonstrate a link between exposure to violent media and symptoms of psychological distress. Such symptoms could be outcomes worth targeting in public health models for developing counter-messages to violent extremism: general clinicians could undertake basic screening before referring patients for in-depth evaluations by specialists. Rather than rush to an international "best practices" approach that characterized early derad-icalization programs despite a lack of outcomes evidence (Aggarwal 2013), a public health approach to counter-messages to violent extremism based on exposure to violent media could proceed cautiously with pilot studies. Clinicians can play a role in counter-messaging by assessing whether their patients' consumption of militant media leads to distress and impairments in social, occupational, or other important areas of functioning.

Practice

The Global Coalition against IS has publicized its goal of "an effective and unified Coalition messaging and counter-messaging effort to oppose Daesh's [a derogatory Arabic term for the Islamic State] narrative and to undermine the appeal of its ideology" (2017b). Cultural mental health experts can aid this effort by adding to the existing knowledge on counter-narratives. Kurt Braddock and John Horgan (2016) have proposed strategies that relate easily to certain psychological mechanisms of persuasion. While their suggestions apply to all militant groups, I have demonstrated their specific applicability to IS's media. For instance, their suggestions to avoid the reinforcement of themes in militant narratives, expose contradictions in these narratives, and disrupt the analogies of these narratives to real-world events counter the persuasion mechanism in which militants impose propositions for audiences. Applied to IS, this could mean avoiding themes that reinforce a love for the afterlife over life on earth or the need to prioritize love for God over love for one's family. To expose contradictions in militant narratives, we can partner with colleagues in area studies such as Middle Eastern, South Asian, or Southeast Asian studies to detect inconsistencies in argumentation. Elsewhere, I've shown that IS glosses over real differences of opinion when citing canonical religious scholars to make claims about the legality of its caliphate under Sharia (Aggarwal 2017). By pointing out these inconsistencies, we can interrogate IS's ability to interpret the Quran and Hadith competently.

To disrupt analogies with real-world events, we can challenge IS's claims of reenacting the Battle of Badr. Islamist militants use this battle to claim that God will deliver a victory against non-Muslims to the outnumbered Muslims in an attempt to forge transnational Muslim solidarity (Halverson, Goodall Jr., and Corman 2011). The Battle of Badr occurred on March 13, 624 CE. A counter-messaging strategy against this analogy could aggregate media of Al-Zarqawi, Al-Baghdadi, and others who have invoked the battle to question how each IS attack is supposed to be another Battle of Badr, which occurred over just a single day. A counter-response that analogies to the Battle of Badr are symbolic, not literal, subverts IS's entire project of producing "allonomous" selves in conformity with its literalist interpretations of the Quran and Hadith. This contradiction could thus raise doubts about the ability of IS's leaders to accurately construct analogies between occurrences in religious texts and real-world events.

Braddock and Horgan (2016) offer two other suggestions that relate to disrupting the contrasts that militants draw: incorporating alternative views of targeted outsiders and challenging the binary structure of these contrasts. Such disruptions will be difficult to accomplish, however, since IS has constructed a polarized identity in competition with out-groups. We saw in chapter 5 with ISI's relationship to other Sunni mujahideen groups that the imposition of a common group identity does not decrease social distance with rivals. For this reason, I am not convinced that counter-messaging to inculcate neutrality or affection with Christians, Shia, and Kurds would be effective among those who identify strongly with IS's in-group norms. Instead, drawing contrasts that expose the gulf in religious interpretations between IS and other Sunni groups—especially those whose reputations for orthodoxy are impeachable, like Sunni scholars at the reputed seminary of Al-Azhar University in Egypt—may counter this persuasion mechanism.

Finally, we should take advantage of persuasion mechanisms that are unique to media platforms. In the same way that Al-Zarqawi exhibited an impressive use of linguistic practices in his speeches, counter-messaging podcasts could also pay as serious attention to style as they do to content. Similar to IS's *nashīds*, counter-messaging songs could cast IS as a targeted out-group with catchy music and rhymes. Finally, counter-messaging videos could demonstrate visual proof of IS members being injured and taken captive to refute claims of their invincibility, as well as the coalition's reconstruction efforts in IS-liberated territories. In all cases, we must try to do no harm by avoiding co-optation from governments who want to use counter-messaging practices without reflecting critically on their policies, such as justifications for the ongoing wars in Iraq or Syria. Those of us working at the crossroads of culture and mental health would do well to remember that we serve our professions best when we critique all aggressors to limit the deaths of innocents, irrespective of their cultural justifications for violence.

***

Ever since President George W. Bush declared the War on Terror in 2001, militant groups around the world have justified violence by treating American military intervention as a threat to an idealized order. In this book, I have shown that we can analyze the psychology of persuasion in militant media through methods from anthropology, psychology, and psychiatry. Mechanisms of persuasion have changed over time, and any science, policy, and practice of counterterrorism communication must keep apace. Militant media also critiques the goals of such intervention and provides a narrative rarely heard in mainstream media, policy, or academic circles. It's time that we treat militant media as an object of study in its own right, from which we can develop and test new theories for real-world impact.

Notes

1. Studying Islamic State Discourse as Mediated Disorder

1. I describe this within each chapter's main text. When I also describe the search strategy for scholarly reproducibility, I include this information in a note. In all cases, I provide references to each text for independent verification.

2. The "Two Rivers" are the Tigris and Euphrates. The Arabic word for "river" here is *furat*, from the Greek "Euphrates."

2. The Organization of Monotheism and Jihad

1. I found this video at https://archive.org/details/AbuJaafarAl-Maqdisi1.

2. I found this video at https://archive.org/details/Aduyu_20150604.

3. Al Qaeda in Iraq

1. This text appears verbatim in the twenty-first issue of Al Qaeda's biweekly *Mu'askar Al-Battār* (*Camp of the Sword*), a periodical of essays on politics and military training. The publication of this text points to the high degree of coordinated communication between OMJ and Al Qaeda even before they announced their merger.

2. I have translated *Al-Battār* as "sword." Many Muslims believe that Muhammad took the sword supposedly used by David against Goliath as booty from the Jewish Banu Qaynuqa tribe during the Battle of Badr (Wheeler 2006). By using this name, Al Qaeda created an analogy between Muhammad's outnumbered army of

believers and insurgents outnumbered by the forces of non-Muslim disbelievers in Iraq.

3. I found this video at https://archive.org/details/wayakoonaldeenkoloholillah 120MB.

4. The Assembly of the Mujahideen Council

1. I found these videos by searching for the group's name in English and Arabic on Internet Archive (https://archive.org/), comparing all videos that were common to both searches and watching all videos that were published online in 2006. I selected the two videos discussed in this chapter for analysis since they exhibit different mechanisms of psychological persuasion, consistent with maximum variation sampling.

2. I found this statement at http://jihadology.net/2006/01/15/statement-from -majlis-shura-al-mujahidin-in-iraq-founding-statement/.

3. I found this video at https://archive.org/details/song-of-terror-main-16.

4. I found this video at https://archive.org/details/iraqwar-song-of-terror.

5. The Islamic State of Iraq, 2006–2013

1. I found this speech at https://archive.org/details/byntn and compared the Arabic audio with the text in Al-Baghdadi (2007) to produce my translation.

2. When I searched for ISI's name in Arabic and English on July 14, 2016, and ordered all results by year on Internet Archive (https://archive.org/), "Vanquisher of the Peshmarga" had the largest number of views at 34,390. The video with the second-largest number of views was titled "Several Releases of the Islamic State of Iraq" at 9,967.

3. I found this video at https://archive.org/details/KaHer0.

4. I found these documents at https://ctc.usma.edu/programs-resources/harmony -program. There is no consensus on case study selection for document analysis (Bowen 2009; Hull 2012). From June through August 2016, I reviewed all documents classified as "AQ and Other Sunni Jihadist Groups in Iraq" by category. From this set, I identified and reviewed 324 documents that pertained to ISI based on the group's logo. I present representative examples of cultural and psychological identity shift in this chapter. My list is available to other researchers through a written request.

6. The Islamic State of Iraq and Syria

1. The goal of the videos in this series is to depict life in ISIS territories. Only one video features Sunni Kurds as ISIS fighters, so I analyze it as a case study of

how ISIS has successfully constructed a common militant identity among groups that speak different languages and with whom there has been historical intergroup competition. Just one video features elderly militants, so I also analyze that video as a unique case study. Many videos feature children and adult men, so I have selected four specimens for each, consistent with the sampling rationale given in chapter 1.

2. I found this speech at http://jihadology.net/2013/06/15/new-audio-visual -message-from-the-islamic-state-of-iraq-and-al-shams-abu-bakr-al-ḥussayni-al -baghdadi-remaining-in-iraq-and-al-sham/ and compared the Arabic audio with the text in Al-Baghdadi (2013) to produce my translation.

3. I found Al-Zawahiri's original speech at www.documentcloud.org/documents /710586-ayman-zawahiri.html#document/p1.

4. I found this video at http://jihadology.net/2013/09/04/al-itiṣam-media -presents-new-video-message-from-the-islamic-state-of-iraq-and-al-sham-a-window -upon-the-land-of-epic-battles-6/.

5. I found this video at http://jihadology.net/2013/09/07/al-itiṣam-media -presents-new-video-messages-from-the-islamic-state-of-iraq-and-al-sham-a-window -upon-the-land-of-epic-battles-7″/.

6. I found this video at http://jihadology.net/2013/11/20/al-itiṣam-media -presents-a-new-video-message-from-the-islamic-state-of-iraq-and-al-sham-a -window-upon-the-land-of-epic-battles-28/.

7. I found this video at http://jihadology.net/2013/12/30/al-itiṣam-media -presents-a-new-video-message-from-the-islamic-state-of-iraq-and-al-sham-a -window-upon-the-land-of-epic-battles-40/.

8. I found this video at http://jihadology.net/2013/08/08/al-itiṣam-media -presents-a-new-video-series-from-the-islamic-state-of-iraq-and-al-sham-a-window -upon-the-land-of-epic-battles-1-and-2/.

9. I found this video at http://jihadology.net/2013/08/11/al-itiṣam-media -presents-new-video-messages-from-the-islamic-state-of-iraq-and-al-sham-a-window -upon-the-land-of-epic-battles-3-4-and-5/.

10. I found this video at http://jihadology.net/2013/11/21/al-itiṣam-media -presents-a-new-video-message-from-the-islamic-state-of-iraq-and-al-sham-a -window-upon-the-land-of-epic-battles-29/.

11. I found this video at http://jihadology.net/2013/12/20/al-itiṣam-media -presents-a-new-video-message-from-the-islamic-state-of-iraq-and-al-sham-a -window-upon-the-land-of-epic-battles-37″/.

12. I found this video at http://jihadology.net/2013/11/15/al-itiṣam-media -presents-a-new-video-message-from-the-islamic-state-of-iraq-and-al-sham-a -window-upon-the-land-of-epic-battles-26/.

13. I found this video at http://jihadology.net/2013/10/19/al-itiṣam-media -presents-a-new-video-message-from-the-islamic-state-of-iraq-and-al-sham-a -window-upon-the-land-of-epic-battles-19/.

14. I found this video at http://jihadology.net/2017/09/03/new-video-message -from-the-islamic-state-the-spelling-teacher/.

7. The Islamic State

1. In writing about the IS period, many researchers continue to use the acronym of its predecessor: ISIS. I retain their original text in quotations.

2. Starting with the seventh issue of *Dabiq*, the fifth issue of *Dâr Al-Islâm* (in French), and the first issue of *Rumiyah* (in English), IS has ranked a "top ten" list of video releases for each issue, which it calls "Select 10." From March through July 2017, I compiled a list of each video that was ranked first, assuming that IS ranked the videos in order of importance. I then watched all videos listed in all issues of *Dabiq* and *Dâr Al-Islâm*, both of which are no longer published. I also watched all videos listed in *Rumiyah* through the eleventh issue (*Rumiyah* remains in print at the time of this manuscript's submission). "My Son Has Preceded Me: A Martyr's Story" was the only video from the list I compiled to feature a father preparing his son for an attack, and "The Caravan of Lights 2" was the only video to show fathers following their sons in martyrdom missions. For this reason, both videos serve as unique case studies of the father–son relationship.

3. I found this video at https://jihadology.net/?s=My+Son+Has+Preceded+Me.

4. I found this video at http://jihadology.net/2017/04/09/new-video-message -from-the-islamic-state-the-caravan-of-light-2-wilayat-ninawa/.

References

Abdul-Rahman, Muhammad Saeed. 2009. *Tafsir Ibn Kathir Juz' 11 (Part 11): At Tauba 93 to HUD 5*. 2nd ed. London: MSA.

Abdulla, Mufid. 2011. "Mahabad—The First Independent Kurdish Republic." *Kurdistan Tribune*, June 12.

Abrahamov, Binyamin. 1992. "Ibn Taymiyya on the Agreement of Reason with Tradition." *The Muslim World* 82 (3–4): 256–73.

Abrams, Philip. 1988. "Notes on the Difficulty of Studying the State." *Journal of Historical Sociology* 1 (1): 58–89.

Abu-Odeh, Lama. 2011. "Crimes of Honor and the Construction of Gender in Arab Societies." *Comparative Law Review* 2 (1): 1–47.

Aggarwal, Neil Krishan. 2012. "Hybridity and Intersubjectivity in the Clinical Encounter: Impact on the Cultural Formulation." *Transcultural Psychiatry* 49 (1): 121–39.

——. 2013. "Mental Discipline, Punishment, and Recidivism: Reading Foucault Against De-radicalisation Programmes in the War on Terror." *Critical Studies on Terrorism* 6 (2): 262–78.

——. 2015. *Mental Health in the War on Terror: Culture, Science, and Statecraft*. New York: Columbia University Press.

——. 2016. *The Taliban's Virtual Emirate: The Culture and Psychology of an Online Militant Community*. New York: Columbia University Press.

——. 2017. "Exploiting the Islamic State–Taliban Rivalry for Counterterrorism Messaging." *Journal of Policing, Intelligence and Counter Terrorism* 12 (1): 1–15.

Aggarwal, Neil Krishan, Andel Veronica Nicasio, Ravi DeSilva, Marit Boiler, and Roberto Lewis-Fernández. 2013. "Barriers to Implementing the DSM-5 Cultural Formulation Interview: A Qualitative Study." *Culture, Medicine, and Psychiatry* 37 (3): 505–33.

Aggarwal, Neil Krishan, Matthew C. Pieh, Lisa Dixon, Peter Guarnaccia, Margarita Alegría, and Roberto Lewis-Fernández. 2016. "Clinician Descriptions of Communication Strategies to Improve Treatment Engagement by Racial/Ethnic Minorities in Mental Health Services: A Systematic Review." *Patient Education and Counseling* 99 (2): 198–209.

Aggarwal, Neil Krishan, and Robert M. Rohrbaugh. 2011. "Teaching Cultural Competency Through an Experiential Seminar on Anthropology and Psychiatry." *Academic Psychiatry* 35 (5): 331–34.

Ahmad, Rabiah, Zahri Yunos, Shahrin Shahib, and Mariana Yusoff. 2012. "Perception on Cyber Terrorism: A Focus Group Discussion Approach." *Journal of Information Security* 3: 231–37.

Ahram, Ariel I. 2002. "Iraq and Syria: The Dilemma of Dynasty." *Middle East Quarterly* 9 (2): 33–42.

Akram, Agha Ibrahim. 2004. *The Sword of Allah: Khalid bin al-Waleed—His Life and Campaigns.* Oxford: Oxford University Press.

Al-'Amari, Al-Faruq. 2004. "*La-ka Allah Yā Fallujah*" ["God Is with You, Oh Fallujah"]. *Mu'askar Al-Battār* 1 (22): 3.

Al-Baghdadi, Abu Bakr. 2013. "Remaining in Iraq and al-Sham." *Internet Archive.* Accessed August 24, 2017. https://ia902602.us.archive.org/22/items/Remaining InIraqAndAlSham/Remaining percent20in percent 20Iraq percent20and percent 20al-Sham.pdf.

Al-Baghdadi, Abu Omar. 2007. "Say I Am on Clear Proof from My Lord." *Institutional Scholarship.* Accessed May 26, 2016. http://triceratops.brynmawr.edu:8080/dspace /bitstream/handle/10066/16500/AOB20070313_2.pdf?sequence=3.

Al-Garrallah, Aiman Sanad. 2010. "Saladin's Chivalry in Arabic 12th Century Poetry." *Cross-Cultural Communication* 6 (4): 9–19.

Al-Mohammad, Hayder. 2011. " 'You Have Car Insurance, We Have Tribes': Negotiating Everyday Life in Basra and the Re-emergence of Tribalism." *Anthropology of the Middle East* 6 (1): 18–34.

Al-Muhājirah, Umm Sumayyah [pseud.]. 2015. "A Jihād Without Fighting." *Dabiq* 1 (11): 40–45.

Al-Rahman, Atiyah. 2005. "ʿAtiyah's Letter to Zarqawi." *Combating Terrorism Center at West Point.* Accessed January 18, 2016. https://ctc.usma.edu/harmony-program /atiyahs-letter-to-zarqawi-original-language-2/.

Al-Rawi, Ahmed. 2018. "Video Games, Terrorism, and ISIS's Jihad 3.0." *Terrorism and Political Violence* 30 (4): 740–60.

Al-Salim, Muhammad ibn Ahmed. 2004. "*La Tadhhabū Li'l-'Irāq*" ["Do Not Go to Iraq"]. *Saut Al-Jihad* 1 (7): 23–24.

Al-Shishani, Murad Batal. 2013. "Syria Emerges as a New Battlefield for Jordan's Jihadists." *Terrorism Monitor* 11 (1): 4–5.

Al-Tamimi, Aymenn Jawad. 2016. " 'The Convoy of Light'—New Nasheed from the Islamic State's Ajnad Media." *Pundicity.* Accessed September 6, 2017. www.aymennj awad.org/2016/10/the-convoy-of-light-new-nasheed-from-the-islamic.

Al-Tamimi, Uthman bin Abd Al-Rahman. 2006. " *ʿIlām Al-Anām Bi-Mīlād Dawla Al-Islām*" ["The Notice to Mankind of the Birth of the Islamic State"]. *Jihadology.* Accessed May 12, 2016. https://azelin.files.wordpress.com/2015/09/shaykh

-uthmc481n-bin-abd-al-rae1b8a5man-al-tamc4abmc4ab-22informing-the
-people-about-the-birth-of-the-islamic-state22.pdf.

"*Al-Taqrīr Al-Ikhbārī Al-Thānī 'Ashara Bi-Shan Kamīn Sirrīyya Al-Falluja*" ["The Twelfth News Statement on the Topic of a Secret Ambush in Fallujah"]. 2004. *Mu'askar Al-Battār* 1 (12): 4.

Al-Zarqawi, Abu Mus'ab. 2003. "*Risāla Ila 'Ashāir Banī Hasan; Yā Qaum Ajībū Dā'ī Allāhi*" ["A Message to the Tribes of the Banu Hasan: Oh Nation, Respond to the Call of God"] (Arabic). In *Al-Kitāb Al-Jāmi' Li-Khutab Wa Kalimāt Al-Shaikh Al-Mu'tazz Bi-Dīni-hi: Abī Mus'ab Al-Zarqāwī*, 17–31. Accessed July 24, 2017. https:// archive.org/details/Abu-Musab-Zarkawi-Speechs.

——. 2004a. "*Ummatī Al-Ghālīyya: Khairu Ummatin Ukhrijat Li'l-Nās*" ["My Beloved Ummah! The Best Ummah Was Produced for the People"] (Arabic). In *Al-Kitāb Al-Jāmi' Li-Khutab Wa Kalimāt Al-Shaikh Al-Mu'tazz Bi-Dīni-hi: Abī Mus'ab Al-Zarqāwī*, 76–90. Accessed July 25, 2017. https://archive.org/details/Abu-Musab-Zarkawi-Speechs.

——. December 28, 2006. "Zarqawi Interview Part One; Zarqawi Interview Part Two; Zarqawi Interview Part Three." *Jihad Unspun.* http://thesis.haverford.edu /dspace/bitstream/handle/10066/5124/ZAR20061228.pdf?sequence=3.

Al-Zarqawi, Abu Musab. 2004b. "*Al-Bay'a Li-Tandhīm Al-Qā'ida Bi-Qayāda Al-Shaykh Usama bin Lādin*" ["The Pledge to the Al Qaeda Organization Under the Leadership of Osama bin Laden"]. In *Al-Kitāb Al-Jāmi' Li-Khutab Wa Kalimāt Al-Shaikh Al-Mu'tazz Bi-Dīni-hi: Abī Mus'ab Al-Zarqāwī*, 173–75. Accessed July 31, 2017. https:// archive.org/details/Abu-Musab-Zarkawi-Speechs.

——. 2004c. "*Risāla Ila Al-Ummah Wa-l-Mujāhidīn Dākhil Al-Fallūjah*" ["A Message to the Ummah and the Mujahideen Inside Fallujah"]. In *Al-Kitāb Al-Jāmi' Li-Khutab Wa Kalimāt Al-Shaikh Al-Mu'tazz Bi-Dīni-hi: Abī Mus'ab Al-Zarqāwī*, 176–79. Accessed August 1, 2017. https://archive.org/details/Abu-Musab-Zarkawi-Speechs.

Al-Zawahiri, Ayman. 2005. ["Zawahiri's Letter to Zarqawi." *Combating Terrorism Center at West Point.* Accessed January 14, 2016. https://ctc.usma.edu/harmony -program/zawahiris-letter-to-zarqawi-original-language-2/.

Allen, Roger. 2000. *An Introduction to Arabic Literature.* Cambridge: Cambridge University Press.

American Psychiatric Association. 1994. *Diagnostic and Statistical Manual of Mental Disorders.* 4th ed. Washington, DC: American Psychiatric Publishing.

——. 2013. *Diagnostic and Statistical Manual of Mental Disorders.* 5th ed. Washington, DC: American Psychiatric Publishing.

Andermann, Lisa, and Kenneth P. Fung. 2015. "Cultural Issues in Women's Mental Health," 287–338. In *Clinical Manual of Cultural Psychiatry.* 2nd ed. Edited by Russell F. Lim. Washington, DC: American Psychiatric Publishing.

Anderson, Jon W. 2003. "New Media, New Publics: Reconfiguring the Public Sphere of Islam." *Social Research* 70 (3): 887–906.

"Ansar Al-Islam Pledges Allegiance to the Islamic State." 2014. *Dabiq* 1 (4): 21–22.

Anthias, Floya, and Nira Yuval-Davis. 1989. Introduction to *Women-Nation-State*, 1–15. Edited by Floya Anthias and Nira Yuval-Davis. New York: Palgrave Macmillan.|

Antoun, Richard T. 1968. "On the Modesty of Women in Arab Muslim Villages: A Study in the Accommodation of Traditions." *American Anthropologist* 70 (4): 671–97.

Appel, Markus, and Barbara Malečkar. 2012. "The Influence of Paratext on Narrative Persuasion: Fact, Fiction, or Fake?" *Human Communication Research* 38 (4): 459–84.

Arberry, A. J. 1996. *The Koran Interpreted: A Translation*. New York: Touchstone. First published 1955 by George Allen & Unwin.

Aretxaga, Begoña. 2002. "Terror as Thrill: First Thoughts on the 'War on Terrorism.'" *Anthropological Quarterly* 75 (1): 138–50.

Asad, Talal. 2003. *Formations of the Secular: Christianity, Islam, Modernity*. Stanford, CA: Stanford University Press.

ash-Shāmī, Abū Maysarah. 2014–2015. "The Qa'idah of Adh-Dhawahiri, Al-Harari, and An-Nadhari, and the Absent Yemeni Wisdom." *Dabiq* 1 (6): 16–25.

Atwan, Abdel Bari. 2015. *Islamic State: The Digital Caliphate*. London: Saqi.

Awan, Akil N. 2007. "Radicalization on the Internet? The Virtual Propagation of Jihadist Media and Its Effects." *RUSI Journal* 152 (3): 76–81.

Awde, Nicholas. 2013. *Women in Islam: An Anthology from the Qu'ran and Hadith*. New York: Routledge.

Bakri, Nada. 2011. "Pro-Assad Rally Shows Syrian Government Can Still Command Support." *New York Times*, October 19.

Baram, Amatzia. 1997. "Neo-Tribalism in Iraq: Saddam Hussein's Tribal Policies 1991–96." *International Journal of Middle Eastern Studies* 29 (1): 1–31.

Barnill, John W. 2014. "The Psychiatric Interview and Mental Status Examination. In *The American Psychiatric Publishing Textbook of Psychiatry*. 6th ed. Edited by Stuart C. Yudofsky, Laura Weiss Roberts, and David J. Kupfer, 3–30. Washington, DC: American Psychiatric Publishing.

Barry, Andrew, Thomas Osborne, and Nikolas Rose. 1996. *Foucault and Political Reason: Liberalism, Neoliberalism, and Rationalities of Government*. Chicago: University of Chicago Press.

Bashir, Shahzad. 2016. "Islam and the Politics of Temporality: The Case of ISIS." In *Time, Temporality and Global Politics*, edited by Andrew Hom, Christopher McIntosh, Alasdair McKay, and Liam Stockdale, 134–49. Bristol, UK: E-International Relations.

Beaumont, Peter. 2014. "How Effective Is ISIS Compared with the Iraqi Army and Kurdish Peshmerga?" *The Guardian*, June 12.

Berger, J. M. 2015a. "The Metronome of Apocalyptic Time: Social Media as Carrier Wave for Millenarian Contagion." *Perspectives on Terrorism* 9 (4): 61–71.

——. 2015b. "Tailored Online Interventions: The Islamic State's Recruitment Strategy." *CTC Sentinel* 8 (10): 19–23.

Berry, John W. 1980. "Social and Cultural Change." In *Handbook of Cross-Cultural Psychology*. Vol. 5. Edited by Harry C. Triandis and Richard W. Brislin, 211–79. Boston: Allyn & Bacon.

——. 1992. "Acculturation and Adaptation in a New Society." *International Migration* 30 (1): 69–85.

——. 1997. "Immigration, Acculturation, and Adaptation." *Applied Psychology* 46 (1): 5–68.

——. 2006. "Acculturation and Identity." In *Textbook of Cultural Psychiatry*, edited by Dinesh Bhugra and Kamaldeep Bhui, 169–78. Cambridge: Cambridge University Press.

REFERENCES

Berry, John W., Ype H. Poortinga, Marshall H. Segall, and Pierre R. Dasen. 1992. *Cross-Cultural Psychology: Research and Applications*. New York: Cambridge University Press.

Bhabha, Homi K. 1996. "Culture's In-Between." In *Questions of Cultural Identity*, edited by Stuart Hall and Paul Du Gay, 53–60. London: Sage.

Bhugra, Dinesh. 2017. "Violent Radicalization." *International Review of Psychiatry* 29 (4): 309.

Bhui, Kamaldeep, Madelyn H. Hicks, Myrna Lashley, and Edgar Jones. 2012. "A Public Health Approach to Understanding and Preventing Violent Radicalization." *BMC Medicine* 10: 16.

Bhui, Kamaldeep, and Yasmin Ibrahim. 2013. "Marketing the 'Radical': Symbolic Communication and Persuasive Technologies in Jihadist Websites." *Transcultural Psychiatry* 50 (2): 216–34.

Bibeau, Gilles. 1997. "Cultural Psychiatry in a Creolizing World: Questions for a New Research Agenda." *Transcultural Psychiatry* 34 (1): 9–41.

Biglan, Anthony, and Dennis D. Embry. 2013. "A Framework for Intentional Cultural Change." *Journal of Contextual Behavioral Science* (3–4): 95–104.

bin Laden, Osama. 2004. "Resist the New Rome." *The Guardian*, January 5.

——. 2005. "*Salām Al-Shaykh Usāma bin Lādin Ila Al-Mujāhidīn Fī Al-'Irāq*" ["The Greetings of Shaykh Osama bin Laden to the Mujahideen in Iraq"]. *Dhirwa Al-Sanām* 1 (1): 4–5.

Bisin, Alberto, and Thierry Verdier. 2001. "The Economics of Cultural Transmission and the Dynamics of Preferences." *Journal of Economic Theory* 97 (2): 298–319.

Bloom, Mia, John Horgan, and Charlie Winter. 2016. "Depictions of Children and Youth in the Islamic State's Martyrdom Propaganda, 2015-2016." *CTC Sentinel* 9(2): 29–32.

Bloom, Mia, Hicham Tiflati, and John Horgan. 2017. "Navigating ISIS's Preferred Platform: Telegram." *Terrorism and Political Violence*, https://doi.org/10.1080/09 546553.2017.1339695.

Borchers, Timothy A. 2013. *Persuasion in the Media Age*. 3rd ed. Long Grove, IL: Waveland.

Borthwick, Bruce M. 1967. "The Islamic Sermon as a Channel of Political Communication." *Middle East Journal* 21 (3): 299–313.

Bourdieu, Pierre. 1977. *Outline of a Theory of Practice*. Cambridge: Cambridge University Press.

Bowen, Glenn A. 2009. "Document Analysis as a Qualitative Research Method." *Qualitative Research Journal* 9 (2): 27–40.

Bowskill, Matt, Evanthia Lyons, and Adrian Coyle. 2007. "The Rhetoric of Acculturation: When Integration Means Assimilation." *British Journal of Social Psychology* 46 (4): 793–813.

Braddock, Kurt, and James Price Dillard. 2016. "Meta-Analytic Evidence for the Persuasive Effect of Narratives on Beliefs, Attitudes, Intentions, and Behaviors." *Communication Monographs* 83 (4): 446–67.

Braddock, Kurt, and John Horgan. 2016. "Toward a Guide for Constructing and Disseminating Counternarratives to Reduce Support for Terrorism." *Studies in Conflict & Terrorism* 39 (5): 381–404.

Brewer, Marilynn B., and Wendi Gardner. 1996. "Who Is This 'We'? Levels of Collective Identity and Self Representations." *Journal of Personality and Social Psychology* 71 (1): 83–93.

Brown, Jonathan A. C. 2009. *Hadith: Muhammad's Legacy in the Medieval and Modern World.* Oxford: One World.

Brown, William J. 2015. "Examining Four Processes of Audience Involvement with Mediae Personae: Transportation, Parasocial Interaction, Identification, and Worship." *Communication Theory* 25 (3): 259–83.

Burke, Peter J. 2006. "Identity Change." *Social Psychology Quarterly* 69 (1): 81–96.

Busse, Heribert. 1968. "The Sanctity of Jerusalem in Islam." *Judaism* 17 (4): 441–68.

Callimachi, Rukmini. 2015a. "ISIS Enshrines a Theology of Rape." *New York Times,* August 13.

——. 2015b. "ISIS and the Lonely Young American." *New York Times,* June 27.

——. 2016. "A News Agency with Scoops Directly from ISIS, and a Veneer of Objectivity." *New York Times,* January 14.

——. 2017. "Not 'Lone Wolves' After All: How ISIS Guides World's Terror Plots from Afar." *New York Times,* February 4.

Carlino, Ludovico. 2012. "Jihadists Exploit Syrian Turmoil as the Islamic State of Iraq Makes a Comeback." *Terrorism Monitor* 10 (23): 7–9.

Carpenter-Song, Elizabeth, Megan Nordquest Schwallie, and Jeffrey Longhofer. 2007. "Cultural Competence Reexamined: Critique and Directions for the Future." *Psychiatric Services* 58 (10): 1362–65.

Cartwright, Elizabeth, and Jerome Crowder. 2017. "Dissecting Images: Multimodal Medical Anthropology." *Medical Anthropology* 36 (6): 515–18.

Cataldo, Giovanni. 2009. "Fighting Terrorism in Cyberspace." In *Modelling Cyber Security: Approaches, Methodology, Strategies,* edited by Umberto Gori, 160–70. Amsterdam: IOS.

Central Intelligence Agency. 2015. "Iraq." *World Factbook.* Accessed October 4, 2015. www.cia.gov/library/publications/the-world-factbook/geos/iz.html.

Chen, Hsienchun. 2012. *Exploring and Data Mining the Dark Side of the Web.* Heidelberg: Springer-Verlag.

Chowdhury, Tamim. 2016. "The Shuhada of the Gulshan Attack." *Rumiyah* 1 (2): 8–11.

Chulov, Martin. 2014. "ISIS: The Inside Story. *The Guardian,* December 11.

Chulov, Martin, and Julian Borger. 2015. "Syria: ISIS Advance on Aleppo Aided by Assad Regime Air Strikes, U.S. Says." *The Guardian,* June 2.

Cialdini, Robert B. 1993. *Influence: Science and Practice.* 3rd ed. New York: HarperCollins.

Cockburn, Patrick. 2015. *The Rise of Islamic State: ISIS and the New Sunni Revolution.* New York: Verso.

Collins, Samuel Gerald, Matthew Durington, and Harjant Gill. 2017. "Multimodality: An Invitation." *American Anthropologist* 119 (1): 142–46.

Comaroff, John L., and Jean Comaroff. 2006. "Law and Disorder in the Postcolony: An Introduction," 1–56. In *Law and Disorder in the Postcolony,* edited by Jean Comaroff and John L. Comaroff. Chicago: University of Chicago Press.

Comas-Díaz, Lillian, and Frederick M. Jacobsen. 1991. "Ethnocultural Transference and Countertransference in the Therapeutic Dyad." *American Journal of Orthopsychiatry* 61 (3): 392–402.

Combating Terrorism Center at West Point. 2006. *Harmony and Disharmony: Exploiting al-Qa'ida's Organizational Vulnerabilities.* West Point, NY: Combating Terrorism Center at West Point.

——. 2015a. "Image Commemorating Abu Dujana Al-Khorasani." *Combating Terrorism Center at West Point.* Accessed December 17, 2015. https://ctc.usma.edu/militant-imagery-project/0344/.

——. 2015b. "Harmony Program." *Combating Terrorism Center at West Point.* Accessed September 30, 2015. https://ctc.usma.edu/harmony-program/.

Comer, Jonathan S., Laura J. Bry, Bridget Poznanski, and Alejandra M. Golik. 2016. "Children's Mental Health in the Context of Terrorist Attacks, Ongoing Threats, and Possibilities of Future Terrorism." *Current Psychiatry Reports* 18 (9): 79.

Conway, Maura. 2012. "From al-Zarqawi to al-Awlaki: The Emergence and Development of an Online Radical Milieu." *Combating Terrorism Exchange* 2 (4): 12–22.

——. 2017. "Determining the Role of the Internet in Violent Extremism and Terrorism: Six Suggestions for Progressing Research." *Studies in Conflict & Terrorism* 40 (1): 77–98.

Cook, David. 2005. "Women Fighting in Jihad?" *Studies in Conflict & Terrorism* 28 (5): 375–84.

Cooper, Helene. 2016. "U.S. Drops Snark in Favor of Emotion to Undercut Extremists." *New York Times,* July 28.

Corera, Gordon. May 5, 2005. "Unraveling Zarqawi's al-Qaeda Connection." *Terrorism Monitor* 2 (24). *The Jamestown Foundation.* www.jamestown.org/programs/tm/single/?tx_ttnews%5Btt_news%5D=332&tx_ttnews%5BbackPid%5D=179&no_cache=1#.ViF0lNb0hCQ.

Cottee, Simon, and Mia Bloom. 2017. "The Myth of the ISIS Female Suicide Bomber." *The Atlantic,* September 8.

Creswell, Robyn, and Bernard Haykel. 2015. "Battle Lines." *New Yorker,* June 8.

Crisp, Richard J., Catriona H. Stone, and Natalie R. Hall. 2006. "Recategorization and Subgroup Identification: Predicting and Preventing Threats from Common Ingroups." *Personality and Social Psychology Bulletin* 32 (2): 230–43.

Curtis, John M., and Mimi J. Curtis. 1993. "Factors Related to Susceptibility and Recruitment by Cults." *Psychological Reports* 73 (2): 451–60.

Dähne, Stephan. 2001. "Qur'anic Wording in Political Speeches in Classical Arabic Literature." *Journal of Qur'anic Studies* 3 (2): 1–13.

Dajani-Shakeel, Hadia. 1976. "Jihād in Twelfth-Century Arabic Poetry: A Moral and Religious Force to Counter the Crusades." *Muslim World* 66 (1): 96–113.

De Castella, Krista, Craig McGarty, and Luke Musgrove. 2009. "Fear Appeals in Political Rhetoric About Terrorism: An Analysis of Speeches by Australian Prime Minister Howard." *Political Psychology* 30 (1): 1–26.

Deci, Edward L., Richard Koestner, and Richard M. Ryan. 1999. "A Meta-Analytic Review of Experiments Examining the Effects of Extrinsic Rewards on Intrinsic Motivation." *Psychological Bulletin* 125 (6): 627–68.

Devereux, George. 2000. "Normal and Abnormal." In *Cultural Psychiatry and Medical Anthropology: An Introduction and Reader,* edited by Roland Littlewood and Simon Dein, 213–89. London: Athlone.

Doornbos, Harald, and Jenan Moussa. 2013. "Blue-Eyed Jihad: An Exclusive Conversation with European Radicals Fighting for an Islamic State in Syria." *Foreign Policy*, August 1.

Douki, S., S. Ben Zineb, F. Nacef, and U. Halbreich. 2007. "Women's Mental Health in the Muslim World: Cultural, Religious, and Social Issues." *Journal of Affective Disorders* 102 (1–3): 177–89.

Dovidio, John F., Samuel L. Gaertner, Alice M. Isen, and Robert Lowrance. 1995. "Group Representations and Intergroup Bias: Positive Affect, Similarity, and Group Size." *Personality and Social Psychology Bulletin* 21 (8): 856–65.

Duderija, Adis. 2011. "Neo-Traditional Salafi Qur'an-Sunna Hermeneutics and Its Interpretational Implications." *Religious Compass* 5 (7): 314–25.

Eggins, Rachael A., S. Alexander Haslam, and Katherine J. Reynolds. 2002. "Social Identity and Negotiation: Subgroup Representation and Superordinate Consensus." *Personality and Social Psychology Bulletin* 28 (7): 887–99.

Eickelman, Dale F. 1967. "Musaylima: An Approach to the Social Anthropology of Seventh Century Arabia." *Journal of the Economic and Social History of the Orient* 10 (1): 17–52.

Eickelman, Dale F., and Armando Salvatore. 2002. "The Public Sphere and Muslim Identities." *European Journal of Sociology* 43 (1): 92–115.

Eisend, Martin. 2009. "A Meta-analysis of Humor in Advertising." *Journal of the Academy of Marketing Science* 37 (2): 191–203.

Ekblad, Solvig, and Sofie Bäärnhielm. 2002. "Focus Group Interview Research in Transcultural Psychiatry: Reflections on Research Experiences." *Transcultural Psychiatry* 39 (4): 484–500.

El Saadawi, Nawal. 2007. *The Hidden Face of Eve: Women in the Arab World.* Translated by Sherif Hetata. London: Zed.

Engineer, Asgharali. 1992. *The Rights of Women in Islam.* New Delhi: Sterling.

Ewing, John A. 1984. "Detecting Alcoholism: The CAGE Questionnaire." *Journal of the American Medical Association* 252 (14): 1905–7.

Ewing, Katherine. 1990. "The Illusion of Wholeness: Culture, Self, and the Experience of Inconsistency." *Ethos* 18 (3): 251–78.

Fahim, Kareem, and Hwaida Saad. 2013. "A Faceless Teenage Refugee Who Helped Ignite Syria's War." *New York Times*, February 8.

Fairclough, Norman. 1992. *Discourse and Social Change.* Cambridge: Polity.

——. 2001. "Critical Discourse Analysis." In *How to Analyze Talk in Institutional Settings*, edited by Alec McHoul and Mark Rapley, 25–38. New York: Continuum.

Faizer, Rizwi. 2014. "Expeditions and Battles." In *Encyclopaedia of the Qur'ān*, edited by Jane Dammen McAuliffe. *Brill Online Reference Works.* Accessed August 10, 2017. http://dx.doi.org/10.1163/1875-3922_q3 _EQCOM_00060.

Faizer, Rizwi S. 1996. "Muhammad and the Medinan Jews: A Comparison of the Texts of Ibn Ishaq's *Kitāb sīrat rasūl Allāh* with al-Waqidi's *Kitāb al-maghāzī.*" *International Journal of Middle East Studies* 28 (4): 463–89.

Farr, Robert M. 1998. "From Collective to Social Representations: *Aller et Retour.*" *Culture & Psychology* 4 (3): 275–96.

Farrall, Leah. 2011. "How Al Qaeda Works." *Foreign Affairs* 90 (2): 128–38.

Farwell, James P. 2014. "The Media Strategy of ISIS." *Survival: Global Politics and Strategy* 56 (6): 49–55.

Feldmann, Theodore B., and Phillip W. Johnson. 1995. "Cult Membership as a Source of Self-Cohesion." *Bulletin of the American Academy of Psychiatry and the Law* 23 (2): 239–48.

Finn, Peter, and Susan Schmidt. 2003. "Al Qaeda Is Trying to Open Iraq Front; Plot Said to Be Hatched in Iran Last February." *Washington Post*, September 7.

Fishman, Brian. 2007. "Fourth Generation Governance: Sheikh Tamimi Defends the Islamic State of Iraq," March 23. *Combating Terrorism Center at West Point.* https://ctc.usma.edu/fourth-generation-governance-sheikh-tamimi-defends -the-islamic-state-of-iraq/.

——. 2009. "Dysfunction and Decline: Lessons Learned from Inside Al Qa'ida in Iraq," March 16. *Combating Terrorism Center at West Point.* https://ctc.usma.edu /dysfunction-and-decline-lessons-learned-from-inside-al-qaida-in-iraq/.

——. 2016. *The Master Plan: ISIS, al-Qaeda, and the Jihadi Strategy for Final Victory.* New Haven, CT: Yale University Press.

Foucault, Michel. 1972. *The Archaeology of Knowledge.* New York: Harper and Row.

——. 1978. *The History of Sexuality.* Vol. 1, *An Introduction,* translated by Robert Hurley. New York: Pantheon.

——. 1991. "Politics and the Study of Discourse." In *The Foucault Effect: Studies in Governmentality,* edited by Graham Burchell, Colin Gordon, and Peter Miller, 53–72. Chicago: University of Chicago Press.

——. 1995. *Discipline and Punish: The Birth of the Prison.* Translated by Alan Sheridan. New York: Vintage.

——. 2008. *Psychiatric Power: Lectures at the Collège de France, 1973-1974.* Edited by Jacques Lagrange and Arnold I. Davidson. Translated by Graham Burchell. New York: Picador.

Freud, Sigmund. 1990. *Five Lectures on Psycho-Analysis.* Edited by James Strachey. New York: W. W. Norton.

"From Hijrah to Khilafah." 2014. *Dabiq* 1 (1): 34–41.

Gaertner, Samuel L., John F. Dovidio, Phyllis A. Anastasio, Betty A. Bachman, and Mary C. Rust. 1993. "The Common Ingroup Identity Model: Recategorization and the Reduction of Intergroup Bias." *European Review of Social Psychology* 4 (1): 1–26.

Gaertner, Samuel L., John F. Dovidio, and Betty A. Bachman. 1996. "Revisiting the Contact Hypothesis: The Induction of a Common Group Identity." *Journal of Intercultural Relations* 20 (3/4): 271–90.

Gaertner, Samuel L., Jeffrey Mann, Audrey Murrell, and John F. Dovidio. 1989. "Reducing Intergroup Bias: The Benefits of Recategorization." *Journal of Personality and Social Psychology* 57 (2): 239–49.

Gaertner, Samuel L., Mary C. Rust, John F. Dovidio, Betty A. Bachman, and Phyllis A. Anastasio. 1994. "The Contact Hypothesis: The Role of a Common Group Identity on Reducing Intergroup Bias." *Small Group Research* 25 (2): 224–49.

Gaines, Atwood. 1992. "From DSM-I to III-R; Voices of Self, Mastery and the Other: A Cultural Constructivist Reading of U.S. Psychiatric Classification." *Social Science & Medicine* 35 (1): 3–24.

Galander, Mahmoud M. 2002. "Communication in the Early Islamic Era: A Social and Historical Analysis." *Intellectual Discourse* 10 (1): 61–75.

Gambhir, Harleen K. 2014. "*Dabiq*: The Strategic Messaging of the Islamic State." *Institute for the Study of War*, August 15.

Gamson, William A., and Hanna Herzog. 1999. "Living with Contradictions: The Taken-for-Granted in Israeli Political Discourse." *Political Psychology* 20 (2): 247–66.

Garamone, Jim. 2016. "Iraqi Leaders Showing Confidence, Optimism in ISIL Fight, Dunford Says." *DoD News*, July 31.

Gardet, Louis. 1991. "Fitna." In *The Encyclopaedia of Islam*, edited by P. Bearman, Th. Bianquis, C. E. Bosworth, E. van Donzel, and W. P. Heinrichs. *Brill Online Reference Works*. Accessed July 31, 2017. http://dx.doi.org/10.1163/1573-3912_islam_SIM_2389.

Gates, Scott, and Sukanya Podder. 2015. "Social Media, Recruitment, Allegiance and the Islamic State." *Perspectives on Terrorism* 9 (4): 107–16.

Geertz, Clifford. 1973. *The Interpretation of Cultures*. New York: Basic Books.

Gelfand, Michele J. 2012. "Culture's Constraints: International Differences in the Strength of Social Norms." *Current Directions in Psychological Science* 21 (6): 420–24.

Gelfand, Michele J., Miriam Erez, and Zeynap Aycan. 2007. "Cross-Cultural Organizational Behavior." *Annual Review of Psychology* 58: 479–514.

Gelfand, Michele J., Lisa Hisae Nishii, and Jana L. Raver. 2007. *On the Nature and Importance of Cultural Tightness-Looseness*. Ithaca, NY: Cornell University School of Industrial and Labor Relations.

Gerges, Fawaz A. 2016. *ISIS: A History*. Princeton, NJ: Princeton University Press.

Gettleman, Jeffrey. 2006. "Abu Musab Al-Zarqawi Lived a Brief, Shadowy Life Replete with Contradictions." *New York Times*, June 9.

Ghabin, Ahmad Y. 1998. "The Quranic Verses as a Source for Legitimacy or Illegitimacy of the Arts in Islam." *Der Islam* 75 (2): 193–225.

Giles, David C. 2002. "Parasocial Interaction: A Review of the Literature and a Model for Future Research." *Media Psychology* 4 (3): 279–305.

Ginges, Jeremy, Scott Atran, Sonya Sachdeva, and Douglas Medin. 2011. "Psychology Out of the Laboratory: The Challenge of Violent Extremism." *American Psychologist* 66 (6): 507–19.

Glassé, Cyril. 2008. *The New Encyclopedia of Islam*. 3rd ed. Lanham, MD: Rowman & Littlefield.

Glasser, Susan B., and Steve Coll. 2005. "The Web as Weapon: Zarqawi Intertwines Acts on Ground in Iraq with Propaganda Campaign on the Internet." *Washington Post*, August 9.

Global Coalition. 2017b. "Countering Daesh's Propaganda." *Global Coalition*. Accessed September 15, 2017. http://theglobalcoalition.org/en/countering-daeshs-propaganda/?lang=en.

——. 2017a. "Daesh Areas of Influence—July 2017 Update." *Global Coalition*. Accessed September 13, 2017. http://theglobalcoalition.org/en/daesh-areas-of-influence-july-2017-update/.

Goldsmith, Leon. 2012. "Alawites for Assad: Why the Syrian Sect Backs the Regime." *Foreign Affairs*, April 16.

Gómez, Ángel, Lucía López-Rodríguez, Hammad Sheikh, Jeremy Ginges, Lydia Wilson, Hoshang Waziri, Alexandra Vázquez, Richard Davis, and Scott Atran. 2017.

"The Devoted Actor's Will to Fight and the Spiritual Dimension of Human Conflict." *Nature Human Behavior* 1: 673–79.

Good, Byron. 1994. *Medicine, Rationality, and Experience: An Anthropological Perspective.* Cambridge: Cambridge University Press.

———. 2012. "Theorizing the 'Subject' of Medical and Psychiatric Anthropology." *Journal of the Royal Anthropological Institute* 18 (3): 515–35.

Good, Byron, and Mary-Jo DelVecchio Good. 1980. "The Meaning of Symptoms: A Cultural Hermeneutic Model for Clinical Practice." In *The Relevance of Social Science for Medicine*, edited by Leon Eisenberg and Arthur Kleinman, 165–96. Dordrecht: D. Reidel.

Good, Byron J., Mary-Jo DelVecchio Good, Sandra Teresa Hyde, and Sarah Pinto. 2008. "Postcolonial Disorders: Reflections on Subjectivity in the Contemporary World." In *Postcolonial Disorders*, edited by Mary-Jo DelVecchio Good, Sandra Teresa Hyde, Sarah Pinto, and Byron Good, 1–40. Berkeley: University of California Press.

Gray, Debra, and Kevin Durrheim. 2013. "Collective Rights and Personal Freedoms: A Discursive Analysis of Participant Accounts of Authoritarianism." *Political Psychology* 34 (4): 631–48.

Groleau, Danielle, Allan Young, and Laurence J. Kirmayer. 2006. "The McGill Illness Narrative Interview (MINI): An Interview Schedule to Elicit Meanings and Modes of Reasoning Related to Illness Experience." *Transcultural Psychiatry* 43 (4): 671–91.

Guarnaccia, Peter J., and Carolina Hausmann-Stabile. 2016. "Acculturation and Its Discontents: A Case for Bringing Anthropology Back into the Conversation." *Sociology and Anthropology* 4 (2): 114–24.

Guarnaccia, Peter J., and Orlando Rodriguez. 1996. "Concepts of Culture and Their Role in the Development of Culturally Competent Mental Health Services." *Hispanic Journal of Behavioral Sciences* 18 (4): 419–43.

Guest, Greg, Arwen Bunce, and Laura Johnson. 2006. "How Many Interviews Are Enough? An Experiment with Data Saturation and Variability." *Field Methods* 18 (1): 59–82.

Hafez, Mohammed M. 2007. *Suicide Bombers in Iraq: The Strategy and Ideology of Martyrdom.* Washington, DC: United States Institute of Peace Press.

"Halab Tribal Assemblies." 2014. *Dabiq* 1 (1): 12–15.

Hallaq, Wael. 2002. " 'Muslim Rage' and Islamic Law." *Hastings Law Journal* 54 (3): 1705–20.

Hallaq, Wael B. 1997. *A History of Islamic Legal Theories: An Introduction to Sunni Usul Al-Fiqh.* Cambridge: Cambridge University Press.

Halldén, Philip. 2005. "What Is Arab Islamic Rhetoric? Rethinking the History of Muslim Oratory Art and Homiletics." *International Journal of Middle East Studies* 37 (1): 19–38.

Halverson, Jeffry R., H. L. Goodall Jr., and Steve R. Corman. 2011. *Master Narratives of Islamist Extremism.* New York: Palgrave MacMillan.

Hanks, W. F. 1989. "Text and Textuality." *Annual Review of Anthropology* 18: 95–127.

Hansen, Helena, Terry M. Dugan, Anne E. Becker, Roberto Lewis-Fernández, Francis G. Lu, Maria A. Oquendo, Renato D. Alarcon, and Manuel Trujillo. 2013. "Educating Psychiatry Residents About Cultural Aspects of Care: A Qualitative Study of Approaches Used by U.S. Expert Faculty." *Academic Psychiatry* 37 (6): 412–16.

Hashim, Ahmed S. 2014. "The Islamic State: From al-Qaeda Affiliate to Caliphate." *Middle East Policy* 21 (4): 69–83.

Haslam, Nick. 2006. "Dehumanization: An Integrative Review." *Personality and Social Psychology Review* 10 (3): 252–64.

Hawton, Keith, Katrina G. Witt, Tatiana L. Taylor Salisbury, Ella Arensman, David Gunnell, Ellen Townsend, Kees van Heeringen, and Philip Hazell. 2015. "Interventions for Self-Harm in Children and Adolescents." *Cochrane Database of Systematic Reviews* 12: CD012013.

Haykel, Bernard. 2003. *Revival and Reform in Islam: The Legacy of Muhammad al-Shawkani.* Cambridge: Cambridge University Press.

Heath, Christian, Jon Hindmarsh, and Paul Luff. 2010. *Video in Qualitative Research; Analysing Social Interaction in Everyday Life.* Thousand Oaks, CA: Sage.

Heath-Kelly, Charlotte. 2016. "Algorithmic Autoimmunity in the NHS: Radicalisation and the Clinic." *Security & Dialogue* 48 (1): 29–45.

Heck, Paul L. 2007. "Sufism—What Is It Exactly?" *Religion Compass* 1 (1): 148–64.

Hegghammer, Thomas. 2006a. "Global Jihadism After the Iraq War." *Middle East Journal* 60 (1): 11–32.

——. 2006b. "Terrorist Recruitment and Radicalization in Saudi Arabia." *Middle East Policy* 13 (4): 39–60.

——. 2008. "Islamist Violence and Regime Stability in Saudi Arabia." *International Affairs* 84 (4): 701–15.

——. 2017. "Introduction: What Is Jihadi Culture and Why Should We Study It?" In *Jihadi Culture: The Art and Social Practices of Militant Islamists,* edited by Thomas Hegghammer, 1–21. Cambridge: Cambridge University Press.

Henrich, Joseph. 2004. "Cultural Group Selection, Coevolutionary Processes and Large-Scale Cooperation." *Journal of Economic Behavior & Organization* 53 (1): 3–35.

——. 2009. "The Evolution of Costly Displays, Cooperation and Religion." *Evolution & Human Behavior* 30 (4): 244–60.

Henrich, Joseph, and Robert Boyd. 2001. "Why People Punish Defectors: Weak Conformist Transmission Can Stabilize Costly Enforcement of Norms in Cooperative Dilemmas." *Journal of Theoretical Biology* 208 (1): 79–89.

Henrich, Joseph, and Francisco J. Gil-White. 2001. "The Evolution of Prestige: Freely Conferred Deference as a Mechanism for Enhancing the Benefits of Cultural Transmission." *Evolution and Human Behavior* 22 (3): 165–96.

Heyman, Josiah M. 2004. "The Anthropology of Power-Wielding Bureaucracies." *Human Organization* 63 (4): 487–500.

Hinton, Devon E., and Ladson Hinton. 2016. "Supplementary Modules: Overview." In *DSM-5 Handbook on the Cultural Formulation Interview,* edited by Roberto Lewis-Fernández, Neil Krishan Aggarwal, Ladson Hinton, Devon E. Hinton, and Laurence J. Kirmayer, 45–55. Washington, DC: American Psychiatric Publishing.

Hoge, Charles W., Christopher G. Ivany, Edward A. Brusher, Millard D. Brown III, John C. Shero, Amy B. Adler, Christopher H. Warner, and David T. Orman. 2016. "Transformation of Mental Health Care for U.S. Soldiers and Families During the Iraq and Afghanistan Wars: Where Science and Politics Intersect." *American Journal of Psychiatry* 173 (4): 334–43.

Hogg, Michael A., and Scott A. Reid. 2006. "Social Identity, Self-Categorization, and the Communication of Group Norms." *Communication Theory* 16 (1): 7–30.

Hogg, Michael A., John C. Turner, and Barbara Davidson. 1990. "Polarized Norms and Social Frames of Reference: A Test of the Self-Categorization Theory of Group Polarization." *Basic and Applied Social Psychology* 11 (1): 77–100.

Horgan, John. 2008a. "Deradicalization or Disengagement? A Process in Need of Clarity and a Counterterrorism Initiative in Need of Evaluation." *Revista de Psicología Social* 24 (2): 291–98.

——. 2008b. "From Profiles to Pathways and Roots to Routes: Perspectives from Psychology on Radicalization into Terrorism." *Annals of the American Academy of Political and Social Science* 618 (1): 80–94.

——. 2009. *Walking Away from Terrorism: Accounts of Disengagement from Radical and Extremist Movements.* New York: Routledge.

——. 2017. "Willingness to Fight and Die." *Nature Human Behavior* 1: 628–29.

Horgan, John, Mia Bloom, Chelsea Daymon, Wojciech Kaczkowsi, and Hicham Tiflati. 2017. "A New Age of Terror? Older Fighters in the Caliphate." *CTC Sentinel* 10 (5): 13–19.

Horowitz, Michael C., and Philip B. K. Potter. 2014. "Allying to Kill: Terrorist Intergroup Cooperation and the Consequences for Lethality." *Journal of Conflict Resolution* 58 (2): 199–225.

Hourani, Albert. 1991. *A History of the Arab Peoples.* London: Faber and Faber.

Howarth, Caroline. 2002. "Identity in Whose Eyes? The Role of Representations in Identity Construction." *Journal for the Theory of Social Behaviour* 32 (2): 145–62.

Huddy, Leonie. 2001. "From Social to Political Identity: A Critical Examination of Social Identity Theory." *Political Psychology* 22 (1): 127–56.

Hull, Matthew S. 2012. "Documents and Bureaucracy." *Annual Review of Anthropology* 41: 251–67.

Hurwicz, Margo-Lea. 1995. "Introduction: Anthropology, Aging, and Health." *Medical Anthropology Quarterly* 9 (2): 143–45.

Iemmi, Valentina, Jason Bantjes, Ernestina Coast, Kerrie Channer, Tiziana Leone, David McDaid, Alexis Palfreyman, Bevan Stephens, and Crick Lund. 2016. "Suicide and Poverty in Low-Income and Middle-Income Countries: A Systematic Review." *Lancet Psychiatry* 3 (8): 774–83.

"In Syria, Crackdown After Protests." 2011. *New York Times*, March 18.

Ingram, Haroro J. 2016. "An Analysis of Islamic State's *Dabiq* Magazine." *Australian Journal of Political Science* 51 (3): 458–77.

"Interview with Abul-'Abbas Ash-Shami, Head of the Islamic Police, Wilayat Ar-Raqqah." 2014. *Islamic State Reports* 1 (2): 7.

"Introduction." 2014. *Dabiq* 1 (1): 3–5.

"The ISIS Papers: A Masterplan for Consolidating Power." 2015. *The Guardian*, December 7.

Islamic State. n.d.-a. "Register to Ensure a Person's Attendance of a Mosque at Dawn and Evening Prayers for One Month (Issued by Hisba Office, Mosul)." *Pundicity.* Accessed August 25, 2017. www.aymennjawad.org/2015/01/archive-of-islamic-state-administrative-documents.

——. n.d.-b. "Call for Allegiance Pledges, Dijla Province." *Pundicity*. Accessed September 8, 2017. www.aymennjawad.org/2016/09/archive-of-islamic-state -administrative-documents-2.

——. 2013. "Educational Regulations Notification Distributed in Aleppo Province." *Pundicity*. Accessed August 25, 2017. www.aymennjawad.org/2015/01/archive -of-islamic-state-administrative-documents.

——. 2014a. "Opening of Schools in Raqqa for Children of English-Speaking Foreign Fighters." *Pundicity*. Accessed August 25, 2017. www.aymennjawad.org/2015/01 /archive-of-islamic-state-administrative-documents.

——. 2014b. "Shari'a Session for Teachers, Raqqa Province." *Pundicity*. Accessed August 25, 2017. www.aymennjawad.org/2015/01/archive-of-islamic-state -administrative-documents.

——. 2014c. "Registering Children in IS-Run Schools in Deir az-Zor City." *Pundicity*. Accessed August 25, 2017. www.aymennjawad.org/2015/01/archive -of-islamic-state-administrative-documents.

——. 2014d. "Quran Memorization Competition (Raqqa Province)." *Pundicity*. Accessed August 25, 2017. www.aymennjawad.org/2015/01/archive-of-islamic -state-administrative-documents.

——. 2014e. "Call On Residents Aged 14 and Above in Villages North of Raqqa to Register Their Names." *Pundicity*. Accessed September 8, 2017. www.aymennj awad.org/2015/01/archive-of-islamic-state-administrative-documents.

——. 2015. "Opening of Kindergarten Centre, Raqqa Province." *Pundicity*. Accessed September 1, 2017. www.aymennjawad.org/2015/01/archive-of-islamic-state -administrative-documents.

——. 2016. "Appointment of Preacher for a Mosque, Ninawa Province." *Pundicity*. Accessed August 25, 2017. www.aymennjawad.org/2016/09/archive-of-islamic -state-administrative-documents-2.

Islamic State in Iraq and al-Sham. 2014. "Statement for the Imposition of the Niqab." *Pundicity*. Accessed August 24, 2017. www.aymennjawad.org/2016/01/ archive-of-islamic-state-administrative-documents-1.

Jakobson, Roman. 1937. *Six Lectures on Sound and Meaning*. Cambridge, MA: MIT Press.

Jamestown Foundation. 2005. "Jihadi Terms and Terminology." *Terrorism Focus* 2 (6). Accessed August 14, 2017. https://jamestown.org/program/jihadi-terms-and -terminology-2/.

Jarrar, Maher. 2004. "The Martyrdom of Passionate Lovers: Holy War as a Sacred Wedding." In *Hadith: Origins and Developments*, edited by Harald Motzki, 317–37. Burlington, VT: Ashgate.

Jayasuriya, Laksiri. 2008. "Constructions of Culture and Identity in Contemporary Social Theorising." *International Journal of Culture and Mental Health* 1 (1): 30–43.

Jessop, Bob. 2001. "Bringing the State Back In (Yet Again): Reviews, Revisions, Rejections, and Redirections." *International Review of Sociology* 11 (2): 149–73.

——. 2010. "Constituting Another Foucault Effect: Foucault on States and Statecraft." In *Governmentality: Current Issues and Future Challenges*, edited by Ulrich Bröckling, Susanne Krasmann, and Thomas Lemke, 56–73. New York: Routledge.

Jones, Seth G. 2013. "Syria's Growing Jihad." *Survival* 55 (4): 53–72.

Kastrup, Marianne, and Unaiza Niaz. 2009. "The Impact of Culture on Women's Mental Health," 463–84. In *Contemporary Topics in Women's Mental Health: Global Perspectives in a Changing Society*, edited by Prabha S. Chandra, Helen Herrman, Jane E. Fisher, Marianne Kastrup, Unaiza Niaz, Marta Rondon, and Ahmed Okasha. West Sussex: John Wiley.

Katzman, Kenneth. 2008. *Al Qaeda in Iraq: Assessment and Outside Links*. Washington, DC: Congressional Research Service.

Katzman, Kenneth, Christopher M. Blanchard, Carla E. Humud, Rhoda Margesson, and Matthew C. Weed. 2015. *The "Islamic State" Crisis and U.S. Policy*. Washington, DC: Congressional Research Service.

"Khilafah Declared." 2014. *Dabiq* 1 (1): 6–11.

Khuri, Fuad I. 1981. "Classification, Meaning, and Use of Arabic Status and Kinship Terms." *International Journal of Sociology of the Family* 11 (2): 347–66.

Kilcullen, David J. 2007. "Countering Global Insurgency." *Journal of Strategic Studies* 28 (4): 597–617.

Kimmage, Daniel, and Kathleen Ridolfo. 2007. "Iraq's Networked Insurgents." *Foreign Policy* 163: 88, 90.

Kirdar, M. J. 2011. *Al Qaeda in Iraq*. Washington, DC: Center for Strategic and International Studies.

Kirmanj, Sherko. 2010. "Challenging the Islamist Politicization of Islam: The Non-Islamic Origins of Muslim Political Concepts." In *Political Islam from Muhammad to Ahmadinejad: Defenders, Detractors, and Definitions*, edited by Joseph Morrison Skelly, 35–50. Santa Barbara, CA: Praeger Security International.

Kirmayer, Laurence J. 2006. "Beyond the 'New Cross-Cultural Psychiatry': Cultural Biology, Discursive Psychology and the Ironies of Globalization." *Transcultural Psychiatry* 43 (1): 126–44.

——. 2007a. "Psychotherapy and the Cultural Concept of the Person." *Transcultural Psychiatry* 44 (2): 232–57.

——. 2007b. "Cultural Psychiatry in Historical Perspective." In *Textbook of Cultural Psychiatry*, edited by Dinesh Bhugra and Kamaldeep Bhui, 3–19. Cambridge: Cambridge University Press.

——. 2008. "Empathy and Alterity in Cultural Psychiatry." *Ethos* 36 (4): 457–74.

Kirmayer, Laurence J., Eugene Raikhel, and Sadeq Rahimi. 2013. "Cultures of the Internet: Identity, Community, and Mental Health." *Transcultural Psychiatry* 50 (2): 165–91.

Kirmayer, Laurence J., Cécile Rousseau, G. Eric Jarvis, and Jaswant Guzder. 2008. "The Cultural Context of Clinical Assessment." In *Psychiatry*. 3rd ed. Edited by Allan Tasman, Jerald Kay, Jeffrey A. Lieberman, Michael B. First, and Mario Maj, 54–66. New York: John Wiley.

Kleinman, Arthur. 1980. *Patients and Healers in the Context of Culture: An Exploration of the Borderland Between Anthropology, Medicine, and Psychiatry*. Berkeley: University of California Press.

——. 1987. "Anthropology and Psychiatry: The Role of Culture in Cross-Cultural Research on Illness." *British Journal of Psychiatry* 151 (4): 447–54.

——. 1988a. *Rethinking Psychiatry: From Cultural Category to Personal Experience*. New York: Free Press.

——. 1988b. *The Illness Narratives: Suffering, Healing, and the Human Condition.* New York: Basic Books.

——. 1996. "How Is Culture Important for DSM-IV?" In *Culture and Psychiatric Diagnosis: A DSM-IV Perspective,* edited by Juan E. Mezzich, Arthur Kleinman, Horacio Fabrega Jr., and Delores L. Parron, 15–25. Washington, DC: American Psychiatric Publishing.

——. 2010. "Four Social Theories for Global Health." *The Lancet* 375 (9725): 1518–19.

Kleinman, Arthur, and Peter Benson. 2006. "Anthropology in the Clinic: The Problem of Cultural Competency and How to Fix It." *PLoS Medicine* 3 (10): e294.

Kleinman, Arthur, Veena Das, and Margaret M. Lock. 1997. Introduction to *Social Suffering,* ix–xxvii. Edited by Arthur Kleinman, Veena Das, and Margaret M. Lock. Berkeley: University of California Press.

Koch, Barbara Johnstone. 1983. "Presentation as Proof: The Language of Arabic Rhetoric." *Anthropological Linguistics* 25 (1): 47–60.

Kristeva, Julia. 2005. *Hatred and Madness.* Translated by Jeanine Herman. New York: Columbia University Press.

Kruglanski, Arie W., Xiaoyan Chen, Mark Dechesne, Shira Fishman, and Edward Orehek. 2009. "Yes, No, and Maybe in the World of Terrorism Research: Reflections on the Commentaries." *Political Psychology* 30 (3): 401–17.

Lacan, Jacques. 1997. *Ecrits: A Selection.* Translated by Alan Sheridan. London: Routledge.

Lahoud, Nelly. 2014. "The Neglected Sex: The Jihadis' Exclusion of Women from Jihad." *Terrorism and Political Violence* 26 (5): 780–802.

Lambert, Helen, and Christopher McKevitt. 2002. "Anthropology in Health Research: From Qualitative Methods to Multidisciplinarity." *British Medical Journal* 325 (7357): 210–13.

Lapierre, Sylvie, Annette Erlangsen, Margda Waern, Diego De Leo, Hirofumi Oyama, Paolo Scocco, Joseph Gallo, Katalin Szanto, Yeates Conwell, Brian Draper, Paul Quinnett, and the International Research Group for Suicide Among the Elderly. 2011. "A Systematic Review of Elderly Suicide Prevention Programs." *Crisis* 32 (2): 88–98.

Lawrence, Bruce. 2005. *Messages to the World: The Statements of Osama bin Laden.* New York: Verso.

Legare, Cristine H., and Mark Nielsen. 2015. "Imitation and Innovation: The Dual Engines of Cultural Learning." *Trends in Cognitive Science* 19 (11): 688–99.

Lehman, Darrin R., Chi-yue Chiu, and Mark Schaller. 2004. "Psychology and Culture." *Annual Review of Psychology* 55: 689–714.

Lemke, Thomas. 2007. "An Indigestible Meal? Foucault, Governmentality and State Theory." *Distinktion: Journal of Social Theory* 8 (2): 43–64.

Levitt, Peggy. 1998. "Social Remittances: Migration Driven Local-Level Forms of Cultural Diffusion." *International Migration Review* 32 (4): 926–48.

Lewis-Fernández, Roberto. 1996. "Cultural Formulation of Psychiatric Diagnosis." *Culture, Medicine, and Psychiatry* 20 (3): 133–44.

Lewis-Fernández, Roberto, Neil Krishan Aggarwal, Sofie Bäärnhielm, Hans Rohlof, Laurence J. Kirmayer, Mitchell G. Weiss, Sushrut Jadhav, Ladson Hinton, Renato Alarcón, Dinesh Bhugra, Simon Groen, Rob van Dijk, Adil Qureshi, Francisco

Collazos, Cécile Rousseau, Luis Caballero, Mar Ramos, and Francis Lu. 2014. "Culture and Psychiatric Evaluation: Operationalizing Cultural Formulation for DSM-5." *Psychiatry* 77 (2): 130–54.

Lipkin, Steven. 1999. "Real Emotional Logic: Persuasive Strategies in Docudrama." *Cinema Journal* 38 (4): 68–85.

——. 2002. *Real Emotional Logic: Film and Television Docudrama as Persuasive Practice.* Carbondale: Southern Illinois University Press.

Littlewood, Roland. 1999. "Qualitative Methods of Research in Cultural Psychiatry." In *Qualitative Methods in Mental Health Research*, edited by R. L. Kapur, 26–43. Bangalore: National Institute of Advanced Studies.

——. 2002. *Pathologies of the West: An Anthropology of Mental Illness in Europe and America.* Ithaca, NY: Cornell University Press.

Lloyd, Stephanie, and Nicholas Moreau. 2011. "Pursuit of a 'Normal Life': Mood, Anxiety, and Their Disordering." *Medical Anthropology: Cross-Cultural Studies in Health and Illness* 30 (6): 591–609.

Long, Austin. 2008. "The Anbar Awakening." *Survival: Global Politics and Strategy* 50 (2): 67–94.

Lu, Francis G., Russell F. Lim, and Juan E. Mezzich. 1995. "Issues in the Assessment and Diagnosis of Culturally Diverse Individuals." In *Review of Psychiatry*, vol. 14, *Assessment and Diagnosis*, edited by John M. Oldham and Michelle B. Riba, 477–510. Washington, DC: American Psychiatric Publishing.

Lund, Crick, Alison Breen, Alan J. Flisher, Ritsuko Kakuma, Joanne Corrigall, John A. Joska, Leslie Swartz, and Vikram Patel. 2010. "Poverty and Common Mental Disorders in Low and Middle Income Countries: A Systematic Review." *Social Science & Medicine* 71 (3): 517–28.

Lynch, Marc. 2010. "Jihadis and the *Ikhwan*." In *Self-Inflicted Wounds: Debates and Divisions Within al-Qa'ida and Its Periphery*, edited by Assaf Moghadam and Brian Fishman, 155–82. West Point, NY: Combating Terrorism Center at West Point.

Mabon, Simon. 2017. "Nationalist Jāhiliyyah and the Flag of the Two Crusaders, or: ISIS, Sovereignty, and the 'Owl of Minerva.'" *Studies in Conflict & Terrorism* 40 (11): 966–85.

Marquis, Christopher. 2004. "Powell Admits No Hard Proof in Linking Iraq to Al Qaeda." *New York Times*, January 9.

Marr, Phebe. 2012. *The Modern History of Iraq.* 3rd ed. Boulder, CO: Westview.

McAuliffe, Jane Dammen. 2006. "The Tasks and Traditions of Interpretation." In *The Cambridge Companion to the Qur'ān*, edited by Jane Dammen McAuliffe, 181–209. Cambridge: Cambridge University Press.

McCants, William. 2015. *The ISIS Apocalypse: The History, Strategy, and Doomsday Vision of the Islamic State.* New York: St. Martin's.

McCary, John A. 2009. "The Anbar Awakening: An Alliance of Incentives." *The Washington Quarterly* 32 (1): 43–59.

McCoy, Terrence. 2014. "ISIS Just Stole $425 Million, Iraqi Governor Says, and Became the 'World's Richest Terrorist Group.'" *Washington Post*, June 12.

Messaris, Paul. 1997. *Visual Persuasion: The Role of Images in Advertising.* New York: Sage.

Messick, Brinkley. 1993. *The Calligraphic State: Textual Domination and History in a Muslim Society.* Berkeley: University of California Press.

Mezzich, Juan, and Giovanni Caracci. 2008. *Cultural Formulation: A Reader for Psychiatric Diagnosis.* Lanham, MD: Jason Aronson.

Mezzich, Juan E., Giovanni Caracci, Horacio Fabrega Jr., and Laurence J. Kirmayer. 2009. "Cultural Formulation Guidelines." *Transcultural Psychiatry* 46 (3): 383–405.

Mills, Stacia, Anna Q. Xiao, Kate Wolitzky-Taylor, Russell Lim, and Francis G. Lu. 2017. "Training on the DSM-5 Cultural Formulation Interview Improves Cultural Competence in General Psychiatry Residents: A Pilot Study." *Transcultural Psychiatry* 54 (2): 179–91.

Mishal, Shaul, and Maoz Rosenthal. 2005. "Al Qaeda as a Dune Organization: Toward a Typology of Islamic Terrorist Organizations." *Studies in Conflict & Terrorism* 28 (4): 275–93.

Mitchell, Timothy. 1991. "The Limits of the State: Beyond Statist Approaches and Their Critics." *American Political Science Review* 85 (1): 77–96.

"MNFT-2007-005315: ISI Personnel Records in Salah Al-Din." 2007. Harmony Document Database. *Combating Terrorism Center at West Point.* Accessed August 15, 2017. https://ctc.usma.edu/v2/wp-content/uploads/2014/12/MNFT-2007-005315 -Orig.pdf.

"MNFT-2007-005318: ISI Personnel Records in Salah Al-Din." 2007. Harmony Document Database. *Combating Terrorism Center at West Point.* Accessed August 15, 2017. https://ctc.usma.edu/v2/wp-content/uploads/2014/12/MNFT-2007-005318 -Orig.pdf.

Moghadam, Assaf. 2003. "Palestinian Suicide Terrorism in the Second Intifada: Motivations and Organizational Aspects." *Studies in Conflict & Terrorism* 26 (1): 65–92.

Monfort, Emmanuel, and Mohammad Hassan Afzali. 2017. "Traumatic Stress Symptoms After the November 13th 2015 Terrorist Attacks Among Young Adults: The Relation to Media and Emotion Regulation." *Comprehensive Psychiatry* 75: 68–74.

Morabia, Alfred. 1978. "Ibn Taymiyya, Dernier Grand Théoricien du Gihād Médiéval." *Bulletin d'Études Orientales* 30: 85–100.

Moscovici, Serge. 1973. Foreword to *Health and Illness: A Social Psychological Analysis,* edited by Claudine Herzlich, ix–xiv. London: Academic.

——. 1990. "The Origin of Social Representations: A Response to Michaels." *New Ideas in Psychology* 8 (3): 383–88.

——. 1994. "Social Representations and Pragmatic Communication." *Social Science Information* 33 (2): 163–77.

Moscovici, Serge, and Ivana Marková. 1998. "Presenting Social Presentations: A Conversation." *Culture & Psychology* 4 (3): 371–410.

Mullins, Daniel A., Harvey Whitehouse, and Quentin D. Atkinson. 2013. "The Role of Writing and Recordkeeping in the Cultural Evolution of Human Cooperation." *Journal of Economic Behavior & Organization* 90S: S141–S151.

Musial, Julia. 2016. " 'My Muslim Sister, Indeed You Are a Mujahidah'—Narratives in the Propaganda of the Islamic State to Address and Radicalize Western Women. An Exemplary Analysis of the Online Magazine *Dabiq*." *Journal for Deradicalization* 9: 39–100.

Nardi, Bonnie. 2015. "Virtuality." *Annual Review of Anthropology* 44: 15–31.

National Academies of Sciences, Engineering, and Medicine. 2017. *Countering Violent Extremism Through Public Health Practice: Proceedings of a Workshop*. Washington, DC: National Academies Press.

National Coordinator for Security and Counterterrorism and the General Intelligence and Security Service. 2017. *The Children of ISIS: The Indoctrination of Minors in ISIS-Held Territory*. The Hague: National Coordinator for Security and Counterterrorism and the General Intelligence and Security Service.

Nesbitt-Larking, Paul, and Catarina Kinnvall. 2012. "The Discursive Frames of Political Psychology." *Political Psychology* 33 (1): 45–59.

Nida, Eugene. 2000. "Principles of Correspondence." In *The Translation Studies Reader*, edited by Lawrence Venuti, 126–40. New York: Routledge.

Nielsen, Mark, Jessica Cucchiaro, and Jumana Mohamedally. 2012. "When the Transmission of Culture Is Child's Play." *PLoS One* 7 (3): e34066.

Nilsson, Marco. 2015. "Foreign Fighters and the Radicalization of Local Jihad: Interview Evidence from Swedish Jihadists." *Studies in Conflict & Terrorism* 38 (5): 343–58.

"NMEC-2007-612449: Analysis of the State of ISI." 2007. Harmony Document Database. *Combating Terrorism Center at West Point*. Accessed August 15, 2017. https://ctc.usma.edu/v2/wp-content/uploads/2013/09/Analysis-of-the-State-of-ISI -Original.pdf.

"NMEC-2007-632533: A List of Some of ISI Expenses During the Year 2006." 2007. Harmony Document Database. *Combating Terrorism Center at West Point*. Accessed July 25, 2016. www.ctc.usma.edu/v2/wp-content/uploads/2014/12/NMEC-2007- 632533-Orig.pdf.

"NMEC-2007-636916: Directive from the ISI Salah-Al-Din Security Office." 2007. Harmony Document Database. *Combating Terrorism Center at West Point*. Accessed August 15, 2017. https://ctc.usma.edu/v2/wp-content/uploads/2013/10/Directive -from-the-ISI-Salah-al-Din-Security-Office-Original.pdf.

"NMEC-2007-636973: Incident Comment from the ISI Ministry of Defense (Dated 5/22/2007)." 2007. Harmony Document Database. *Combating Terrorism Center at West Point*. Accessed August 16, 2017. https://ctc.usma.edu/v2 /wp-content/uploads/2013/09/Incident-Comment-from-the-ISI-Ministry-of -Defense-Dated-5-22-2007_Original.pdf.

"NMEC-2007-637001: Letters to the Leadership of ISI About Issues of Single-Party Control." 2007. Harmony Document Database. *Combating Terrorism Center at West Point*. Accessed August 16, 2017. https://ctc.usma.edu/v2/wp-content /uploads/2013/09/Letters-to-the-Leadership-of-ISI-about-Issues-of-Single -party-Control-Original.pdf.

"NMEC-2007-637011: Incident Comment from the ISI Ministry of Defense (Dated 6/2/2007)." 2007. Harmony Document Database. *Combating Terrorism Center at West Point*. Accessed August 16, 2017. https://ctc.usma.edu/v2/wp-content /uploads/2013/09/Incident-Comment-from-the-ISI-Ministry-of-Defense -Dated-622007_Translation.pdf.

"NMEC-2007-657829: PI for Hatim Ahmed Hamdan Al Shamrani." 2007. Harmony Document Database. *Combating Terrorism Center at West Point*. Accessed August 15, 2017. https://ctc.usma.edu/v2/wp-content/uploads/2013/09/PI-for-Hatim -Ahmed-Hamdan-Al-Shamrani-Original.pdf.

"NMEC-2007-657925: ISI Template for Suicide Operation Pledge." 2007. Harmony Document Database. *Combating Terrorism Center at West Point.* Accessed August 16, 2017. https://ctc.usma.edu/v2/wp-content/uploads/2013/09/ISI-Template-for-Suicide-Operation-Pledge-Original.pdf.

"NMEC-2007-657926: ISI Border Emirate Statement of Responsibility." 2007. Harmony Document Database. *Combating Terrorism Center at West Point.* Accessed August 15, 2017. https://www.ctc.usma.edu/v2/wp-content/uploads/2013/09/ISI-Border-Emirate-Statement-of-Responsibility-Original.pdf.

Nordland, Rod. 2017. "Lebanese Army, Hezbollah and Syrian Army Declare Cease-Fire with ISIS." *New York Times,* August 27.

"Notification for Kurds to Leave Raqqa City." n.d. Archive of Islamic State Administrative Documents. *Pundicity.* Accessed August 18, 2017. www.aymennjawad.org/2015/01/archive-of-islamic-state-administrative-documents.

O'Callaghan, Derek, Nico Prucha, Derek Greene, Maura Conway, Joe Carthy, and Pádraig Cunningham. 2014. "Online Social Media in the Syria Conflict: Encompassing the Extremes and the In-Betweens." Paper presented at the 2014 IEEE/ACM International Conference on Advances in Social Networks Analysis and Mining, Beijing, August 17–20.

O'Halloran, Kay L., Sabine Tan, Peter Wignell, John A. Bateman, Duc-Son Pham, Michele Grossman, and Andrew Vande Moere. 2016. "Interpreting Text and Image Relations in Violent Extremist Discourse: A Mixed Methods Approach for Big Data Analytics." *Terrorism and Political Violence,* https://doi.org/10.1080/0954 6553.2016.1233871.

Office of the United Nations High Commissioner for Refugees. 2017a. "Iraq Emergency." *UNHCR.* Accessed July 21, 2017. www.unhcr.org/en-us/iraq-emergency.html.

——. 2017b. "2017 Syria Emergency." *UNHCR.* Accessed July 21, 2017. www.unhcr.org/en-us/syria-emergency.html.

Onorato, Rina S., and John C. Turner. 2004. "Fluidity in the Self-Concept: The Shift from Personal to Social Identity." *European Journal of Social Psychology* 34 (3): 257–78.

Onwuegbuzie, Anthony J., and Kathleen M. T. Collins. 2007. "A Typology of Mixed Methods Sampling Designs in Social Science Research." *The Qualitative Report* 12 (2): 281–316.

"Open Letter to Dr. Ibrahim Awwad Al-Badri, Alias 'Abu Bakr Al-Baghdadi.'" 2014. *Open Letter to Al-Baghdadi.* Accessed September 6, 2017. www.lettertobaghdadi.com.

Pantucci, Raffaello. 2013. "British Fighters Joining the War in Syria." *CTC Sentinel* 6 (2): 11–15.

Patton, Michael Quinn. 2002. *Qualitative Research and Evaluation Methods.* 3rd ed. Thousand Oaks, CA: Sage.

Pelletier, Ian R., Leif Lundmark, Rachel Gardner, Gina Scott Ligon, and Ramazan Kilinc. 2016. "Why ISIS's Message Resonates: Leveraging Islam, Sociopolitical Catalysts, and Adaptive Messaging." *Studies in Conflict & Terrorism* 39 (10): 871–99.

Penrice, John. 2004. *A Dictionary and Glossary of the Koran.* Mineola, NY: Dover. First published 1873 by Henry S. King.

Perešin, Anita. 2015. "Fatal Attraction: Western Muslimas and ISIS." *Perspectives on Terrorism* 9 (3): 21–38.

Perešin, Anita, and Alberto Cervone. 2015. "The Western Muhajirat of ISIS." *Studies in Conflict & Terrorism* 38 (7): 499–509.

Perrin, Andrew J. 2005. "National Threat and Political Culture: Authoritarianism, Antiauthoritarianism, and the September 11 Attacks." *Political Psychology* 26 (2): 167–94.

Perry, Samuel P., and Jerry Mark Long. 2016. " 'Why Would Anyone Sell Paradise?': The Islamic State in Iraq and the Making of a Martyr." *Southern Communication Journal* 81 (1): 1–17.

Pfefferbaum, Betty, Pascal Nitiéma, Rose L. Pfefferbaum, J. Brian Houston, Phebe Tucker, Haekyung Jeon-Slaughter, and Carol S. North. 2016. "Reactions of Oklahoma City Bombing Survivors to Media Coverage of the September 11, 2001, Attacks." *Comprehensive Psychiatry* 65: 70–78.

Phillips, Brian J. 2014. "Terrorist Group Cooperation and Longevity." *International Studies Quarterly* 58 (2): 336–47.

Pollock, Sheldon. 2009. "Cosmopolitan and Vernacular in History." *Public Culture* 12 (3): 591–625.

Post, Jerrold. 2005. "When Hatred Is Bred in the Bone: Psycho-Cultural Foundations of Contemporary Terrorism." *Political Psychology* 26 (4): 615–36.

Post, Jerrold, Ehud Sprinzak, and Laurita M. Denny. 2003. "The Terrorists in Their Own Words: Interviews with 35 Incarcerated Middle Eastern Terrorists." *Terrorism and Political Violence* 15 (1): 171–84.

Prins, Annabel, Michelle J. Bovin, Derek J. Smolenski, Brian P. Marx, Rachel Kimerling, Michael A. Jenkins-Guarnieri, Danny G. Kaloupek, Paula P. Schnurr, Anica Pless Kaiser, Yani E. Leyva, and Quyen Q. Tiet. 2016. "The Primary Care PTSD Screen for DSM-5 (PC-PTSD-5): Development and Evaluation Within a Veteran Primary Care Sample." *Journal of General Internal Medicine* 31 (10): 1206–11.

"Propagating the Correct Manhaj." 2014. *Islamic State Reports* 1 (1): 2–4.

Qutbuddin, Tahira. 2008. "Khutba: The Evolution of Early Arabic Oration." In *Classical Arabic Humanities in Their Own Terms: Festschrift for Wolfhart Heinrichs*, edited by Beatrice Gruendler and Michael Cooperson, 176–273. Leiden, South Holland, Netherlands: Brill.

Rabiger, Michael. 2015. *Directing the Documentary*. 6th ed. New York: Focal Press.

Rabinow, Paul, and William M. Sullivan. 1987. "The Interpretive Turn: A Second Look." In *Interpretive Social Science: A Second Look*, edited by Paul Rabinow and William M. Sullivan, 1–30. Berkeley: University of California Press.

Rahmaan, Yasiin. 2016. "Feminist Edges of Muslim Feminist Readings of Qurʾanic Verses." *Journal of Feminist Studies in Religion* 32 (2): 142–48.

Rassler, Don, Muhammad al-ʿUbaydi, and Vera Mironova. January 31, 2017. "CTC Perspectives—The Islamic State's Drone Documents: Management, Acquisitions, and Diy Tradecraft." *Combating Terrorism Center at West Point*. https://ctc.usma.edu/posts/ctc-perspectives-the-islamic-states-drone-documents-management-acquisitions-and-diy-tradecraft.

Redfield, Robert, Ralph Linton, and Melville J. Herskovits. 1936. "Memorandum for the Study of Acculturation." *American Anthropologist* 38 (1): 149–52.

Renshon, Stanley, and John Duckitt. 1997. "Cultural and Cross-Cultural Political Psychology: Toward the Development of a New Subfield." *Political Psychology* 18 (2): 233–40.

Riley, David S., Melissa S. Barber, Gunver S. Kienle, Jeffrey K. Aronson, Tido von Schoen-Angerer, Peter Tugwell, Helmut Kiene, Mark Helfand, Douglas G. Altman, Harold Sox, Paul G. Werthmann, David Moher, Richard A. Rison, Larissa Shamseer, Christian A. Koch, Gordon H. Sun, Patrick Hanaway, Nancy L. Sudak, Marietta Kaszkin-Bettag, James E. Carpenter, and Joel J. Gagnier. 2017. "CARE Guidelines for Case Reports: Explanation and Elaboration Document." *Journal of Clinical Epidemiology*, https://doi.org/10.1016/j.jclinepi.2017.04.026.

Robinson, Francis. 1993. "Technology and Religious Change: Islam and the Impact of Print." *Modern Asian Studies* 27 (1): 229–51.

Rose, Nikolas, and Peter Miller. 1992. "Political Power Beyond the State: Problematics of Government." *British Journal of Sociology* 43 (2): 173–205.

Rosowsky, Andrey. 2011. "Heavenly Singing: The Practice of Naat and Nasheed and Its Possible Contribution to Reversing Language Shift Among Young Muslim Multilinguals in the UK." *International Journal of the Sociology of Language* 212: 135–48.

Rothenberger, Liane, Kathrin Müller, and Ahmed Elmezeny. 2018. "The Discursive Construction of Terrorist Group Identity." *Terrorism and Political Violence* 30 (3): 428–53.

Rousseau, Cécile, Toby Measham, and Marie Bathiche-Suidan. 2008. "DSM IV, Culture and Child Psychiatry." *Journal of the American Academy of Child and Adolescent Psychiatry* 17 (2): 69–75.

Roy, Olivier. 2004. *Globalized Islam: The Search for a New Ummah.* New York: Columbia University Press.

Ryan, Michael. 2013. *Decoding Al-Qaeda's Strategy: The Deep Battle Against America.* New York: Columbia University Press.

Ryan, Tracii, Andrea Chester, John Reece, and Sophia Xenos. 2014. "The Uses and Abuses of Facebook: A Review of Facebook Addiction." *Journal of Behavioral Addictions* 3 (3): 133–48.

Saddhono, Kundharu, Nugraheni Eko Wardani, and Chafit Ulya. 2015. "Sociopragmatic Approach on Discourse Structure of Friday Prayer's Sermon in Java and Madura Island." *Journal of Language and Literature* 6 (1): 26–30.

Said, Behnam. 2012. "Hymns (Nasheeds): A Contribution to the Study of the Jihadist Culture." *Studies in Conflict and Terrorism* 35 (12): 863–79.

Sajadpour, Karim. 2013. "Iran's Unwavering Support to Assad's Syria." *CTC Sentinel* 6 (8): 11–13.

Sanger, David E., and Eric Schmitt. 2017. "U.S. Cyberweapons, Used Against Iran and North Korea, Are a Disappointment Against ISIS." *New York Times*, June 12.

Saris, A. Jamie. 1995. "Telling Stories: Life Histories, Illness Narratives, and Institutional Landscapes." *Culture, Medicine, and Psychiatry* 19 (1): 39–72.

"Saudi Arabia's Ambitious Al-Qaida Fighter." 2005. *Dateline NBC*, July 11.

Scheper-Hughes, Nancy, and Margaret Lock. 1987. "The Mindful Body: A Prolegomenon to Future Work in Medical Anthropology." *Medical Anthropology Quarterly* 1 (1): 6–41.

Schimmel, Annemarie. 1987. *And Muhammad Is His Messenger: The Veneration of the Prophet in Islamic Piety*. Chapel Hill: University of North Carolina Press.

Schmitt, Eric. 2013. "Worries Mount as Syria Lures West's Muslims." *New York Times*, July 27.

——. 2015. "A Raid on ISIS Yields a Trove of Intelligence." *New York Times*, June 8.

——. 2016a. "U.S. Secures Vast New Trove of Intelligence on ISIS." *New York Times*, July 27.

——. 2016b. "Pentagon Expects Mosul Push to Unlock Trove of ISIS Intelligence." *New York Times*, October 22.

Schmitt, Eric, and Anne Barnard. 2016. "Senior ISIS Strategist and Spokesman Is Reported Killed in Syria." *New York Times*, August 30.

Schulz, Richard, and Jutta Heckhausen. 1999. "Aging, Culture and Control: Setting a New Research Agenda." *The Journals of Gerontology: Series B* 54B (3): 139–45.

Serjeant, R. B. 1964. "The 'Constitution of Medina.'" *Islamic Quarterly* 8 (1): 3–16.

Shane, Scott. 2006. "Zarqawi Built Global Jihadist Network on Internet." *New York Times*, June 9.

——. 2016. "The Enduring Influence of Anwar Al-Awlaki in the Age of the Islamic State." *CTC Sentinel* 9 (7): 15–19.

Shane, Scott, and Ben Hubbard. 2014. "ISIS Displaying a Deft Command of Varied Media." *New York Times*, August 30.

Sheikh, Hammad, Angel Gómez, and Scott Atran. 2016. "Empirical Evidence for the Devoted Actor Model." *Current Anthropology* 57 (S13): S204–S209.

Shelton, Mary Lou, and Ronald W. Rogers. 1981. "Fear-Arousing and Empathy-Arousing Appeals to Help: The Pathos of Persuasion." *Journal of Applied Social Psychology* 11 (4): 366–78.

Sherlock, Ruth. 2013. "Syria: How Jihadist Group Jabhat al-Nusra Is Taking Over Syria's Revolution." *The Telegraph*, February 8.

Shields, Stephanie. 1975. "Functionalism, Darwinism, and the Psychology of Women." *American Psychologist* 30 (7): 739–54.

Shtuni, Adrian. 2015. "Ethnic Albanian Foreign Fighters in Iraq and Syria." *CTC Sentinel* 8 (4): 11–14.

Shweder, Richard A. 1999a. "Why Cultural Psychology?" *Ethos* 27 (1): 62–73.

——. 1999b. "Cultural Psychology—What Is It?" In *Cultural Psychology: Essays on Comparative Human Development*, edited by James W. Stigler, Richard A. Shweder, and Gilbert Herdt, 1–44. Cambridge: Cambridge University Press.

Siegel, Pascale Combelles. 2008. "Islamic State of Iraq Commemorates Its Two-Year Anniversary." *CTC Sentinel* 1 (11): 5–7.

Silke, Andrew. 2003. "The Psychology of Suicidal Terrorism." In *Terrorists, Victims, and Society: Psychological Perspectives on Terrorism and its Consequences*, edited by Andrew Silke, 93–108. Chichester: John Wiley.

Sinha, Chris. 2000. "Culture, Language, and the Emergence of Subjectivity." *Culture & Psychology* 6 (2): 197–207.

Slater, Michael D. 1997. "Persuasion Processes Across Receiver Goals and Message Genres." *Communication Theory* 7 (2): 125–48.

Smith, Lindsay, and Arthur Kleinman. 2010. "Emotional Engagements: Acknowledgement, Advocacy, and Direct Action." In *Emotions in the Field: The Psychology and Anthropology of Fieldwork Experience*, edited by James Davies and Dimitrina Spencer, 171–87. Stanford, CA: Stanford University Press.

Smyth, Phillip. 2013. "From Karbala to Sayyida Zainab: Iraqi Fighters in Syria's Shi'a Militias." *CTC Sentinel* 6 (8): 28–32.

Soares, Benjamin, and Filippo Osella. 2009. "Islam, Politics, Anthropology." *The Journal of the Royal Anthropological Institute* 15: S1–S3.

Sprusansky, Dale. 2014. "Understanding ISIS: Frequently Asked Questions." *Washington Report on Middle East Affairs* 33 (7): 19–20.

Stack, Liam. 2015. "Islamic State Blows Up Temple at Palmyra Ruins in Syria." *New York Times*, August 24.

Staples, James, and Tom Widiger. 2012. "Situating Suicide as an Anthropological Problem: Ethnographic Approaches to Understanding Self-Harm and Self-Inflicted Death." *Culture, Medicine, and Psychiatry* 36 (2): 183–203.

Steenbergen, Jo Van. 2016. *Caliphate and Kingship in a Fifteenth-Century Literary History of Muslim Leadership and Pilgrimage.* Leiden, South Holland, Netherlands: Brill.

Stenersen, Anne. 2008. "The Internet: A Virtual Training Camp?" *Terrorism and Political Violence* 20 (2): 215–33.

——. 2014. "Gathering Data Through Court Cases: Implications for Understanding Visual Messaging." In *Visual Propaganda and Extremism in the Online Environment*, edited by Carol K. Winkler and Cori E. Dauber, 33–54. Carlisle, PA: Strategic Studies Institute and U.S. Army War College Press.

Stern, Jessica, and J. M. Berger. 2015. *ISIS: The State of Terror.* New York: HarperCollins.

Sternthal, Brian, and C. Samuel Craig. 1973. "Humor in Marketing." *Journal of Marketing* 37 (4): 12–18.

Stetkevych, Jarsolav. 1986. "Name and Epithet: The Philology and Semiotics of Animal Nomenclature in Early Arabic Poetry." *Journal of Near Eastern Studies* 45 (2): 89–124.

Stewart, Devin J. 1990. "Sajʿ in the "Qurʾān": Prosody and Structure." *Journal of Arabic Literature* 21 (2): 101–39.

——. 2004. "Muhammad b. Jarir al-Tabari's *al-Bayan ʿan Usul al-Ahkam* and the Genre of Usul al-Fiqh in Ninth Century Baghdad." In *Abbasid Studies: Occasional Papers of the School of Abbasid Studies, Cambridge, 6–10 January 2002*, edited by James Montgomery, 321–49. Leuven (Belgium): Peeters.

Stiglitz, Joseph, and Linda Bilmes. 2008. *The Three Trillion Dollar War.* New York: W. W. Norton.

Stillman, Norman. 1979. *The Jews of Arab Lands: A History and Source Book.* Philadelphia: Jewish Publication Society of America.

Suleiman, Yasir. 1995. "Arabic Linguistic Tradition." In *Concise History of the Language Sciences: From the Sumerians to the Cognitivists*, edited by E. F. K. Koerner and R. E. Asher, 28–38. Oxford: Elsevier Science.

——. 2003. *The Arabic Language and National Identity: A Study in Ideology.* Edinburgh: University of Edinburgh Press.

"Syria: 'Hundreds of Thousands' Join Anti-Assad Protests." 2011. *BBC News*, July 2.

Taarnby, Michael, and Lars Hallundbaek. 2008. *Fatah al-Islam: Anthropological Perspectives on Jihadi Culture.* Madrid: Real Instituto Elcano.

Tajfel, Henri. 1970. "Experiments in Intergroup Discrimination." *Scientific American* 223 (5): 96–102.

——. 1974. "Social Identity and Group Behavior." *Social Science Information* 13 (2): 65–93.

Todd, Jennifer. 2005. "Social Transformation, Collective Categories, and Identity Change." *Theory and Society* 34 (4): 429–63.

Triandis, Harry C. 1989. "The Self and Social Behavior in Differing Cultural Contexts." *Psychological Review* 96 (3): 506–20.

Tripp, Charles. 2002. *A History of Iraq*. 2nd ed. Cambridge: Cambridge University Press.

Tsfati, Yariv, and Gabriel Weimann. 2002. "www.terrorism.com: Terror on the Internet." *Studies in Conflict & Terrorism* 25 (5): 317–32.

Turner, John C. 1982. "Towards a Cognitive Redefinition of the Social Group." In *Social Identity and Intergroup Relations*, edited by Henri Tajfel, 15–40. Cambridge: Cambridge University Press.

Turner, John C., and Penelope J. Oakes. 1986. "The Significance of the Social Identity Concept for Social Psychology with Reference to Individualism, Interactionism and Social Influence." *British Journal of Social Psychology* 25 (3): 237–52.

Turner, John C., Penelope J. Oakes, S. Alexander Haslam, and Craig McGarty. 1994. "Self and Collective: Cognition and Social Context." *Personality and Social Psychology Bulletin* 20 (5): 454–63.

Turner, John C., and Katherine J. Reynolds. 2001. "The Social Identity Perspective in Intergroup Relations: Theories, Themes, and Controversies." In *Blackwell Handbook of Social Psychology: Intergroup Processes*, edited by Rupert Brown and Samuel L. Gaertner, 133–52. Oxford: Blackwell.

U.S. Department of Defense. 2015a. "Iraqi Security Forces Defeat ISIL Attack on Ramadi," March 13. *U.S. Department of Defense*. www.defense.gov/Portals/1/features/2014/0814_iraq/Iraqi-Security-Forces-defeat-ISIL-attack-on-Ramadi.pdf.

——.2015b. "ISF Clears Pathway to Bayji Oil Refinery," May 15. *U.S. Department of Defense*. www.defense.gov/Portals/1/features/2014/0814_iraq/docs/20150515_-_Media_Release_-_ISFBOR.pdf.

——. 2016. "Statement by Secretary of Defense Ash Carter on the Liberation of Dabiq," October 16. *U.S. Department of Defense*. www.defense.gov/News/News-Releases/News-Release-View/Article/975074/statement-by-secretary-of-defense-ash-carter-on-the-liberation-of-dabiq.

——. 2017. "Iraqi Security Forces Liberate Mosul," July 10. *Operation Inherent Resolve*. www.inherentresolve.mil/News/Article/1241247/iraqi-security-forces-liberate-mosul/.

U.S. Department of State. 2004. "Foreign Terrorist Organization: Designation of Jama'at al-Tawhid wa'al-Jihad and Aliases," October 15. *Internet Archive*. web.archive.org/web/20060420083621/http://www.state.gov/r/pa/prs/ps/2004/37130.htm.

U.S. Department of State Office of the Spokesperson. 2015. "Ministerial on Information Sharing to Counter Foreign Terrorist Fighters," February 18. *U.S. Department of State*. https://2009-2017.state.gov/r/pa/prs/ps/2015/02/237575.htm.

Ünsal, Hadiye. 2016. "On the Revelation Circumstances and General Emphases of Sūrat Al-Aḥzāb: An Analysis Within the Scope of Textual and Non-Textual Context." *Ilahiyat Studies* 7 (1), https://doi.org/10.12730/13091719.2016.71.140.

"Until It Burns the Crusader Armies in Dabiq." 2014. *Dabiq* 1 (1): 3–5.

van Knippenberg, Daan, Nathalie Lossie, and Henk Wilke. 1994. "In-Group Prototypicality and Persuasion: Determinants of Heuristic and Systemic Message Processing." *British Journal of Social Psychology* 33 (3): 289–300.

Vergani, Matteo, and Ana-Maria Bliuc. 2015. "The Evolution of the ISIS's Language: A Quantitative Analysis of Language of the First Year of *Dabiq* Magazine." *Sicurezza, Terrorismo e Società* 2 (2): 7–20.

Vu, Tuong. 2010. "Studying the State through State Formation." *World Politics* 62 (1): 148–75.

Wagemakers, Joas. 2014. "A Terrorist Organization That Never Was: The Jordanian 'Bay'at al-Imam' Group." *Middle East Journal* 68 (1): 59–75.

"Wala and Bara, O Women." 2017. *Rumiyah* 1 (6): 22–24.

Walton, Douglas. 2007. *Media Argumentation: Dialectic, Persuasion, and Rhetoric*. Cambridge: Cambridge University Press.

Wan, Ching. 2012. "Shared Knowledge Matters: Culture as Intersubjective Representations." *Social and Personality Psychology Compass* 6 (2): 109–25.

Wasserstein, David J. 2013. "Ibn Ḥazm and al-Andalus." In *Ibn Ḥazm of Cordoba: The Life and Works of a Controversial Thinker*, edited by Camilla Adang, Maribel Fierro, and Sabine Schmidtke, 69–86. Leiden, South Holland, Netherlands: Brill.

Watt, W. Montgomery. 1961. *Muhammad: Prophet and Statesman*. Oxford: Oxford University Press.

Weaver, Mary Anne. 2006. "The Short, Violent Life of Abu Musab al-Zarqawi." *Atlantic Monthly* 298 (1): 87–101.

Weber, Max. 1991. "Politics as a Vocation." In *From Max Weber: Essays in Sociology*, edited and translated by H. H. Gerth and C. Wright Mills, 77–128. Oxon, UK: Routledge. First published 1946 by Free Press.

Wehr, Hans. 1976. *A Dictionary of Modern Written Arabic*, edited by J. Milton Cowan. Ithaca, NY: Spoken Language Services.

Weimann, Gabriel. 2004. *www.terror.net: How Modern Terrorism Uses the Internet*. Washington, DC: United States Institute of Peace.

Weine, Stevan, David P. Eisenman, La Tina Jackson, Janni Kinsler, and Chloe Polutnik. 2017. "Utilizing Mental Health Professionals to Help Prevent the Next Attacks." *International Review of Psychiatry* 29 (4): 334–40.

Weiss, Michael, and Hassan Hassan. 2015. *ISIS: Inside the Army of Terror*. New York: Regan Arts.

Weltman, David, and Michael Billig. 2001. "The Political Psychology of Contemporary Anti-Politics: A Discursive Approach to the End-of-Ideology Era." *Political Psychology* 22 (2): 367–82.

Wheeler, Brannon. 2006. *Mecca and Eden: Ritual, Relics, and Territory in Islam*. Chicago: University of Chicago Press.

White House Office of the Press Secretary. 2014a. "Statement by the President," August 7. *Obama White House Archives*. https://obamawhitehouse.archives.gov/the-press-office/2014/08/07/statement-president.

——. 2014b. "Statement by the President on Iraq," August 11. *Obama White House Archives.* https://obamawhitehouse.archives.gov/the-press-office/2014/08/11/statement-president-iraq.

——. 2014c. "Statement by the President on Airstrikes in Syria," September 23. *Obama White House Archives.* https://obamawhitehouse.archives.gov/the-press-office/2014/09/23/statement-president-airstrikes-syria.

Whiten, Andrew, Christine A. Caldwell, and Alex Mesoudi. 2016. "Cultural Diffusion in Humans and Other Animals." *Current Opinion in Psychology* 8 (1): 15–21.

Whitley, Rob, and Mike Crawford. 2005. "Qualitative Research in Psychiatry." *Canadian Journal of Psychiatry* 50 (2): 108–14.

Whitlock, Craig. 2004. "Grisly Path to Power in Iraq's Insurgency." *Washington Post,* September 27.

Wignell, Peter, Sabine Tan, Kay L. O'Halloran, and Rebecca Lange. 2017. "A Mixed Methods Empirical Examination of Changes in Emphasis and Style in the Extremist Magazines *Dabiq* and *Rumiyah.*" *Perspectives on Terrorism* 11 (2): 2–20.

Winnicott, Donald. 1949. "Hate in the Counter-Transference." *International Journal of Psycho-Analysis* 30 (1): 69–74.

Witte, Kim, and Mike Allen. 2000. "A Meta-analysis of Fear Appeals: Implications for Effective Public Health Campaigns." *Health Education and Behavior* 27 (5): 591–615.

Yardley, Lucy. 2000. "Dilemmas in Qualitative Health Research." *Psychology & Health* 15 (2): 215–28.

Young, Allan. 1981. "When Rational Men Fall Sick: An Inquiry into Some Assumptions Made by Medical Anthropologists." *Culture, Medicine, and Psychiatry* 5 (4): 317–35.

Zelin, Aaron. 2014. "The War Between ISIS and al-Qaeda for Supremacy of the Global Jihadist Movement." *Research Notes: The Washington Institute for Near East Policy* 20: 1–11.

——. 2015. "Picture or It Didn't Happen: A Snapshot of the Islamic State's Official Media Output." *Perspectives on Terrorism* 9 (4): 85–97.

——. 2016. "The Islamic State's Territorial Methodology." *Research Notes: The Washington Institute for Near East Policy* 29 (1): 1–24.

Zubaida, Sami. 2002. "The Fragments Imagine the Nation: The Case of Iraq." *International Journal of Middle Eastern Studies* 34 (2): 205–15.

Index